TRUE NORTH RISING

WHIT FRASER

My fifty-year journey with the Inuit and Dene leaders who transformed Canada's North

RANDOM HOUSE CANADA

PUBLISHED BY RANDOM HOUSE CANADA

 Published in 2023 by Random House Canada, a division of Penguin Random House Canada Limited, Toronto. Originally published in 2018 in Canada by Burnstown Publishing House, Burnstown. Distributed in Canada and internationally by Penguin Random House Canada Limited, Toronto.

www.penguinrandomhouse.ca

Library and Archives Canada Cataloguing in Publication

Title: True north rising / Whit Fraser.
Names: Fraser, Whit, author.
Description: Previously published: Burnstown, Ontario: Burnstown Publishing House, 2018.
Identifiers: Canadiana (print) 20220257787 | Canadiana (ebook) 20220257795 | ISBN 9781039005594 (softcover) | ISBN 9781039005600 (EPUB)
Subjects: LCSH: Fraser, Whit. | LCSH: Canada, Northern—History. | LCSH: Indigenous peoples—Canada, Northern—Social conditions. | LCSH: Indigenous peoples—Canada, Northern—Government relations. | LCSH: Journalists—Canada, Northern—Biography. | LCSH: Canada, Northern—Biography. | LCGFT: Autobiographies.
Classification: LCC FC3963.1.F73 A3 2023 | DDC 971.9/03092—dc23

Text design: Dylan Browne
Cover design: Dylan Browne
Image credits: Jayson McIvor / Getty Images
Printed in Canada

10 9 8 7 6 5 4 3 2 1

Penguin
Random House
RANDOM HOUSE CANADA

In memory of Andrew and Austin

CONTENTS

BUILDERS

PREFACE

Beginning as a reporter with CBC Northern Service in 1967, and more through luck than good management, my travels over fifty years have taken me across the North, to every town and village from Labrador to Alaska, to the oil and gas exploration and mining sites, and across traplines and waterways too numerous to mention. My northern perceptions were later sharpened as chair of the Canadian Polar Commission and as executive director of Inuit Tapiriit Kanatami, Canada's national Inuit organization.

Some of the coldest places I encountered and some of my warmest friendships emerged while I covered the Mackenzie Valley Pipeline Inquiry under Justice Thomas Berger. Over four pivotal years in the mid-1970s, the inquiry became much more about overcoming racism and building a better society than it was about laying a steel pipe through the permafrost.

It is more than time for me to tell the stories of the remarkable Indigenous-language broadcasters who provided the daily radio and TV coverage of the hearings. They were more than just gifted communicators. Their knowledge of their language and their people inspired a generation of young Indigenous leaders and profoundly changed the future of northern broadcasting.

I watched and reported as bright young men and women, including Mary Simon—my future wife and Canada's future governor general—fought for cultural survival and identity for First Nations, Inuit, and Métis. More often than not, my favourite stories are the ones that didn't make the news, or the stories that I wish hadn't made the news—like the time, after listening to unbearably racist testimony, I threw down my CBC reporter's notebook and asked to be sworn in as a witness at the Berger Inquiry. People not only demanded that I be fired as a result, but that I be banished, along with my whole family, from the Northwest Territories.

Over the years many of my colleagues have described me as a natural storyteller. This memoir puts that flattering judgment to the test.

Yet I want to do more than tell colourful stories. I also want to bring what I can to the discussion of the critical issues we are facing today: reconciliation and climate change. And I want to pay tribute to the remarkable men and women who have shaped the North over the past fifty years, among them Stephen Kakfwi, who was sexually abused as a child at a Catholic residential school but brought the Pope to the Northwest Territories—twice. And John Amagoalik. In the 1950s, the government of Canada, attempting to assert Arctic sovereignty, forcibly relocated young John and his family, along with other Inuit, from their home in northern Quebec to Resolute Bay, 1,400 kilometres north in the High Arctic. In 1999, John led the movement that changed the map of Canada with the creation of the new territory of Nunavut.

My hope is that this book will allow people who have never been fortunate enough to go north to feel a little closer to knowing its people and their culture and history. For those who have travelled the North and those who live there, I hope this book does justice to your experiences and your place in history.

This is my way of saying thanks for sharing so much of it with me.

Discovery

Where's Frobisher Bay?

I

COLONIAL JUSTICE

White Men in Black Robes

I will remember the look in Tootalik's eyes forever.

His was a face weathered and leathered from a lifetime of travelling across the frozen reaches of Arctic tundra and sea ice. Anyone, even a northern novice from the south like me, could tell by his stained clothing and sealskin knee-high footwear that he was a seasoned hunter. Yet the situation he faced filled him with panic and confusion.

He had to be asking himself: Why am I here? What have I done? Why is this uniformed Mountie guarding me? I imagine what was most frightening to him was standing in front of these white men in long, flowing black robes in this room with so many flags.

Why are they looking at me that way? What are they saying?

The white men in front of him included a judge, two lawyers, another man who was writing down everything that anyone said, the Mountie who'd arrested him and one broadcast reporter—me.

What did we know of his life? None of us understood Inuktitut. He couldn't speak to us. He couldn't tell his story. What's more, none of us had lived his life, venturing far out onto the sea ice by dog team, confronting and hunting polar bears, building iglus to survive Arctic blizzards, and then, following trail markers invisible to the southern eye, finding the way back home.

Tootalik's crime? He was accused of hunting a female polar bear with young.

Bizarre when you think about it. He was charged with practising the ancient skill that had allowed Inuit to survive for thousands of years. In his own culture, what he and his three companions had done was the feat of great hunters. The statement of fact submitted by the prosecutor ignored all of that, concentrating instead on the white man's laws and justice:

> On or about 14th April 1969 the accused, an Eskimo (Tootalik E4-321) and his Eskimo companion, Argvik Anvil, both of whom live at Spence Bay, Northwest Territories, proceeded by dog sled northwest of Spence Bay to a point several miles off the coast of the Boothia Peninsula on the sea ice northwest of Pasley Bay, Northwest Territories, in search of polar bears to shoot for their hides. They sighted three polar bears together—two smaller bears, approximately the same size, and a larger bear.

The statement appeared to recognize Inuit traditions only once, by acknowledging that rather than kill the bears themselves, Tootalik and Argvik waited for their friend Mathias Munga and his deaf son, Oomeemungnak Munga, to arrive. The prosecutor's charge continued: "They wanted Oomeemungnak to have the first shot. If he were successful in killing a bear, he would gain the hide, which he could then trade with the local fur trader."

Oomeemungnak did take the first shot, and it was a memorable one. That single bullet took down the larger bear and one of the smaller ones. To be clear, this second one was not a tiny cuddly cub but a medium-sized bear, measuring over five feet in length. The statement continued: "The other small bear ran away but was chased back to the area by the accused's dog." Tootalik then shot it.

In the Inuit world—then, still today and for a thousand years before—the hunters would have been praised for their skill. But in the 1960s, Spence Bay, now Taloyoak, and all other Arctic settlements were in a kind of legal twilight zone, where the white man's rules had to be obeyed. Which meant that Tootalik wasn't a great hunter; he was an accused criminal.

If Tootalik had questions in his mind, there were questions in mine as well. Foremost among them: Why is this guy even here?

A reporter as young and inexperienced as I was back then wasn't usually inclined to question the courts or search for ulterior motives. Nothing in my background had prepared me for this.

It had been only two and half years since Ted Morris, the station manager at CBC Frobisher Bay (now Iqaluit)—who had barely said hello after hiring me as an announcer-operator—verbally hit me between the eyes. "You're going to be our news reporter. We have a newscast here every evening at 5:30, Monday to Friday."

I wanted to protest that I was only there to read what was placed in front of me, play music and keep all the on-air switches in the right places. But less than forty-eight hours earlier, I had been discharged from the Royal Canadian Air Force (RCAF), where I had been well trained to keep my mouth shut and take orders. So I made my way, obediently, to the "news desk," which sat beside racks of old 78 rpm records. All that was on it was a telephone, an Underwood typewriter and a collection of unfiled albums and tapes.

My stomach was churning. Seven hours from now, I was supposed to deliver a newscast, five to seven minutes long. Had I known where the washroom was, I might have gone there to throw up.

Many times over the following years, in every kind of situation, I would tell my colleagues, "I might not have been a good reporter, but I was a lucky one." Case in point: my panic and despair were soon interrupted by a voice. "Can I use the phone?"

I turned from staring at a typewriter with no paper in it to see the familiar face of Bob Evans, a television reporter for *CBC News Magazine*, one of the corporation's flagship network programs through the 1960s and '70s.

After he finished his short call, I introduced myself and confessed my predicament, concluding with the simple admission, "I don't know what to do."

I'll never forget his smile. "I know Morris," he said, referring to my new boss. Bob didn't elaborate, he simply proceeded to give me a crash course in journalism:

"Use your tape recorder. A few thirty-second clips of people speaking will fill your time faster than writing your own copy, and people will find it more interesting. Write the news simply, make it fair, and always make sure it's the truth. Ask questions, talk to the police officers and the regional administrator, develop your list of contacts."

He only spent ten or fifteen minutes with me, in which he also passed on one or two tips he'd picked up that he thought would make a good local story. But that night at 5:30, I was on the air. "Here is the CBC Eastern Arctic News . . ." I intoned as though I was Earl Cameron, then the anchor of the *National*. Eventually, I was even able to appreciate Morris for throwing me in at the deep end of a very cold pool.

And now, here I was in Spence Bay, on the Boothia Peninsula in the central High Arctic, looking at Tootalik's face, listening to the lawyers, and I knew just enough to realize this was a story with legs.

A year earlier, in April 1969, Tootalik and his three companions had returned home to Spence Bay with several hundred pounds of meat and four polar bear hides on their qamutiks or sleds—the mother and young bears, and a single bear Argvik had killed. The hides alone were worth several hundred dollars.

The lone RCMP constable in Spence Bay, Hank Moorlag, had no reason to suspect any laws had been broken. But days later his special constable, an Inuk named Adam Tootalik (no relation), reported that local hunters had shot two small polar bears.

Constable Moorlag went to check, first to Mathias Munga's house, where two hides were bundled up and stored in a shed, and then to Tootalik's house, where one of the smaller bear hides was on the porch. In the constable's testimony, he said he thought the smaller hides were about four feet long from nose to tail. Later evidence proved that in fact they were both over five feet long.

Moorlag asked the hunters to come to the police station, and, using his special constable as an interpreter, listened as they told their story, including where, when, how and who had shot the bears. Then he arrested them.

In addition to his flat-brimmed brown stetson, an Arctic Mountie like Hank Moorlag wore many hats in the 1960s. He was a "human flagpole," as such Mounties often put it, asserting Canada's sovereignty along with upholding its laws. He was also the ex-officio territorial game officer, and that's the hat he wore when he charged the men under the Northwest Territories game ordinance. Then he brought them before Justice William Morrow of the NWT Territorial Court, which was being convened in the Spence Bay schoolhouse. It was unusual for the chief justice of the territorial court to hear a charge under the game ordinance. However, just as the Mounties wore more than one hat, judges wore more than one robe.

At the time, Morrow was on a circuit performing custom adoption cases, but as he wrote in his memoir, *Frontier Justice*: "The Mountie said he had three cases under the game ordinance that he wanted 'disposed of quickly.' He asked if I would hear three guilty pleas." Morrow recalled that the three hunters "agreed to all of the facts."

Indeed, it was the three hunters who provided all of the facts, and no one asked whether in doing so, they had also incriminated themselves. No lawyer or judge raised the matter of basic legal or Aboriginal rights.

In Morrow's memoir, there is a hint he felt some discomfort. "I regretted having no lawyers present." He expressed added reservations about the wording of the game ordinance.

"This worried me because *with young* was a phrase that some legal cases have interpreted to mean pregnancy. I then set aside the guilty pleas and reserved judgment and told Moorlag and the baffled hunters that they would hear from me."

A week later, Morrow reopened the case in Yellowknife with learned lawyers present, but no accused. It was my introduction to a remarkable legal, cultural and colonial collision.

To simplify the matter, Tootalik was the only hunter now on trial. The Crown attorney had set aside the charges against Argvik Anvil and Mathias Munga pending the outcome.

Oomeemungnak, the young man who had killed two polar bears with the one remarkable shot, was not charged. This was, to my mind at least, the one semblance of common sense that prevailed. The Yellowknife trial concentrated on the game ordinance and the size of the bears. The court heard expert evidence from game officials who stated that a cub would usually remain with the mother for two years, and even longer if she did not become pregnant.

When Mark de Weerdt, the defence attorney, spoke, he gestured with his hands so that his long black robe flowed in rhythm with his words as if to emphasize his arguments, questioning the size and age of the smaller bears and the precise wording of the NWT game ordinance. The Crown attorney, Orval Troy, always seemed to be losing his hands up the sleeves of his robes, but he was careful to get every detail of the measurements of the smaller bears on the record. (Both were skilled and competent lawyers, and both would become judges of the Court of the Northwest Territories. De Weerdt would later replace the man on the bench in front of him as chief justice of the NWT court.)

For a full day the lawyers argued the extent to which size did or did not matter and parsed the confusing wording of the game law. Then de Weerdt threw a curve into the proceedings by challenging whether Canada had jurisdiction over the area where the bears had been shot, which was out on the sea ice beyond the three-nautical-mile territorial limit. Morrow once again adjourned the case for two months until he could find his way back to Spence Bay.

In mid-January 1970, I was the lone broadcast reporter on the cold six-hour flight across the frozen land and sea ice to the central High Arctic. There was lots of time to talk while we were in the air, and I recall the suave and capable Mark de Weerdt saying that I should be prepared to hear more about Canada's Arctic sovereignty and jurisdiction after we landed.

The old DC-3 droned northward, hour after hour, at an altitude of four or five thousand feet. On such flights, I loved passing the time by looking out the window, gazing at the captivating land below me. I was always struck by the changing geography as the treeline disappeared into a world of black and white, snow and ice framed by outcrops of rock and gravel beds swept bare by the northern gales.

We were perhaps three or four hundred kilometres from our destination when below me, along the frozen reaches of the Arctic coast and ocean, I saw one tiny black spot against the stark white of the ice and snow. From this altitude, this tiny speck looked to be no more than a half-inch long, but it was recognizable—one lone Inuit hunter on a snowmobile, towing a laden qamutik.

Here was a human being, hundreds of kilometres—and several days' travel—away from any settlement, alone in the depth of an Arctic winter, pursuing a living. I remember marvelling at the strength and confidence it must take to survive in such extreme conditions and feeling a deep respect for Inuit and their ability to survive in that hard, cold country.

That image and that respect were with me later in the day as I studied Tootalik's face in court. On any other day, it could have been Tootalik I'd seen beneath the airplane, but on this day, he was here, standing straight and strong in a far different and still more frightening world.

Of the thousands of stories that I would cover in every part of the North, few images have stayed in my mind as vividly as that hunter standing silently in front of Justice Morrow. Most of all, he looked bewildered. Was he laughing inside at these "crazy white men," a common expression among bewildered Inuit trying to understand these strange men from another world who had just landed on the ice in that DC-3 airplane? Or was he petrified? I would soon be wondering whether he was set up. Beginning in the 1920s, the Canadian government had a strong, consistent policy about asserting Canada's Arctic sovereignty. From the mid-1960s to the mid-1980s, it seemed like a bureaucratic obsession. Had someone somewhere read a police report and seized the moment?

As he'd told me he would on the flight, de Weerdt focused on the sovereignty issue, claiming that Tootalik hadn't broken any regulations because he'd shot the bear on the sea ice beyond Canada's three-mile coastal jurisdictional limit. The Crown attorney found his best offence on a map of Canada posted on the wall of the schoolroom turned courthouse; it was one that most Canadian students (of a certain age) will recall, displaying Canada's provinces and territories in different colours with thick black lines extending east and west from our border with the United States out into the Atlantic and Pacific oceans and also stretching northward to the North Pole, marking Canada's Arctic boundaries.

This is the "sector theory," argued Troy, and it defines Canada's jurisdiction. De Weerdt's three-mile-limit argument was not applicable because the bears were shot inside those lines, which means they were shot in Canada. Even if Tootalik had been able to follow all the legal language, his trial now had nothing to do with the age or size of the young bears. It had become an argument about sovereignty and jurisdiction.

To no one's surprise, Morrow ruled against de Weerdt's "no sovereignty" defence and found Tootalik guilty. He set a ten-dollar "nominal" fine but also ordered the hides to be forfeited, which hit the hunters hard financially—the hides were worth several hundred dollars. (Put in the context of the period, that was more than the monthly salary of a well-paid CBC reporter.)

What's more, Canada's sovereignty had been tested and upheld in the territorial court. The belief that Canada had been well served prevailed among all of those who wore robes and uniforms.

De Weerdt was quick to appeal. Three months later, and almost a year after the bears were shot, Justice Harry Maddison of the Yukon, sitting as an NWT Court of Appeal judge, rode the DC-3 back to Spence Bay from Yellowknife with the same lawyers and court clerks, and me for the CBC, in tow.

The hearing took barely a day. In it, de Weerdt reverted to his original defence, arguing about the size and age of the bears and the confusing wording of the game laws. And for the first time Tootalik testified, with the parish priest interpreting for him. Tootalik said he knew very little about the game laws, but that no one should hunt a female polar bear with small cubs. He held out his hands three feet at most apart, indicating the size of a smaller-than-average husky dog. Further, he said it would be wrong to hunt a female bear when she was in a den with cubs. The two smaller bears Tootalik and Oomeemungnak shot were over five feet, and while no one in 1969 would ever suggest an "Eskimo" could be an expert witness, Tootalik estimated that would make them about three years old.

A hundred-page transcript of the appeal exists, and towards the end of it, Justice Maddison expresses concern about the hunters' comprehension of the situation, given that no official translator was present, just the parish priest. And he was right; the appeal didn't bring greater understanding to either the accused or the community.

At the end of the day, Maddison told Tootalik and the community of Spence Bay that he needed to take some time to decide. Three months later, in July 1970, he issued a clear decision in seventeen paragraphs. In part, he wrote: "If an offense was committed, there is no doubt on the facts that the accused was a party to it. The question for my determination is whether the hunting of this female polar bear, which was accompanied by smaller bears, comes within the Game Ordinance."

In short, Maddison had doubts. The laws were at best ambiguous, and as he was unable to find concise wording and meaning, he overturned the lower court's ruling, meaning Tootalik was innocent. He also ordered the forfeited polar bearskins to be returned.

What happened later reinforced my doubts about whose justice was begin upheld. Justice Morrow was highly respected for his sharp mind and compassion for the North. In his memoir, he expressed doubts about the lack of clarity in the wording of the game law when he first heard the case in Spence Bay, but chose not to simply throw the whole case out at the beginning.

Morrow was also a fellow of Calgary's Glenbow Museum. In his memoir, he implied that he believed the case was of great national significance, writing that he had recommended the institution purchase the hides "as a memento to our case in Spence Bay." He also likely advised that the proceeds go to Tootalik and the other hunters, and de Weerdt soon became a marketing agent, as a telegram sent to the lawyer reveals: "Because of the extreme mental anguish involved and the historic value of the skins, the price is now one thousand dollars for the larger skin and seven hundred dollars for each of the smaller hides." That was about four times the going rate for such skins, and the museum paid.

When all else fails, there is still "poetic justice."

Tootalik's polar bear case was not the only issue testing Canada's Arctic sovereignty at that time. Before, during and long after the trial, Canada and the US were quarrelling over the Arctic at the highest levels. Richard Nixon had just moved into the White House. Pierre Elliott Trudeau was Canada's prime minister. The two men despised each other, and their fight over sovereignty was being played out with the voyage of the *Manhattan*.

This ship was an American three-hundred-metre oil tanker retrofitted for Arctic travel, making it the largest icebreaker ever built. In August and September of 1969, the US government sent it on a trip through the Northwest Passage to challenge the Canadian claim that all Arctic Archipelago waters were its "internal waters." Despite some changes of direction, the *Manhattan* completed its journey, delivering a token barrel of oil from Alaska's Prudhoe Bay to the eastern seaboard of the US.

Canada asserted its sovereignty by sending the Canadian Coast Guard icebreaker *John A. MacDonald* to accompany the tanker. Another two US Coast Guard icebreakers joined in, and it was anything but smooth sailing as the ships confronted massive fields of sea ice. (It's a reminder for us just how much of that ice has since disappeared due to climate change. Today, fifty years later, cruise ships sail those same waters unobstructed.)

My favourite part of the *Manhattan* story occurred when a group of Inuit hunters from Resolute Bay in Lancaster Sound ventured by snowmobile and dog team out onto the ice. They barricaded the massive ship until the US captain, Rodger A. Steward, asked permission to pass. One small step for Inuit sovereignty!

In the CBC archives, there is a wonderful, flag-waving documentary by one of my journalistic heroes, Norman DePoe, reporting from the deck of the *John A. MacDonald*. The black-and-white film captures the huge ice pans caving and collapsing under the prow of the Canadian ship as it crosses in front of the US ships, clearing a passage. In his distinctive gravelly voice, DePoe describes almost mockingly how helpless the Americans appear and then concludes, as the ice separates and open water fills the frame, "The gutsy little Canadian icebreaker, *Sir John A. MacDonald*, shows them how it's done—Canadian style."

DePoe was the CBC's top dog at the time, but he didn't forget the needs of the smallest stations. Every few days, when he could find a clear ship-to-shore radio link, he would file a report to our newsroom in Yellowknife. How I would have loved to be on that ship, with that reporter, instead of having to cover it from my "listening post" in Yellowknife 2,400 kilometres away.

I was, however, on-site in 1985 when the US next challenged Canada's Arctic sovereignty with the voyage of the *Polar Sea*. Once again, the Americans underlined their refusal to accept Canada's claim to Arctic waters by sending a US Coast Guard icebreaker from Greenland to Alaska without asking permission or even formally notifying Canada. The journey caused no end of embarrassment for Canada's Progressive Conservative government and its leader, Brian Mulroney.

A final footnote about Tootalik the hunter.

The first chief justice of the NWT Supreme Court was a man called Jack Sissons. William Morrow succeeded him. Both judges shared the rather macabre practice of commissioning Inuit carvings to commemorate the cases they heard: murders, stabbings, strangulations. In one case, at the end of the trail Justice Sissons commissioned the man he'd convicted of murder to make carvings of the proceedings.

In 1969, Justice Morrow asked the renowned carver Abraham Kingmiaqtuq to make a carving of Tootalik aiming his rifle at three polar bears. That carving is now held in a Sissons-Morrow collection maintained by the NWT Department of Justice, which staff apparently refer to as "The S&M collection."

2

LEFT OR RIGHT?

Survival of the Fastest

I was about two-thirds of the way down a jagged cliff on the shore of Ungava Bay when I first saw the polar bear. No more than ten feet separated us. He was below me, facing away, and then his head snapped back over his shoulder and we were staring at each other eye to eye.

He was a big male, lean and powerful, and I was a guy who'd stepped out that morning without a gun. I'm sure I didn't startle him; more likely he was lying in wait. A few seconds earlier in my walk, I'd made a simple choice and turned to my right. Had I gone left, I would have put my back to him, and I probably wouldn't have known what hit me. But because I turned right, I saw him first and from above.

I know people who have almost drowned who say their lives flash before them. Nothing from my past went through my mind. All I was thinking about was how to get out of there, how to make sure this wasn't "Whit's end."

Similar serendipitous which-way-to-turn decisions have guided my northern journey over more than fifty years, a journey that has taken me to every town and village from Labrador and Arctic Quebec, across all of Nunavut and the Northwest Territories, to the coast of Alaska and farther north through the High Arctic Islands to the pole. This journey has also brought me to outpost camps, mining sites and oil drilling platforms, traplines and fish camps, and even to lonely and almost forgotten graves.

That's a lot of ground—and a lot of ice and snow—to cover, but it's not the territory or even the polar bear adventures that stand out. It's the remarkable people I encountered along the way and what they have accomplished in what, in the scheme of things, is a very short time.

I was in the tiny CBC newsroom in Yellowknife, pecking away on an old typewriter, when a twenty-five-year-old Inuk walked in and pulled up a chair beside me.

"Hi," he said. "My name is Tagak Curley and I am leading a movement to demand an Eskimo land claim settlement."

This was 1971.

"What the hell is a land claim?" I asked.

This first talk of land claims was the beginning of the end of the northern colonial era. In some parts of the North, governments were still identifying Inuit with numbers instead of last names. My friend Abe Okpik would lead the campaign to give the people back their names.

People had been relocated thousands of kilometres to strange surroundings and expected to survive because they were, after all, "Eskimos." Another friend, John Amagoalik, would later seize on Tagak Curley's dream of a land claim and go on to become the Father of Nunavut.

I can still remember John's words to Justice Thomas Berger, during the exhaustive Mackenzie Valley Pipeline Inquiry: "The north has been labelled as the 'last frontier.' Some look at it as something which needs to be conquered, explored and exploited. It has been called a 'warehouse of resources.' To us it is home."

Amagoalik's northern vision emerged in the title of Berger's historic report, *Northern Frontier, Northern Homeland.*

On a personal level that Inquiry connected me with four remarkable and unforgettable people who became like brothers to me: Jim Sittichinli, a Gwich'in Dene; Louie Blondin, only twenty when I met him, and paraplegic; Abe Okpik; and Joe Tobie (whom I'll tell you more about soon).

When the director of the CBC Northern Service, Andrew Cowan, gave me the assignment to spend years covering the pipeline inquiry, he told me that it was more than a great story. I was about to enter a classroom that would provide me with the vital education I had missed. He was right. The pipeline proposal was, after all, a $6-billion proposition, with complex engineering, environmental and energy equations all connected to the social sciences and humanities, which would affect all the people of the North, particularly the Indigenous peoples. From my perspective, by the time it had run its course, Berger's inquiry ended an era of rampant bitterness and racism across the North, crucially aided by the skilled efforts of our Indigenous broadcasters.

There were other transformative events. I watched young Inuit, First Nations, and Métis leaders, including the woman

I would later wed, Mary Simon, shed tears of joy when Canada's first ministers enshrined their rights in the Canadian Constitution.

I witnessed more tears of joy when, after years of broken promises, one sacred promise was kept and Pope John Paul II landed in Fort Simpson. That was the same town where, fifteen years earlier, the local council and mayor tried to ban me from reporting on Berger's pipeline inquiry because I had taken a stand and supported the Indigenous position: no pipeline until the land claims are settled.

My own successes or failures have always been determined by which way I turned—left or right—exactly as it happened when I ran into that polar bear.

That day had started as a picture-perfect early July morning in 2002—warm, sunny and with just enough of a breeze to discourage the savage northern mosquitoes and black flies.

My wife, Mary Simon, and I were visiting her brother Johnny's family at their summer fishing camp on the rugged coast of Ungava Bay at Black Point, almost at the northern boundary of Arctic Quebec and Labrador. Johnny and his family had camped there every July for over forty years.

The most practical geographic feature of the place is a small sheltered cove that protects the boats against unpredictable winds and the treacherous Ungava Bay tides, which average about thirteen metres here. About a kilometre inland, beyond the rocks, the cove opens into meadows wide enough for a short homemade gravel airstrip, which allows Johnny, one of the most accomplished and storied Arctic bush pilots, to land his small Cessna.

Scattered among the grassy meadows are outlines of ancient campsites, suggesting that the area was popular long before Johnny "discovered" it. Over the years, the camp has become a collection of little shacks or shanties to accommodate Johnny's growing family, spread out on a narrow spit of land. What keeps Johnny and his clan coming back to Black Point every July is the spectacular Arctic char fishing.

The char is always there to be caught—whether you're using a fishing rod or net. The tides make net fishing a simple and rather effortless proposition that involves laying the net out across the rocks on the shoreline when the tide is out. As the water rises, so does the net, in a nature-controlled twelve-hour fishing cycle. By the time the tide falls again, that net always yields fresh Arctic char. Sometimes it is only a few, sometimes a dozen or more. Cleaned, filleted and dried char is called pitsiq, and it's a mainstay of the Inuit diet.

On this particular morning, I woke early and decided to go for a short walk, while everyone else, perhaps a dozen adults and children in all, was still sleeping. I knew Mary and her sister Sara had been catching fish with a net stretched on the shore of the little cove. I also knew that some days they were catching more kelp than fish, so I decided to tend the net, clean out the seaweed and reset it.

This is a rugged coast, with no easy path to the beach. From the cabins to the water, it was about a ten-metre drop almost straight down to the bottom of a gully, but the jagged rocks offered natural steps downward.

Halfway to the bottom I paused on a bit of a ledge to ponder the best path. I took a few steps left, but that way didn't look so easy. I stepped back along the ledge, turned right, took one or two more steps down—and instantly froze. I could see the entire length of the polar bear's massive body, and then he was staring me in the eye.

I knew better than to have put myself in this terrifying situation. I had been in the North long enough to know the dangers. Even if I was going only a few hundred metres from camp, for a walk or to fish off the point, I always carried a rifle. But this morning had been so peaceful, and I hadn't wanted to wake either Johnny or my other brother-in-law, William Tagoona, to fetch a rifle from one of their cabins.

My only thought now was not to panic. As if in slow motion, I moved back up the rock face, almost on all fours, using my hands and feet to find safe and sure footing. If I slipped, that was it for me. I was so focused I didn't look back once, and I reached the top of the rock face in a retreat that took sixty heart-pounding seconds.

William and Sara's cabin was no more than thirty metres away. A few dozen strides and I was through the door, calling, "There's a bear, a big Nanook! And he's right there in the gully!" Sara came awake with a shriek, but William ignored me—later he said he thought I'd shouted "in the gulf"—and rolled over to go back to sleep.

Then his wife yelled, "It's here!" That woke him up. A few years earlier, a black bear had burst into their cabin in the middle of the night. William had shot that bear square in the face. He needed no reminders to keep a loaded rifle close by, in this case, under his bed.

Suddenly, he was on his feet and the .30-06 rifle was in his capable hands. We stepped outside. The bear had stalked me up the rock wall and was directly in front of us, less than fifteen metres away. Perhaps the buildings gave him pause, but his body language said he was mean and hungry. His head down, weaving from side to side, the bear began to move slowly forward.

In a split second, William raised his rifle and fired. The bear reeled backward, the shot almost ripping his jaw off. Somehow, he stayed on his feet. He ran back to the gully, down the cliff face, across the dry cove bottom where the boats were beached, then up the other side of a rocky outcrop no more than a hundred metres away. William looked at me, almost apologetically, and said, "I really didn't want to have to kill him."

At that moment Carson, William's twelve-year-old son, arrived beside us with his rifle. His father told him to put the bear out of his misery. He did, with one quick and deadly shot to the heart.

Now everyone was streaming out of the cabins. The last to appear was Mary, who wanted to know what all the racket was about. Johnny, always ready with a one-liner for any situation, said, "While you were sleeping, your husband almost became tomorrow's pile of bear shit."

Later in the day, William and I skinned the bear. We are not biologists, but we knew this one had been starving. Not only was his stomach empty, but there was not an ounce of fat on his body. That summer, as with most recent summers, Ungava Bay had been free of ice, making it difficult for bears to hunt seals.

Carson claimed the hide to make a new seat for his snowmobile. That was okay with me. I needed no reminders. But as William and I peeled away the hide, we talked about how life and death can be as simple as a choice to turn left or turn right.

Had I followed my initial instinct and stayed left, I would have been trapped in the bottom of the gully, between two steep rock walls. The bear would have been behind me. As Johnny said, tomorrow's bear shit!

That night in the cozy little cabin, in the brief sunset-to-sunrise twilight that defines a summer night in the Far North, Mary snuggled closer than usual. "What if I had lost you today?" It wasn't meant to be, I said, but even as I reassured her, I considered the amazing twists and turns of fate and circumstance that had brought us both to this place and would shape and guide our lives in the years to come.

I'll tell you more about Mary later. But first, another question: How does a kid from Nova Scotia, a kid whose own mother once said he didn't have enough education to get through high school, find his way into such a remarkable family and such a remarkable place?

3

WHERE'S FROBISHER BAY?

Always Trust Your Gut

Remarkably, as children, both Mary and I had shared an attraction to old shortwave radio sets. One of the first times I heard Mary Simon speak, at a university gathering, she recalled living in a tent at the height of a bitterly cold Arctic winter. Every evening, gathered around a small wood stove, she and her grandmother would tune in to the BBC World Service on shortwave radio. Sometimes, she said, they would listen to marvellous music sung by Greenlandic choirs.

The evening ritual was much the same in my own childhood home in Pictou County, Nova Scotia. There was always a radio playing somewhere in the house that my family (my sisters and I, and our mum and dad) shared with my grandmother. She had one of those old floor models in a finely finished wood cabinet, and she was fascinated with any program that brought her news and images of the Far North. On winter evenings, especially, she'd always take time to listen to

CBC's northern broadcasts, one of her favourites being *Northern Messenger*.

The show was on every night, delivering letters over the air to and from people receiving treatment for tuberculosis in hospitals in the south. The announcers also read out letters to sailors and airmen at the weather stations, to Hudson's Bay clerks, Mounties, and others who worked in the North.

Most of those tiny Arctic settlements and outposts received mail only once a year when the resupply ship arrived from the south. Others got service every month or two, depending on the limited number of air flights. *Northern Messenger* gave them the most basic news from home—births, deaths, illnesses and other events. Then came the northern weather for places like Eureka, Isachsen and Resolute; mind-boggling temperatures, blizzard warnings, forecasts of forty-five below zero. Fahrenheit! That one radio program was the Facebook—the social network—of the Arctic in the 1950s, a lifeline to the rest of Canada. I loved tuning in with Grammy, both of us being pretty interested in other people's mail.

In hindsight, high school was like the radio. I tuned in to what interested me—English, history and social studies—and tuned out what didn't, especially algebra and geometry. An encounter with my grade nine math teacher helped me chart my course. Mr. McClellan was a former colonel who had served in the Second World War and who didn't have much time for a smartass.

When he began putting up equations, $X = 2$, $Y = 3$ and so $X \times Y = 6$ on the board, I asked him, "Why use X and Y, why not just the numbers?"

In my later years in journalism, I would learn that there are no "wrong questions," but with Mr. McClellan any question was the wrong one. It went downhill from there.

My marks in the subjects I liked were better than average. But math? I was hopeless, an ineptitude that caught up to me in senior high. If I wanted to graduate, I had to pass math, but I couldn't take the senior-level class because I'd failed the previous year.

I appealed for a second chance, for probation, for anything, because I knew what was at stake. If I wasn't in this math class then I wasn't in school, and if I wasn't in school, I was in serious trouble with my mother, who worked sixteen hours a day raising us, and my father, a tradesman. They constantly pushed my sisters and me to get the education and find the opportunities they had missed.

There was no reprieve. I was out. It was September 1960 and I was seventeen years old. I stood in the schoolyard, contemplating my next move.

Which way to turn? It was my first left-or-right decision. I did know one thing. If I turned right and went directly home, I'd have to face my parents. If I went left, I could get on the bus, go to New Glasgow, three kilometres away, and start looking for a job. My survival instinct told me that if I was employed when I came home, it would soften the inevitable disappointment and wrath of my parents. I turned left.

New Glasgow, the hub of Pictou County, hasn't changed much in fifty years; it remains home to about ten thousand people and its two parallel main streets, Provost and Archimedes, are lined with a collection of shops and small businesses. I planned to make the loop of the whole downtown, checking with every business to see if it had any job openings.

At the top of the town, on the bank of the East River, next to the tracks, is a historic building that, at the time, housed the Hector Publishing Company, named for the ship that had brought the first Scottish settlers to the region nearly two hundred years earlier. It was the first and only stop I made that day.

When I reflect on it now, I recognize that those were good days and simpler times. Imagine today walking into a business and asking if you could see the manager about a job, and instead of being told to send a resumé by email, you get in to see them. That's what happened to me. After I made my request, the polite receptionist said, "Just a moment," stuck her head into a small, cluttered cubicle, and then turned to me, saying, "Mr. Cameron will see you now."

James M. Cameron was a large, balding man with piercing eyes, buried under large, bushy eyebrows—perhaps the most intimidating person I've ever met. He was also a pillar in the local business and political community, an author and a local historian.

He asked just what I had in mind. Behind a small door in his tiny office, I could hear the clashing rhythms of the printing presses. Printing fascinated me, and I asked about the possibility of becoming an "apprentice."

"We do not need apprentices in the print shop," he said, "but what about radio?" On the floor above where we sat was the Hector Broadcasting Company, a.k.a. CKEC New Glasgow.

Cameron picked up a copy of *Time* magazine off his desk. He ran his big finger down a column, then passed it to me and said, "Read that."

I was seventeen. I am not sure I'd ever held a copy of *Time* in my hands before, but without hesitation, I started to read.

I hadn't gone on for more than half a minute when he stopped me.

"Okay, let's go upstairs and see what you sound like on tape."

Five minutes later, I was in the radio studio, reading wire copy from the Canadian Press, with Cameron listening on the other side of the glass. What remains most clear in my mind, even after all these years, is how badly my young hands were shaking. I smoothed the copy on the table and tried to sound the way I thought people on the radio should sound, deep and authoritative.

When I finished, JM (the staff called him that, but never to his face) pointed me into a small studio. He hit playback. It was the first time I had heard my voice on a recording. I didn't recognize it.

"I can use you here," he said. "We will start you off part-time, but first you have to learn the board and operations. I don't pay for the training time. That's about two weeks. Then part-time. After a few months we'll see how you do and look at full-time. Part-time is fifteen dollars a week, full-time is twenty-five a week."

I accepted, happily, and started my training that afternoon. All I could think about on the fifteen-minute bus ride home was that I not only had a job but also I was going to be on the radio.

I remember my mother's surprise when she heard the news, standing over the wood-burning stove in the kitchen and making dinner. "So you can't go to school because you failed math, which means you don't even have enough education to finish high school, and yet you're going to work in the radio station?" Regrettably, in all my years as a broadcast journalist, I never quite matched my mother's ability to put issues in perspective. But I was smart enough to read in her tone that she was pleased, and so was my father.

The next day, I was on the radio. It turns out that "training" meant making all my mistakes live on air. "Part-time" translated into a few hours in the morning, nine to noon, or three to five in the afternoon, or the night program, seven to midnight.

I was earning barely enough to cover my bus fare, but I was working and I was learning. However, the senior announcers at the station warned me that I was about the twentieth young guy to be hired in the last five or six years. "Don't count on that full-time job," they cautioned.

They were right. One day a new apprentice was hired, and on the next, JM gave me the bad news. "I'm sorry, laddie, I just don't think you're suited to radio."

I was heartbroken—washed up at seventeen.

I spent that winter doing odd jobs, peeling and stacking pulpwood, even going house to house peddling windows and doors. The summer of 1961 found me standing at attention in Saint-Jean-sur-Richelieu, Quebec, as a newly minted member of the RCAF. It paid twenty-five dollars a week, plus room and board.

Within a year I was posted to Summerside, Prince Edward Island. A year later, at the age of twenty, I married my teenage sweetheart, Dianne Linden. A year after that we had a baby daughter we named Rhonda and, within a few more months, another child was on the way.

I didn't make more than two hundred dollars a month. Like most young families in the military in the early 1960s, we couldn't make ends meet. Part-time jobs with moving companies, bartending, anything with flexible hours, were part and parcel of an airman's existence.

Then one day a knock on our tiny third-floor apartment turned financial desperation into financial chaos. Encyclopedia salesmen. A couple of the sharpest-talking, smoothest con men imaginable talked their way into our apartment and, within an hour, had us convinced that the road to prosperity for ourselves and our children, born and yet unborn, was waiting for us within the pages of the *Encyclopaedia Britannica*.

I can still see us signing those pink and yellow contracts to purchase multiple volumes, from *A* to *Z*, for the "low, low" price of seventeen dollars a month, ad infinitum.

The next day, we recognized reality. How could we pay seventeen dollars a month? This was not a smart move, and we certainly weren't going to get any smarter with a room full of leather-bound books when we had no money and a baby without a proper pee pot.

There was but one answer: I would have to get way more regular part-time work. I called the closest radio station, CJRW. I spoke to the owner/manager, Bob Schurman, who turned out to be one of the most gifted broadcasters I was ever to meet. He set up an audition with his program manager, who handed me some wire copy to read. My hands still shook, but my voice must have sounded calm. A few days later, I called back as instructed, and Schurman offered me work, every evening from nine to midnight and Sunday afternoons. More than that, he would pay me a dollar an hour, slightly more than minimum wage. I was delighted. That extra twenty dollars a week gave us a shot at making ends meet.

What's more, I never did have to pay for that encyclopedia. It turns out the slicksters had signed up dozens of young air force families in the same week. Our base commander stepped in and told us that if we didn't want the books because we couldn't afford them, then we shouldn't accept delivery. We took his advice and never heard another word about it. More than that, I was back in radio, with an owner who said it was where I belonged.

At my air force day job, I got tremendous support. The men who were my bosses—the corporals, sergeants, warrant officers—were all veterans. They had learned years earlier how to separate the large issues from the small. They took me off shift work so I wouldn't miss any time on air. One old veteran, our section commander, Squadron Leader Gordon Hendron, would gently (and always in private) point out my frequent on-air pronunciation errors, especially of French names.

When the time came for me to ask for a discharge to join the CBC, to a person they supported me and helped me navigate the red tape it took to get a release. But I almost blew that chance.

"Hey there, Fraser," shouted Corporal Ivan Curley, as I hurried across the hangar floor to my work station at 8:30 one morning. "I got a message for you."

I stopped, wondering what this was about.

The corporal continued, "Last night my brother and I were driving home. He's a big shot with the CBC, on the island for his father-in-law's funeral. He heard you reading the news and he wants to meet you. He'll be here today at one o'clock. He'll meet you in the parking lot outside the main door."

I couldn't believe my good fortune. I had now been in the air force for six years, and at my part-time CJRW job for two, and I had been discovered. What luck! But as the morning progressed, I began to have second thoughts. This was coming from Ivan Curley, one of the most notorious pranksters on the base. Surely this was his latest joke. I could visualize the feisty little PEI Irishman rubbing his hands in glee as he and a dozen others hid around the corner while I paced back and forth waiting for Mr. CBC. I wouldn't fall for it. This joke would be on them. Instead, I took my lunch hour to run an errand in downtown Summerside, about eight kilometres from the base.

Near the west end of the main drag, Water Street, I watched a man walking towards me. He was clearly out of place. Nobody in Summerside is this well dressed, I thought. It was the suit, such a nice deep-grey suit, which must have cost a hundred dollars, never mind the sharp tie and the shoes. As he got closer, it occurred to me that this fellow looked a lot like Corporal Curley.

I stared at him as he passed, thinking, My God, is that him? Mr. CBC? What if this is not a joke? I hurried back to base, parked my old car, and hustled to the front of the number five hangar.

There he was. The very well-dressed Austin Curley, administrative officer for CBC Northern Service, was waiting for me. Here was my guardian angel and saviour.

He had many questions, but two I clearly remember: "Would you like to work for the CBC?"

Yes!

"Would you be willing to move north, to Frobisher Bay?"

Yes, certainly. (Though I didn't know where it was until I looked it up on the map later.)

It didn't happen right away. It took four or five months to work out the arrangements. The CBC hadn't sent announcers' families north with them before, so there were costs and accommodations to be resolved. I also had to secure a release from the air force. But by April 1967, with my belongings packed into two cardboard boxes, I was on the ten-hour DC-4 flight bound for Frobisher Bay, two thousand kilometres north of Montreal. Dianne and the children would join me in a few months, once I passed my probation.

I'm not sure, even today, if I had any idea what I was getting into.

4

JONAH KELLY—E7-262

I Am Not a Dog

Jonah Kelly stood out among the other reporters gathering in the Ottawa Government Conference Centre on a November morning in 1981. Prime Minister Pierre Trudeau had invited the premiers of the provinces and territories and the leaders of Canada's Indigenous organizations to a crucial meeting about the repatriation of the Constitution.

Jonah, an Inuktitut-speaking CBC Northern Service broadcaster, understood more about what was at stake for his audience when it came to such a repatriation than the rest of us in the media throng covering the event. He was also better dressed.

Jonah Kelly's voice was familiar, enduring and influential among the thirty thousand Inuit living in the North at the time. From relaying messages back and forth between people confined to distant southern hospitals and their families in the most remote Arctic settlements, to reporting, interpreting and educating Inuit on national and international events, he had become a cultural bridge and a lifeline connecting two very different worlds.

On this day and at this historic event, those of us at CBC and the other networks were often left to fill air—a half-hour or sometimes longer—when the leaders decided to go into in camera sessions to discuss strategy. The French and English networks had their constitutional experts and pundits on hand, eager to pontificate upon Canada's constitutional future. But Jonah carried the live Inuktitut broadcast on his own. He had no experts and pundits to lean on. While brilliant young Inuit negotiators were in the room—including John Amagoalik, Mary Simon and Charlie Watt—they were either at the table or in strategy meetings, leaving Jonah to paddle and bail his kayak at the same time.

It didn't matter. Jonah was his own best expert. His version of the story came down to a couple of simple questions: Will the rights of Indigenous peoples, which were enshrined in the British North America Act and the Royal Proclamation of 1763, be lost if the Constitution "comes home" without explicit recognition of those rights? Of even greater concern, would Aboriginal rights be written out of a renewed and "patriated" Canadian Constitution altogether?

As part of the CBC National TV News Specials team, I was assigned the "Aboriginal angle." It made sense, given that my broadcasting roots were in the North. I knew the players and I could at least help explain the complexities. I remember watching Jonah, at the edge of the press pool, doing his live solo broadcast for a half-hour or more at a stretch, ad libbing and never appearing bewildered or stumped. There were no hesitations, just a smooth flow as he described the setting, the stakes and the Inuit strategy to his audience across the Arctic.

I'd first met Jonah on a bitterly cold day in April 1967 as he was picking out records for one of his radio programs. He wore his jet-black hair in a Beatles mop and hid his eyes with a pair of dark sunglasses—and though he was not much more than twenty years old at the time, he was already considered an old hand at the CBC, having started not quite a year earlier.

Back then our radio station, CFFB, was as barebones as broadcasting can be. It was on the ground floor of what had once been a three-storey military barracks and office complex built by the United States as a Strategic Air Command base at the onset of the Cold War. When the Americans pulled out, the Canadian government inherited it, and it became known simply as the Federal Building. Through the 1960s and '70s, it was both the workplace and the living quarters of nearly all the government employees in town. It would then serve another twenty years as a residence for high school students from across the eastern Arctic.

The CBC occupied no more than six hundred square feet in the building, chopped up into a tiny control room, a sound studio, a record library, a manager's office and a technical workshop. Of the six broadcasters who worked there, Jonah was the only Inuk. Everyone else was from the south, and no one seemed to stay longer than two years, nor were they expected to.

This was at a time when the CBC Northern Service had committed itself to delivering programming in the local "Eskimo language." Ted Morris, the station manager who threw me into the deep end of news, told me he'd hired Jonah because "he was open, affable, eager, and educated. He was everyone's friend and he was also bilingual, capable of thinking and feeling in Inuktitut and English."

For Jonah, this was home. Back in the mid-1950s, his parents had moved their ten children to Frobisher Bay. They knew there were schools there, and they had the foresight to see that their children would need to be educated to live in this "modern" world. Jonah finished grade nine at Sir Martin Frobisher School and then went to high school at Camp Borden, a military base in Ontario, boarding with a family there. He was among the few Inuit youth of his day who were spared the pain and anguish associated with the residential school system.

By the time I got to Frobisher Bay in 1967, the town had a population of about fifteen hundred—three-quarters Inuit and one-quarter Qallunaat (white), from southern Canada or Europe. Entertainment was scarce. Practical jokes were daily fare to maintain our sanity—and sometimes a hint that sanity had taken its leave.

One bitterly cold morning I watched Jonah carry a bucket of snow into the booth where we did our broadcasts. He placed it near the floor heater.

"What's that for?" I asked.

"You'll see," he said.

A couple of hours later it was my turn at the microphone. In the middle of some great pronouncement of mine, I felt the heart-stopping shock of ice water pouring down over my head and back. The screams and curses that went out over the airwaves were matched by the roar of Jonah's laughter. I promised payback.

Some time later, I recruited the help of our technician. As Jonah began the opening to his show, we slipped quietly into the booth alongside him and removed all the turntables, tape players and radio receivers. Jonah was left with only a single live mic and one hour to fill. He just laughed. When he came out of the studio after the end of his show, he was still laughing. "That was a good one—you guys really got me."

I asked, "What in the world did you talk about for a full hour?"

"Oh, it was easy," he said. "I just told everybody what you guys did, and explained how a radio station works, where our material comes from and where you come from, and what it is like working here." To Jonah, everything was an opportunity to educate and inform, even being the butt of a practical joke.

At the time, Jonah referred to himself as an "Eskimo," but he was also one of the leading voices for change, insisting that people should be identified as Inuit and not by someone else's slang word. Most of all, not by a number.

Early in our friendship, Jonah confided to me that his destiny was shaped shortly after he was born in a hunting camp on southern Baffin Island, near the present community of Kimmirut. That's when a government official recorded him as Jonah E7-262. He despised the very idea that Canada would label any of its citizens with numbers and then justify the action with a contrived "for recording accuracy" excuse. The disc number was introduced in 1941. It was literally a round, brown leather disc stamped with the number and the image of the crown, and it was meant to be sewn into clothing or worn around the neck. By the 1960s, very few people did either. But on the CBC, we kept on identifying people by number, still party to colonization.

The *E* signified the person was born in the eastern Arctic; Inuit born in the western Arctic had a *W* disc number. Jonah's number 7 indicated that he was born in southern Baffin Island; Lake Harbour is how it was then described on the maps. The 262 was simply the next number in the sequence as a new birth was recorded.

When Jonah joined CBC, communication across the Arctic was primitive. Most communities had no telephone service. Mail and air service were sporadic, perhaps once a week or, for the tiny settlements, even once a month. Television was something only people in southern Canada had. The link with the outside world was shortwave radio. Beginning with his hiring in 1966, Jonah was the star and the principal messenger. He recognized that radio was the best possible tool to expose injustice and inequality, so he never missed an opportunity to question authority about the despised disc number. Until change came along in the early 1970s, he'd direct this question to Inuit and non-Inuit politicians alike: "Why do we have numbers when everyone else has a name? Are we like dogs?"

Was he a crusading reporter? Was he too editorial and opinionated in his broadcasts? The fact is none of us ever knew for sure; no one in management or at an editor's desk spoke or understood Inuktitut. We trusted that Jonah was smart enough to respect the boundaries of fair comment that guide all reporters.

In 1970, the government of the Northwest Territories stopped identifying people with numbers and appointed the prominent Inuit leader Abe Okpik to survey every family across the Arctic and record each family's preferred surname. Jonah made sure through his broadcasts that people knew when Okpik would be in their community and how important this matter was. And at last he got rid of his hated number.

We were working side by side in Ottawa at the 1981 constitutional conference, when Jonah became quite amused by the way the CBC's makeup artist, shapely in a striking hot-pink jumpsuit, consistently ensured that nobody had a "shine" on camera. I remember him watching from a few feet away as she applied paint or powder to me, and how hilarious he thought this was. He even included it in his broadcast, describing the scene to the folks back home, becoming more and more animated the longer he talked. I would be lying if I said I understood what he was saying, but the tone and building hilarity in his voice were unmistakable. He had Inuit names for all of us who worked with him, usually something appropriate to our physical makeup. The small guy would be Mikeouq and the thin guy Sudluk. To make sure he had my attention, he clearly emphasized the pet name he'd given me: Queneuq, a reference to my emerging pot belly and chubby cheeks.

My ears perked up, and then the Inuktitut patter stopped. There was a short pause as he shifted to English and three words came out slowly and clearly: "Make Out Lady!"

As the director counted the last few seconds to my cue, I whispered something to the makeup artist, and she went directly over to Jonah. In the middle of his joking commentary, she began plying him with both her makeup and her considerable sex appeal. I watched that big brown friendly face grow increasingly red. For once Jonah had difficulty finding words in either language, no doubt wondering if his wife and childhood sweetheart, Lizzie Siniq, was watching.

At one time or another, all of us who have been broadcasters have been accused of "making it up." Jonah never made up facts, but he did often have to invent words to tell the story.

Many of the key issues and words in his stories had no Inuktitut equivalent—words like nuclear bomb, satellite or commercial. Jonah was a language purist who didn't think it was right to just use the English words. His Inuktitut-speaking colleagues and fellow broadcasters were always impressed by his ability to find and apply clear and understandable Inuktitut words and phrases.

Ann Hanson, a former commissioner of the Northwest Territories, remembers the quick discussions and one-on-one meetings she'd have in the hallway searching for relevant Inuktutit terms to convey an idea. William Tagoona, another veteran Inuit broadcaster, says, "Almost every modern term [now] has an acceptable Inuktitut word, and many of them are because of Jonah. For example, a satellite is Qummuktitausimajuq—something put up in space. A TV commercial is Tususaarutik, something to make one want. A nuclear bomb is Qaqtaqtualuk Nungusuitulik. William says that literally translates to "big bomb with consequences of no end." I would say the Inuktitut version offers more clarity than the English.

Jonah was only sixty-six when he died in the spring of 2012, of a heart condition complicated by diabetes. I was out of the country and couldn't make it to his funeral. But two months later I had the chance to remember Jonah and honour his memory in the very building where we met. As part of a summer program called Students on Ice, I was in Iqaluit with about a hundred youths; twenty-five of them were Inuit, but others came from around the world. As I was winding up a storytelling session in the old cafeteria of the Federal Building, I pointed to the door and told them, "From just down that corridor came the best radio broadcast I have ever heard."

I paused. "It was coverage of the assassination of Martin Luther King Jr. in 1968."

As soon as I mentioned Dr. King, two of the students who were from Memphis, Tennessee, sat up straight with a puzzled look in their eyes. What could be the connection between the great American civil rights leader and this run-down old building in northern Canada?

I told them that when Dr. King was shot, the CBC and the other major Canadian networks went into full live coverage. So those of us in Frobisher Bay had some time on our hands. Jonah instantly recognized the parallels between the struggles of Inuit in the Far North and the injustices against Black Americans that were at the heart of the civil rights movement. The common denominator was the colonial mentality. Jonah felt compelled to do his own major news special, recording it on tape and sending it to Montreal for broadcast.

In our makeshift studio that doubled as a technician's workshop, Jonah had none of the tools available to his southern counterparts—no wire copy and no experts offering insights on this looming US national crisis. Undaunted, he recorded news reports from the static-filled shortwave radio signals from the American Forces Network and the CBC's International Service. Colleagues at CBC Montreal sent him background material via telegram, each word pasted to a transmission page where sentences ended with the word "stop."

Then, for several hours, Jonah locked himself in the studio. Minutes before his local deadline, he emerged with two taped one-hour programs—one that would go to air immediately and another that station manager Ted Morris had to get to Montreal for the shortwave service. Morris remembers, "As luck would have it, an unscheduled DC-3 stopped for fuel en route to Montreal. We cadged a ride for our hot tape with delivery instructions. The next night CBC Northern Service aired the program all over the Arctic."

All of us at the station listened and realized what Jonah had done. So did the audience. He had captured King's story in a way that not only Inuit but also non-Inuit understood. He had translated King's famous "I Have a Dream" speech, with his words in Inuktitut fading in and out of King's great oratory, matching all the passion and emotion, especially in the part where Dr. King talked of a time when his little children "will not be judged by the color of their skin but by the content of their character." More than providing a basic news story's "who, what, why, when and where," Jonah had captured the emotion of the assassination and linked it to the struggle for self-determination in the North.

A couple of days later, an Anglican missionary came in from a remote settlement demanding news about the King assassination, saying, "I heard two hunters talking about it in the Hudson's Bay post. They found out from Jonah Kelly."

As I recounted the story to this diverse group of students, I realized that it had happened over forty years earlier, and I could barely speak for the lump in my throat. Their faces told me they got it. They connected north and south, white, Black and Inuit. Maybe, like me, they felt another spirit in the room.

For Jonah and me, our proudest moment together was on April 1, 1999, when we hosted the inauguration ceremonies for the creation of the new territory of Nunavut. It was the last time we would do a live broadcast together, and it was also my final broadcast ever. We had both left CBC and were on the air for the Inuit Broadcasting Corporation.

Jonah Kelly was recognized for his outstanding work with an honorary degree in journalism from Nunavut Arctic College in 1989, the CBC President's Award in 1991, and the National Aboriginal Achievement Award in 2002. He also received numerous awards for community service. Ted Morris recalls a different kind of award that Jonah received: the respect of his listeners. "When I visited Lake Harbour, south of Frobisher Bay, in deep winter of the late '60s," he says, "I noticed the whole town went black at two p.m. The diesel generators were turned off for an hour because they were creating static and the townsfolk couldn't hear Jonah Kelly. When Jonah went off the air, the power came back on."

5

JOE TOBIE

Treasured Hunts

Joe Tobie was the guy who taught me to hunt and butcher caribou. And though Joe was a highly skilled trapper, I was the one who once showed him the quickest way to dispatch an elusive wolverine.

Joe was a contradiction. He was a broadcaster who valued silence as much as, or perhaps more than, talk, even though he had a better grasp of language than anyone at CBC Northern Service, now simply called CBC North. Joe was equally fluent in two Dene languages, Dogrib and Chipewyan, and he could easily converse in Cree and Slavey. He was also fully fluent in English, and if necessary, he could reach back into a closed chapter of his childhood and find the words to make himself understood in French.

I met Joe in 1969 when I transferred from Frobisher Bay to CBC Yellowknife. He was one of those people who could put you at ease with just a warm handshake and a smile. At the time, his confidence, his incredible on-air presence and his remarkable grasp of languages made him the biggest star on the CBC Mackenzie network, which included the main station in Yellowknife and about twenty communities around Great Slave Lake and down the Mackenzie Valley to the Arctic coast. He was number one at the CBC, and he didn't even work there full-time—his day job was as a translator for Health Canada.

He translated for doctors and nurses in the communities and at the Yellowknife hospital, and twice a week he hosted a public service broadcast on behalf of Health Canada, where he would explain, in both Dogrib and Chipewyan, the importance of good health, nutrition and sanitation. All of it was key information at the time. Most houses were small, and few had running water or flush toilets. More than the golden age of radio, it was the golden age of the honey bucket.

Joe's health broadcast also announced, at least twice a day, a list of sexually active citizens who needed to contact the health department or the community nurse. Such were the standards of privacy and community confidentiality in the late 1960s. We referred to those announcements as the community clapboard.

Saturday afternoons, Joe became a CBC performer, hosting the best two-hour country music program in the North. It was typical old-time radio, featuring a few requests and birthday messages, but mostly the old songs that everybody liked, regardless of their language. Does "Back in the Saddle Again" ring a bell?

In 1975, when I was appointed to head up the team of broadcasters providing daily coverage on the Mackenzie Valley Pipeline Inquiry, Joe was the first person I asked to join me. He said yes immediately, and we sat together through every session of that two-year inquiry in every community in the Mackenzie Valley, the Yukon and major cities across Canada.

We worked side by side for more than five years, but our friendship wasn't focused on broadcasting and we rarely talked shop when we slipped away from the studio to drink beer at the old Gold Range, about three buildings up the street from the radio station. Joe would often bring me a cut of caribou from one of his weekend hunting trips. When I told him how much I appreciated it and how much the family enjoyed the meat, he invited me to join him. I took him up on it, but I thought that our first hunting trip would be my last, not because I was squeamish, but because it completely wore me out.

There were three of us: Joe, his twelve-year-old son, James, and me. We travelled by pickup truck along a series of roads that had been plowed over the frozen lakes towards the Bluefish River hydro dam, about sixty-five kilometres from Yellowknife. Joe's Dene friends had told him caribou were migrating through the area. As a Dene hunter, Joe and his family could shoot as many caribou as they needed in any given year. As a non-native NWT resident, I was able to buy a licence with five tags, more than enough to feed my small family.

It was early winter, so the days were short, with no more than five or six hours of daylight. About midday we spotted a few caribou close to the edge of the lake we were crossing. Joe politely pointed to the one he would shoot, a cow, leaving me my choice of the others. I foolishly picked out the biggest bull.

We fired almost simultaneously, and two animals dropped. Joe ripped off a second shot and downed the third one. As I began to silently congratulate myself on such a fine shot, my big bull jumped back up. He staggered for a moment, clearly wounded, but before I could get another shot away, he was running with big, powerful leaps towards the shore and then almost straight up the rocky cliffs overhanging the frozen lake.

There was that tough-luck smile on Joe's face. "You'll have to go after him."

I ran through the snow hoping to get a second shot, but the caribou had disappeared. I had no choice but to follow him up the steep bluff. In most places the snow was waist deep, and the big bull didn't even break a trail for me. All he left were widely spaced holes in the snow marking his leaps and bounds.

After several hundred metres, I reached a narrow ledge. The caribou was lying there, close enough for me to hear his breathing and to see the clouds of steam from his nostrils hanging in a frozen cloud above his head. The animal was as exhausted as I was.

I dropped to my knees and snapped the rifle to my shoulder, but with my heart pounding, my lungs heaving and my hands shaking from exhaustion, I couldn't hold it steady. As I lowered the barrel towards the bull caribou, my shaking hand accidentally hit the trigger and the bullet went flying a few feet over his head.

The big animal lurched to his feet, found his second wind, and shot further up the bluff and out of sight. I followed, wading ever more slowly through waist-deep snow. After another few hundred metres, I came to another ledge, where once again I found the caribou lying down looking at me.

We stared at each other, eye to eye, for several minutes. I didn't want to make the same mistake, and it seemed that as long as I didn't move, neither would he. When my heart stopped pounding, I removed my heavy gloves, checked my rifle, aimed carefully and shot him through the head, killing him instantly.

This wasn't the first time I'd shot an animal. Growing up in Nova Scotia, I had hunted deer with my father. The practice was to bleed the animal where it fell, then drag it out of the bush, tie it across the hood of the car and drive home by the longest route, to give everyone a chance to view the fine trophy. But here there was no way to drag this heavy creature down the slope, over huge boulders and through snow three feet deep.

I was pondering my situation when Joe's son James arrived. "Dad said to see if you need help."

Needing help was an understatement! I confessed to the boy that I hadn't skinned an animal in the wild before. We'd always hung them in the barn.

"Do you watch your father skin caribou?" I asked.

"Oh yes."

"Well, James, you tell me what he does."

And so he began giving me instructions, repeating the steps he had already learned from his dad. Together we cleaned, skinned and quartered the caribou.

It took us two trips each, up and down the rock face, to get the caribou down from the cliff. Thankfully, as we broke a trail, it got easier.

Joe met us at the bottom, where he had also been busy. He had both his caribou gutted, skinned, quartered and packed in the back of his truck. As we loaded the rest, I was grateful to be bringing meat home to my family, but for days after, I felt the agony of the ordeal; every muscle and joint of my body ached.

Those years we worked together in the early to mid-1970s were a politically explosive period across the Northwest Territories. Our reporting often centred on quarrelling among the Indian Brotherhood of the Northwest Territories (later the Dene Nation), the NWT Métis Association, and the federal and territorial governments. Sometimes the battle lines were drawn along racial and organizational lines—the Dene and Métis on one side, the governments on the other. Just as frequently, there was infighting between the two Indigenous organizations or among political factions within each.

Joe and I would help each other. I passed on my knowledge and interpretation of what the governments were doing or, just as often, not doing. He kept me informed of Dene politics and interpreted the words, and the nuances, of the Dene languages so that I knew what was being said.

Like Jonah had done for the Inuit audience, Joe had to grapple with technical terms, such as how to translate pipeline, oil well and space shuttle into Dene languages. This was not a new challenge for him, as he had already become quite an expert in developing and adapting words and phrases to explain English-language medical and health terms.

When the Russian satellite Kosmos 954 fell on our heads in the gripping cold winter of 1978, we knew we had a major story on our hands. Pieces of the satellite were scattered over hundreds of kilometres, some within forty kilometres of Yellowknife. The first question was whether the satellite's reactor had burned up entering the atmosphere, or if there were radioactive pieces out on the ice of Great Slave Lake. And if there were, what was the risk?

For the first couple of days, it seemed every radio and TV station in the world wanted a piece of the story. But once the major national and international TV networks got their people on the ground in Yellowknife, we went back to covering the local angles and concerns, which revolved around the health threat for residents and the wildlife that so many of them depended on.

In the middle of the pandemonium, I was directed by the CBC station manager to go to the Canadian military's northern region headquarters, where the brass were very upset with Joe's reporting. When I arrived one of the senior officers came straight to the point: "We believe Joe Tobie is causing unnecessary public panic and concern."

"How is Joe Tobie causing panic?" I wanted to know.

"The way he is translating this situation," replied the officer, explaining that in the Native languages Joe's translation of "radioactivity" was "poison air."

I couldn't believe my ears. For two days and nights, in a dozen or more reports, I had repeatedly used the word "radioactive," always wondering, Do people really understand what it means? Joe had answered my question.

I told the army bigwig, "Not only do I support Joe Tobie, but tonight in my report, I am going to use the same terminology. You can't see radioactivity or smell it or feel it. 'Poison air' seems to be a very accurate way of describing it."

Professionally, Joe was a steady nine-to-five, Monday-to-Friday worker, with his roots firmly planted in the traditional Dene economy—hunting, trapping and fishing. He lived in Dettah, a small Dogrib village across Yellowknife Bay. It was about a thirty-kilometre drive around the bay in summer and fall, over very bad gravel roads.

For several years, the government had tried unsuccessfully to relocate the people of the village to Yellowknife. The bureaucrats had some limited success, basically by withholding services including electricity, schooling and road maintenance. Still, most residents stayed in the village, including Joe and his wife, Helen.

In 1970, the North's centennial year, Queen Elizabeth came to town. Chief Joseph Sangris asked Her Majesty through his trusted interpreter (none other than Joe Tobie) if she could provide the community with electricity. Did she pass on the message? No one knows except Her Majesty, but the chief's request marked a turning point.

The territory's government had moved from Ottawa only three years earlier. Yellowknife became the new capital instead of Fort Smith. Several families in Dettah who refused to move were getting increasingly vocal. Slowly, services returned, including a two-room school, electricity and improvements to the road system. Even the winter road across the frozen Yellowknife Bay on Great Slave Lake began to get regular plowing and maintenance.

That ice road cut Joe's daily commute by two-thirds. Every year in late November he would be the first out on the lake with his steel pick, sounding the ice for thickness. He would be seen doing the same thing in April when it began to thaw, and every year he was the first and last to cross.

Whether he was checking life-and-death ice thickness or broadcasting, Joe was not one to make mistakes and never one to boast about his accomplishments. I had known Joe for several years before I learned he had been a Canadian dog-racing champion at a time when the national competitions were held in Edmonton. He only smiled when I asked him about it, saying, "Yes, I won a couple of times, but I also lost." The last time he competed, defending his title, he told me he was in the lead after the first two days but didn't race on the final day. "I was just too hungover."

A week after my first caribou hunt with Joe, he came over to my desk in the newsroom. "We are out of caribou meat," he said, "and I am going hunting tomorrow. Do you want to come?"

I asked, "How the hell can you be out of caribou meat already? We shot three last week."

"I gave it to the elders," he explained. "There are a lot of old people in the village."

And so the next day we were off again, heading northeast of Yellowknife to a place called Victory Lake. The first forty kilometres, to Tibbitt Lake, we drove by truck, and then we travelled another forty or so by snowmobile, over frozen lakes and barely discernible portages through the bush.

Joe showed me how to find the trail markers—just a slash on a tree about four feet above the ground. He left nothing to chance. A couple of times every hour, he would reach inside his parka and take out a well-worn topographical map, check our surroundings and confirm our location on the map, then look for the next marker.

We were travelling with only the one snowmobile. I had thought about what might happen if we were to break down, but I knew there was no cause to worry. For one thing, we had tools and Joe had the skills to make basic repairs. More importantly, we were equipped to survive, with sleeping bags, a tarp for a tent, axes, extra food, and above all Joe's knowledge and experience on the land.

We found a small herd of about a dozen caribou on a small lake. They were relatively easy pickings, and we each dropped three or four before the remaining animals scattered. This time, it was one of Joe's caribou that staggered to its feet and began running towards the bush.

"Well," I smiled, "you're going to have to go after it."

He strapped on his snowshoes, slipped into a small backpack with his knives, and headed out, soon a tiny dot on the frozen lake. Then he disappeared into the bush. I set about the skinning process. I finished the first animal, no sign of Joe. I started on the second, then the third. Still no sign of him. The day was wearing on, so I moved on to the next and then the next. I was wondering what my best course of action would be if Joe was not back by dark, when I saw him coming towards me, moving slowly with his back bent.

He had tracked the wounded animal for about two hours before he caught up and was able to finish him with one shot. He'd cleaned the carcass out, boned much of it to bring down the weight, fashioned a backpack from the hide, and then carried the meat from the whole animal back. Given that he didn't stand more than about five foot eight and weighed maybe 160 pounds, his hiking several miles in snowshoes with about a hundred pounds on his back was an impressive feat. Not bad for a radio announcer. We packed the quarters, ribs, heads and skins onto large toboggans, lashed them tight, then towed them back behind the snowmobile.

Another winter morning, Joe and I had the good fortune to witness one of the great wildlife spectacles of the Arctic—indeed, of the world. We had travelled about fifteen kilometres beyond the end of the road on two snowmobiles, each hauling a toboggan, and were slowly picking our way across a rough portage through deep snow.

As we came down the slope onto a lake a good fifteen kilometres long, there in front of us we saw the whole Bathurst caribou herd in full migration. There were animals by the tens and tens of thousands, running at a moderate pace, somewhat alarmed by our presence but not panicked. It never crossed our minds to start shooting. This was something to witness.

We swung our snowmobiles in a wide arc around the back end of the herd and began driving parallel to the caribou, travelling about twenty kilometres an hour. It took us more than ten minutes to reach the front of the animals—that migrating herd was at least eight kilometres long. At the time wildlife experts estimated the herd at 300,000 animals. Neither of us had ever seen anything like it.

We let the herd pass, still in awe, and then we got down to the business of hunting the stragglers. I don't know how many we shot that day, but it was certainly all we could skin and haul. The community freezer in Joe's little village was again well stocked.

In the years after I left Yellowknife, working on Parliament Hill and later in Alberta, I returned north countless times to cover stories for the *National*. Many of these trips afforded me a visit with Joe. One story was about long-overdue changes in the northern education system, which until then had generally ignored Indigenous values and traditions.

We were going to visit a small school in a town called Rae-Edzo, now Behchokǫ̀, about a hundred kilometres from

Yellowknife. I asked Joe to join us, knowing he had friends there. He always liked to get out of the studio and do some community reporting, but we also wanted to spend the day together.

We were speeding along the frozen gravel of the Mackenzie Highway when we spotted a black dot moving far ahead of us.

"What's that?" I asked. "A raven?"

"Too big for a raven—maybe a bear," Joe said.

"Too small for a bear," I replied, as we continued to speed along. Then, for the first time in my life, I learned that Joe Tobie could get excited.

"It's a wolverine!" he shouted, bouncing in his seat. "A wolverine! Get him, get him! He's worth four hundred bucks!"

We were now almost on top of the animal, which was running full speed on the left shoulder, apparently thinking that it could outrun a Ford LTD station wagon down a straight gravel road.

It was wrong. I put the front wheel over its head, killing the animal faster than any steel trap or bullet. As I picked it up, I could feel its broken neck. I stowed it in the back of the station wagon, on top of our gear.

As we drove away, I looked in the rear-view mirror and spotted the wide eyes of my TV crew from Ottawa. Finally, one of them blurted out, "Joe, are you sure this thing is dead?"

Joe's face creased in a thin smile. "I hope so," he said.

When we got to the school, the principal apologized that his cultural teacher was away.

I asked, "If he were here, would he do a lesson in skinning a wolverine?"

"Of course," said the teacher, "but where would we ever get a wolverine?"

"Well," I said, "not only do I have a wolverine in the car, but I brought you a great substitute teacher as well."

The classroom was outdoors and the temperature was minus twenty-five, but the kids stood quietly in a circle to watch as Joe Tobie, with a surgeon's skill, began at the claws and gently stripped the fur from the animal, all the time telling the children, in their language, about the wolverine's place in their culture, including the fact that the animal is seen as an enemy.

A single wolverine, he explained, can destroy a hard-working trapper's whole season. They rob the traps and are cunning enough to avoid being caught themselves.

When I asked Joe later what he'd done with the four hundred bucks from the pelt, he simply replied, "Easy come, easy go." It turned out that when he got home and showed it to his wife, Helen, one of Yellowknife's most sought after seamstresses, she'd grabbed it right out of his hand.

"Joe," she said, "that is just what I need." That very day Helen had got an order to sew a new parka for someone who specified they wanted wolverine trim on the hood.

As well as I thought I knew Joe, and as close as our friendship had become, it was only after many adventures together that I met the real man. We'd been hunting at Victory Lake. We had shot a few animals and were taking a lunch break around a big fire. Our tea was hot. The bannock Helen had baked for us was tasty and we were enjoying the solitude and bright sunshine.

It was not uncommon for us to have long periods of silence, but Joe suddenly broke this one.

"I was born here," he said.

"Pardon?" I asked. I thought he was generalizing. "What do you mean you were born here?"

"Right here," he said. "Where we are having tea. This is where I was born. Our tents and cabins were here. That's why I like to come here." He continued, "See that little point there going out on the lake?"

We were facing south to get the warmth of the winter sun. It was, in fact, a very pretty spot, likely even more beautiful in the summer months.

"Yes, I see it," I said.

"There is a little girl buried there. She was about five years old when she died, and she was my friend and playmate. When I was about seven, I was taken away and sent to a residential school in Fort Resolution. I never saw my parents again." He fell silent.

By this time, we had known each other for close to ten years. We had travelled together to every part of the Northwest Territories and all across Canada reporting and covering the Mackenzie Valley Pipeline Inquiry—we knew and shared secrets that we will keep right to the end—and yet he'd waited until now to tell me in a few short sentences this remarkable story of a very painful childhood.

He never again mentioned the residential school. I never learned if he was ill-treated. But I knew, in that moment, I had been given the privilege of becoming a confidant to a fine gentleman and a friend.

Even today, when I hear of the abuses and the injustices of those residential schools, my mind goes back to that sunlit clearing on Victory Lake so far from any town and village. I try to imagine a time in the late 1940s when the authorities took a small boy from his parents, who would never see him again.

Some people would become bitter and resentful against all white people over that kind of pain and injustice. There are people like that, and I understand why they would feel that way. But that was not Joe Tobie's way.

6

NORTHERN LIGHTS AND WINE

At Life's Crossroads

Her name was June and she used to work behind the bar at the Canadian Legion in Yellowknife. I am not sure if I ever knew her last name, but I'll never forget her warm eyes and gentle manner. She was the kind of person who puts the tender in bartender.

The last time I saw her, in the late fall of 1981, she was not pouring drinks, but rather dishing up food on an offshore oil drilling rig in the Beaufort Sea. She was working behind the steam table, and the man she was serving was Canada's prime minister, Pierre Trudeau.

Trudeau was there to visit a Dome Petroleum oil rig in the Beaufort Sea off Tuktoyaktuk, promoting his government's controversial National Energy Program. At the time Canadian taxpayers were paying eighty cents of every dollar that was spent on northern oil and gas exploration. The goal (and the gamble) was to tap the huge potential of the Arctic regions. It never happened, and here we are decades and half-a-dozen prime ministers later, and the quest for those Arctic riches continues.

I was in that oil-rig food line, two or three people behind Trudeau, reporting on this northern visit for the *National*. When June saw me, she dropped her ladle.

"Whit!" she said. "You made it! I am so happy for you!"

And then she was around the counter hugging me, and I was hugging her back. I'm not sure what the people around us thought, but I didn't care. She was a special person and seeing her brought back a critical turning point in my young life. Ten years earlier, June had poured me a double rye with a small splash of water.

Some people take time to become an alcoholic. Not me. I was a natural, right from the beginning, and had had trouble with alcohol since my teenage years. Back then, I believed that the only problem I had with alcohol was figuring out how to get a steady supply of it. One imperative drove me: When can I have the next drink?

I still remember June looking at me as I wrapped my hand around that glass of rye. I got it halfway to my lips, then set it back on the bar. She already knew what I was starting to figure out. I was a twenty-nine-year-old wreck.

I remember slowly pushing it back towards her. "I can't do it, June. I've got to get help."

She said, "Yes, you should."

I knew I had to make a life-changing decision, but I didn't know which way to go. In the deepest recesses of my heart and head, I knew that if I didn't stop drinking immediately, that very day, I wouldn't have another chance at recovery and redemption.

In the days and weeks and months that followed, I never went back to see June. I never went back to thank her. I still regret that. It should have been easy to just drop by; a half-dozen times every day—on the way to work, on the way home, on errands or visiting friends—I had to fight with the steering wheel of my old car to turn it away from the friendly sanctuary of the Legion's downstairs bar on Yellowknife's 50th Avenue. I would joke to friends that my old car had been programmed to go to that location. Of course, it was me who'd been programmed.

My last day as a drunk was a Saturday in 1971. I'd gotten up early and had been drinking all morning, at first alone and then with a neighbour who eventually passed out. By midafternoon, I should have been out of it too, but instead, I was in the middle of realizing that the drinking had to end.

I kept plotting how to get out of the house, but for once I didn't have the energy to start another confrontation with my wife. Dianne knew that if I went out, she would be alone again until the middle of the night when I would come staggering in, and she was not buying my story that I had to go out for a few minutes.

I couldn't do the fight, but I could lie. Right after supper, I told Dianne I was going for help. I cleaned myself up, went out the door, and instantly headed for the Legion without confrontation or shouting. How clever.

It's not like I hadn't been warned about the impact of my drinking. A year earlier, Health Canada was doing a national study of the health of Canadians. Several thousand people were randomly chosen in every part of the country. I don't recall how many people were chosen in Yellowknife, but I was one of them. We would each get a thorough medical exam, and from those results, Health Canada would be able to create a picture of the nation's health.

I was leaving the school auditorium that was being used as a temporary examination room after my checkup when a boyish-looking doctor asked if he could have a word with me. He led me behind a curtain, where he told me that what he was about to say was not part of the study—it was an off-the-record discussion just between us. I was a reporter. I knew what "off the record" meant. Then he laid it out. I was under thirty and already a physical wreck.

My blood pressure was at a dangerous level. I was seriously overweight. Smoking had aggravated my chronic bronchitis to the point where I had very little lung capacity. I couldn't take a deep breath without breaking into uncontrollable coughing. He said, "You can't maintain this lifestyle. If you do, you will kill yourself at a very young age."

Little did he know the level to which I could take denial. How could there be a problem? Didn't I just get another promotion? Didn't I just get great praise from my boss and didn't he put it in writing? What about that great story I broke last week, the one the national radio news made such a fuss about? Besides, look at how many great friends I have.

In the early years, booze was fun; yesterday's drunken antics were the next morning's laugh. Nothing was serious, neither the drinking nor me.

One time while I was in Frobisher Bay, Ted Morris decided that we needed to have a different kind of early evening program, which he called *Northern Lights and Wine*. He insisted that we play soft music, violins and light classics—a poor programming decision in a frontier town where only 10 percent of the population were non-Inuit, and Inuit mostly favoured country music, folk and rock, in that order.

Back then, I had convinced myself that I was a much better broadcaster after a few stiff ones, thinking that I was more relaxed and entertaining. I frequently stopped at the old navy mess for a couple of bracers before my shift. One evening I "overcompensated" by a couple of ounces. When it came time for me to host *Northern Lights and Wine*, what came over the air was loud fiddles and me shouting, "Good evening! Forget *Northern Lights and Wine*. We are going for something a little stronger . . ."

Thankfully, Ted was out of town or I would have been fired. For a while after that, I kept my head down, waiting for the embarrassment to blow over. It became my pattern: a screw-up, followed by remorse, followed by resolving "never again," followed by another screw-up.

Back then I told myself I was having great fun, but the truth is that I can't remember any real fun or enjoyment. I can't remember it because it wasn't there. What remains real are guilt and remorse, and memories of waking up so many times knowing that once again I'd embarrassed myself and my family, and probably my friends, and thrown away money that we needed for food and household bills.

There were out-of-control months when I tried to drink and stay sober at the same time. I switched from beer to wine, then to hard liquor. I would change from rum to scotch and finally to rye, somehow trying to convince myself that the real problem was the flavour, not the alcohol content.

In the spring of 1970 or 1971 (see how well I remember those times?), I was driving home after a long day of work and an even longer night of drinking. In my booze-soggy mind, I rationalized that driving would be okay if I drove slowly, staying in first or second gear. Four or five blocks from my house, I saw in my headlights a man in a uniform with a raised arm. I slammed on the brake and lurched to a stop. The car stalled. I hadn't disengaged the clutch.

I rolled down the window.

"Get out of the car, sir," he said.

"I can't," I replied.

"Sir, I am asking that you get out of the car."

To which I responded, "I can't get out of the car because I am too drunk."

One more time he said, "Get out of the car," and then he said something I didn't expect.

"You are driving an unregistered vehicle. Your plates are expired, and I am going to drive you home." And it was true. My plates had expired, just hours before he stopped me.

The constable, whose name I did not know, helped me into the police car, wrote me a ticket, and told me to appear before the justice of the peace in the morning to face a charge of driving an unregistered vehicle.

The justice of the peace imposed the routine $10 fine and $3.50 in court costs, payable forthwith. I didn't have the money. I asked for fifteen minutes to go to the bank. He said pay now or spend three days in jail. I avoided a cell only because one of the lawyers in attendance loaned me the $13.50.

I knew how lucky I had been. A drunk-driving charge would likely have led to my dismissal from the CBC. Not to mention that I could have injured or killed someone—though at the time I barely gave any thought to that. Here was my paradox.

The drinking constantly put my job on the line, but the job facilitated and justified the boozing.

For example, my decision to move to the North made it easier to drink. There were always gatherings, conferences, dinners and other functions offering a story and, more importantly, free booze. Many people at the time (and I was among them) regarded the North as the last frontier, which meant a place for hard, constant, two-fisted drinking. Sadly, as I see it through my clearer eyes today, not a lot has changed. Alcohol remains a scourge of the North.

Part of my recovery is not to preach or condemn, but the facts speak for themselves. The rate of violent crime in the North is ten times the national average, and alcohol is a factor in 90 percent of those crimes. Sexual abuse of youth is also ten times the national average; the same for youth suicide. Treatment facilities, rehab programs and counselling initiatives are virtually non-existent in most communities.

It is undeniable that rapid growth, cultural dislocation and the horrifying physical, mental and sexual abuse inflicted through the residential schools have left a damaged society. Read the testimony from people who appeared before the Truth and Reconciliation Commission (TRC). You can't deny that it is anything but the cruellest part of Canada's history. And alcohol has been an almost constant theme in that story.

It's part of my story too. I hardly ever considered the toll on my family of all those days, nights and lost weekends. Dianne endured with three small children, while I worked to drink and drank to work.

I can still remember sitting at my kitchen table trying to clear my head, when I heard, on the kitchen radio, the familiar voice of Rex Loring on the *World at Eight*. "In the Northwest Territories," he said, "blah blah . . . Yellowknife . . . blah blah . . . Natives . . . development . . ." Then came the chilling words: "For a report here is Whit Fraser in Yellowknife."

It was terrifying: I had no recollection of gathering, writing or filing that story. It was as much news to me as to anyone else. But there I was. It was my voice I was hearing.

This happened not once, but twice. Both times I rushed to the CBC to get to the newsroom before my co-workers. I would find the script on the cluttered desk and look it over. There was barely a word spelled correctly, yet my delivery was more than passable. I would listen again to the tape as all the while my mind was racing. *Where did this story come from? Did I make it up? Is it true?*

Then came the stomach-churning process of checking with whoever was named or quoted in the story. I'd call them up and ask, "Did you hear the piece?"—waiting for them to say, "What kind of idiot are you, misquoting me like that?" Or even to issue an outright denial. Thankfully it never happened.

There's also a mystery that I have never been able to solve: there was nothing in my childhood that should have led to my condition. As a kid, I was never abused. Both my parents gave me unconditional love. They guided me rather than disciplined me, and outright punishment was not part of my upbringing.

When I was a young man, I remember my hard-working and loving mother ironed my underwear. Because of the places my father took me and the lessons he taught me, I had the skills to hunt with Joe Tobie and fish with Mary's brothers. I was at home in the northern wilderness because my dad made sure I could shoot a rifle, paddle a canoe, chop a tree and light a fire.

My drinking was my own doing. But perhaps it was the love I got as a kid that eventually allowed me to accept that my life was out of control and to do something about it. So let me go back to the moment I put my rye and water back on the bar in front of June the bartender.

The next morning was a Sunday. Before 10 a.m., two old drinking pals were at my door. One was a colleague from CBC and the other a prominent Yellowknife lawyer. They were already well in their cups and carrying a case of beer; they'd had beer for breakfast and one more for dessert. I didn't let them in the door.

"I am not drinking," I said. "I quit, and what's more I am going to get help." They laughed and left.

I thought it would be a good idea if I just got out of town. It was a beautiful day. Dianne packed a big picnic basket, the three kids and the dog into the car, and we all went for a family outing.

I drove past the ever-popular Prelude Lake campground, knowing that temptations would abound at the half-dozen campsite and picnic tables frequented by the city's partiers. I drove all the way to Tibbitt Lake, at the end of the road that extends east of Yellowknife, believing no one would be there. I was about to learn my first lesson, on my first day sober: there is no escape from alcoholic opportunity.

As we unloaded the car and walked towards the lake, I heard a familiar voice: "Whit Fraser, you old son-of-a-bitch, come and have a drink." Was I hallucinating?

Was that my old friend from Frobisher Bay? It was, and he was sitting in a folding lawn chair with what appeared to be two or three cases of wine stacked beside him. He was holding a bottle in his hand. No glass, just sipping straight from the bottle.

"Come and have a drink." He motioned with his arm.

"Get back in the car," I said to everybody. In seconds I was spinning my wheels out of there. We found a pretty spot with a lichen-covered rock by the side of the road. We had our peaceful family picnic and I made it through day one. Ten years later, I was ten years sober and standing on an oil rig hugging the bartender who'd encouraged me to get help.

June had only spoken those three words to me when I said I had to get help: "Yes, you should!" But it was her action that spoke volumes. Most bartenders serve the drink and move away. She had stood directly in front of me, keeping her eye on a guy she realized was pumping his handcart to hell.

Though I never went back to the Legion bar to thank her, I'll say it now. *Thank you, June.*

7

WARM MEMORY FROZEN IN TIME

The Lull Before the Storm

Fifty years later I can still hear it. A church bell—the purest sound I have ever heard. Its source was the steeple of a tiny Arctic church, and angels themselves could not have produced anything sweeter.

In the midwinter of 1970, I was covering a series of visits by government officials across the central and High Arctic, one of those unending "consultation tours" that were not consultation at all, but rather, here's-what-we-have-decided-will-be good-for-you-because-it's-good-for-us community briefings. Were it not for the bell, I would not even recall the story.

The temperature was minus forty or colder. I would later learn from Abe Okpik that long before Mr. Celsius or Mr. Fahrenheit, Inuit measured the cold by the sounds under their feet. We can all do that. When it's a bit below freezing, the snow crunches sometimes quite loudly as you walk or run. Below that, there are varying levels of "squeaky cold." At minus forty, your footsteps produce a high-pitched squeak as your toes bend through the step. At minus forty and colder, the squeak is at its highest and shortest.

Despite the cold, that evening in Holman, now Ulukhaktok, on Victoria Island on the western High Arctic coastline of the Northwest Territories, begged for a walk, under waves of magnificent northern lights and stars. The sound under my feet was so high pitched it was like the squeaking of little mice.

The difference between photojournalists and radio reporters is simple. When photojournalists go for a walk, they usually carry a camera. When this radio reporter went for that walk, he left the thirty-pound tape recorder behind.

But when I'd gone about a kilometre from the community, I wished I had brought that bulky old machine. In the clear night, I could see the lights of the tiny houses, the schoolhouse and other buildings, and most clearly the lights from the old runway that passed so close by the village it often doubled as the main street. Then in the middle of this stillness, a church bell rang, and I stopped breathing for a few seconds.

It rang again and again, an ancient sound that seeped right into my body and soul. Who was ringing the bell and why? Perhaps it was the parish priest, or someone else from the village, dressed for the extreme cold, standing beneath the glorious brass bell, fur mitts wrapped around its frozen rope as they pulled down slowly and purposefully.

There was no pattern. Sometimes there was only a single peal followed by a long silence, as though to allow time for it to find its way to the heavens to reverberate among the northern lights. Other times a series of two and three chimes added rhythm to the spectacular dancing columns of blue-green, yellow and red aurora that seemed to be trying to touch, even taste, the snow-white landscape.

If it was a special occasion, I didn't know what it was. Had there been a death in the village, we would have known, and the meeting would have been postponed or cancelled. I like to think that whoever rang the bell had simply heard the snow beneath their sealskin kamiks and decided it was a good night for the church bell.

Across this world, there are cities with great symphonies and the most gifted performers and musicians. In Ottawa, of course, the carillon from Parliament Hill can take a nation's breath away.

Maybe someday, somehow, on a clear winter's night—when the northern lights are at their brightest and there's nary a breath of breeze—a few of the people from those distant cities will have the chance to stand at the edge of Ulukhaktok in the very high Arctic when it is minus forty and hear the purest and sweetest sound. And marvel, as I did, at the magic of a single bell sounding in a tiny place beneath the northern lights.

Turbulence

"There Should Be No Pipeline Until the Land Claim Is Settled"

8

BULLDOZERS AND BIG DISHES

What's a Land Claim?

It was the federal government's own political and bureaucratic bulldozer approach towards Indigenous peoples that both dug and buried the first trench in the great northern pipeline debate and Aboriginal rights movement of the 1970s. Aboriginal rights in the country that became Canada were protected in British and, by constitutional extension, Canadian law by the Royal Proclamation of 1763. But during the turbulent 1970s, no one in the government of Canada was willing to recognize that fact or even discuss Aboriginal rights. And neither were the settlers serving corporate interests in the North.

Indigenous legal activists have brought us a long way since then. Consider that it was only recently that the Supreme Court of Canada ruled that the federal government has a legal and constitutional obligation to consult Indigenous peoples confronted with large-scale developments on their traditional lands.

Government policy papers released in 1969 and 1970 woke a sleeping giant that became the northern Aboriginal rights movement. A century or more of policies that perpetuated inequality, discrimination and marginalization across Indigenous lands and communities reached the breaking point.

The 1969 White Paper, called *Statement of the Government of Canada on Indian Policy*, was actually a government assimilation policy that outlined objectives for social and economic "equality" while proposing to eliminate the Department of Indian Affairs and Northern Development—the only voice Indigenous peoples had in the federal government of the day. The reaction from Indigenous peoples in Canada, as well as many in the larger society, was immediate, forceful and effective. Almost overnight, the National Indian Brotherhood, under George Manuel, became a potent political force.

Yet despite the growing protests and mounting legal challenges, the same government and department, only months later, in November 1969, released a second White Paper, also under the auspices of a young and aggressive cabinet minister, Jean Chrétien. In a speech to the Council of the Northwest Territories, the largely appointed legislative assembly, Chrétien declared that the vast, untapped riches of the North would be "developed in the interests of all Canadians."

Titles tell a story. In June 1968, Chrétien, a thirty-four-year-old from Shawinigan, Quebec, was chosen to join the first cabinet of Pierre Trudeau as minister of Indian affairs and northern development. That title—those two tasks on the same business card—tells us everything we need to know about the political push that led to the boom in northern resource development. Chrétien's marching orders were clear. Manage Indian affairs but, above all, develop the North.

Chrétien did change the North. He cast the die at the Elks Hall in Yellowknife, once the town's favourite dance hall and recently converted into the territorial legislative assembly. He had come north, White Paper in hand, to jump-start the heavy equipment of northern development. Along with his declaration about developing the riches of the North for "all Canadians," he promised oil and gas pipelines down the Mackenzie River Valley and a highway that would extend from Fort Simpson all the way to the Arctic coast.

The two hundred or more people who crowded into the Elks Hall heard not a word from Chrétien about how Indigenous peoples would share the economic benefits and royalties from this great policy declaration. But they applauded anyway. Yellowknife was, after all, a mining town. People there understood development and felt they were part of the new and exciting "last frontier." More significantly, very few "Indians" or "Eskimos," as they were still called back then, were even invited to the event.

For a young reporter, new in the job, this was a very big story, and it suddenly seemed much bigger because it put me shoulder to shoulder with Norman DePoe, the biggest name in Canadian journalism at the time. He had come north to cover the event for CBC's the *National*. A kind and thoughtful man, Norman was also a legendary drinker. When we'd said hello the night before, during Chrétien's stopover in Fort Smith, on the Alberta border, I thanked him again for his help on the *Manhattan* saga.

We shared a bottle of rye whiskey and compared the stories we were filing. Norman's was an advance piece on Chrétien's upcoming speech. Mine was about a group of young Dene leaders who had been meeting in the Anglican Church basement to put a plan together to form the Indian Brotherhood of the Northwest Territories (destined to become the Dene Nation). After we filed our stories—mine to Yellowknife and his to Toronto—and poured one more glass, he predicted that, over the long haul, my story would have the greater impact on the North.

Norman was more than a great reporter. He was also a prophet. And he knew when to throw a colleague a lifeline. The next day I was supposed to do a live broadcast of a long-anticipated announcement on the future of the Northwest Territories. Norman agreed to co-host it, giving the broadcast solid credibility and journalistic depth.

Chrétien's speech was loudly and resoundingly applauded by the mainly white audience inside the Elks Hall. But outside it, in the tiny communities along the Mackenzie River and across the Arctic coast, Chrétien succeeded in escalating northern Indigenous discontent.

No doubt the 1968 discovery of a massive oil deposit at Prudhoe Bay in Alaska shaped Chrétien's policy paper. It certainly had a profound, immediate impact on Canadian energy policy. The geography and geology said if there was oil at Prudhoe, there was also oil and gas east of there, in the coastal waters of the Canadian Beaufort Sea. And, as a result, Canada got into the Arctic oil play with both feet and an open wallet.

The oil industry made a clear and forceful case for subsidization. Exploration in the Arctic was expensive. Industry would not underwrite national energy priorities. If the government, lured by the promise of Arabian-sized oil fields, wanted exploration, the government had better be prepared to pay for it.

And it was. Soon the federal government began pouring hundreds of millions of dollars into the North, most of it as tax incentives to oil and exploration companies, which were given an 80 percent write-off on every dollar they spent in the Arctic. Canadian taxpayers backed the High Arctic oil play that was clearly visible from the windows of every airplane flying across the vast region. Long lines of mobile work camps pulled along by caterpillar tractors crawled across the tundra or sea ice, reaching the most remote reaches of the High Arctic Islands. Straight lines and square patterns, cutting across the landscape, showed where explosives, deep in the ground or underwater, had been detonated to reveal the geologic formations.

While they were discovering significant deposits of both oil and gas, the explorers showed little respect for the land's traditional lifestyles or livelihoods. Soon, resentments festered and fermented, tapping into a deep history of colonial exploitation of the north. Similar drilling activity was underway in the Beaufort Sea, where Dome Petroleum was building islands to serve as drilling platforms rather than use ships or floating rigs.

Battle lines, Native rights versus development, were now drawn across the frozen ground.

One of the most dramatic physical signs of all this activity were the massive round faces of the communication satellite dishes across the horizon. I remember taking a long flight to one of the most remote of the Arctic drilling sites with Charles

Hetherington, president of Panarctic Oils. "We told the government directly," he said, "that if they wanted Arctic exploration, we needed daily communications with the rest of Canada and the world." It was a simple matter of safety, logistics, economics and management.

At the time, no one realized how important these communication networks would be for Indigenous organizations and the political future of northern Canada. Suddenly, young Indigenous leaders in remote villages and towns could speak to one another. The tool that the oil companies had demanded to make exploration possible was the same tool that allowed these leaders to begin organizing and communicating with one another.

In the autumn of 1971, I was banging away with four fingers on an old Olympic typewriter in my Yellowknife newsroom—maybe a hundred square feet and cluttered with papers, old scripts, tape recorders, editing machines and stacks of audiotape reels—when a thin young man in a striped shirt walked in the door. Tagak Curley took a seat beside my desk, introduced himself, and told me he was "organizing the Eskimos" to demand a land claim settlement.

I had at least heard of him; he was a member of the NWT Indian-Eskimo Association that had been set up by the federal government to provide advice on social and cultural matters. It had no powers and answered directly to the government. It's fair to say that although its members were serious about change, the organization was little more than federal window dressing. But as I told him, I didn't know what the hell a land claim settlement was.

We talked for some time. It was clear to Tagak and a few others that Inuit were under siege. He recognized the impact the Dene had made with the Indian Brotherhood. New measures and independent voices needed to be heard. I put the microphone under his chin and that night aired a short piece on another organization entering the development debate—another perspective in the gathering clash of development versus rights.

Tagak got his message out in a way that he had been unable to do before, and most importantly, he was heard far beyond the political and business circle he had wanted to hear him. People in every northern community were also able to respond to his ideals and debate his vision among themselves, as cold but exciting winds of change began to blow across the Arctic.

The more development money and investors poured in, the more a growing vocal Indigenous community protested; a new, potentially vicious circle shaped the Arctic. The more the Dene, Inuit and Métis protested, the more determined the developers became to protect their investments.

Four simple and ill-considered words from the mouth of the commissioner of the Northwest Territories, Stuart Hodgson, helped spark Indigenous unrest just as much as Ottawa's assimilation policies. "I am the government," he declared.

His nickname, which he wore with pride, was Omingmak—the Muskox. It suited his bull-like approach to life, to work and to northern development. The implication was clear. Hodgson was saying, I am the government because this is a colony of Ottawa and I'm the guy in charge. And on one level he was right. He was the head of a territorial legislative advisory council and nothing happened without his approval. His connections and the unwavering support of Minister Chrétien and Prime Minister Trudeau made his position appear even stronger. Often it was not clear whether Hodgson was doing Trudeau and Chrétien's bidding, or whether it was the other way around.

In his time, most of the day-to-day management of the North remained in the hands of the commissioner. Until 1967, the Northwest Territories had been administered out of Ottawa. Hodgson had moved "his" government in a charter airplane to Yellowknife. He had a handful of employees and responsibility for an area amounting to one-third of Canada, populated by about thirty thousand people in fifty communities. From 1967 to 1979, he micromanaged and controlled the Northwest Territories with a combination of personality, persuasion and an iron fist.

There can be no denying that his ramrod personality lifted the North higher in the national and political consciousness. He cut a swath that left some in the media and on his staff with the impression that the federal minister and deputy minister of northern affairs worked for him. Rather than the other way around. Hodgson, a public servant, travelled by chartered jet plane; if the plane or the pilots or the company he had leased it from didn't please him, he would simply get another.

He persuaded the Queen and members of the Royal Family to make more than one visit to the North. On his routine commissioner's tours, he always brought along influential people, such as publisher Mel Hurtig and author Mordecai Richler, and writers from major newspapers like the *Toronto Star*, Vancouver *Province*, *Edmonton Journal* and *Globe and Mail*. There was always room for local media too. Were it not for

Hodgson, I would never have set foot in many of the most remote northern communities or seen first-hand the High Arctic oil play.

"Stu," as he was widely known, took a high level of personal satisfaction in showcasing the vast oil and gas discoveries in the High Arctic Islands. He revelled in the uncapping of a gas well at Rae Point as it released a blazing blowtorch two hundred metres into the clear, cold Arctic air. An impressive photo op for sure, but one that may have backfired because it also allowed Indigenous peoples to see physical evidence of the great untapped resources that lay beneath their lands.

And Hodgson was inconsistent in dispensing his favours. To me he never appeared comfortable in Dene communities. He generally resisted meeting band chiefs and councils, preferring instead to meet mayors and business leaders—depending on them to speak for the needs of the Dene communities within their boundaries.

I recall once, in the early 1970s, arriving with him in Wrigley, on the east bank of the Mackenzie River. The young chief, Gabe Hardisty, wanting to offer some local culture, pride and spirit, had arranged for a colourful dog team and toboggan to transport the commissioner from the landing strip into the tiny community of only a few hundred people. Hodgson was pissed off, saying he didn't want to smell another dirty old dog team, and jumped into a pickup truck instead.

But above the treeline and in the Arctic coastal communities, Hodgson was at ease. He found a visit to an iglu a great joy. He would take two or three weeks every year to visit Inuit communities, meeting with hunters and trappers' groups, community councils and leaders. He revelled in fixing the local problems, giving direction and providing money for biggish-ticket items such as a new water truck, a garage or a new schoolhouse.

Hodgson would sweep through the local carving shop, pointing out sculptures and other artwork, and ordering his assistant to arrange payment and packing. These he gave as gifts to visiting dignitaries, from politicians to royalty, or as donations to his dream of a northern heritage centre in Yellowknife.

My big knock against Stuart Hodgson is that he stayed in the job too long. I told him that directly some years after he stopped being commissioner, when circumstances had taken us both in different directions. In his first five years, he was a builder and promoter with no equal. No one could have accomplished more when it came to bringing the Arctic and the Northwest Territories to the attention of the nation. But in the years of crisis over northern development, he didn't stand up for northerners. He was openly critical of the strength and force of the Indigenous organizations, and he was publicly silent about an angry racist reaction, called White Power North of Sixty, to the growing Indigenous political movement. You would be hard-pressed to find many references to this organization today, but its leaders and spokespeople promoted a pull-yourself-up-by-your-bootstraps approach to life, believing that everybody should get only what they worked for. The concept of Aboriginal rights or title to lands based on historic ownership and law counted for nothing with them.

For months in the mid-1970s, White Power North of Sixty was in the local headlines and sometimes in the national papers. In my view, it did serve a purpose—it brought into full view the bitter racial divide that was never far beneath the surface.

In 1973, twenty-seven oil companies formed Canadian Arctic Gas and filed an application to build a pipeline down the Mackenzie River Valley. The Indian Brotherhood vowed to use whatever means possible to stop the pipeline. It did not rule out violence. The Dene were joined in opposition to the pipeline by Inuit, the Métis, and a growing environmental and political lobby across Canada. A new era, with new players with ancient roots, began to take shape.

There was turbulence well beyond the Mackenzie Valley and Northwest Territories too. The economic, social, environmental and political stakes concerning northern development were just as high or higher in Quebec, and protest and anger were growing across the country.

In 1971, Premier Robert Bourassa had announced phase one of the James Bay hydro project. It was, in the plainest terms, Quebec's economic blueprint for the next century. The plan required that several of the great northern Quebec rivers be dammed or diverted. Eight massive generation stations would be constructed. There would be construction jobs by the tens of thousands for Quebecers and an assured supply of clean hydro power for generations to come. Moreover, Quebec would have energy to export, which would pay the $13-billion price tag, a figure that at the time seemed unimaginable.

The project would flood an area in northern Quebec twice the size of Prince Edward Island. There were no consultations and no regard for Inuit and Cree who lived in the area and depended for their living on the land and its animals. In 1971, after all, the notion of Aboriginal rights or title had barely surfaced anywhere on the wide Canadian horizon.

That the Cree and Inuit of northern Quebec were most certainly going to take the province to court to block the development worried the federal government. So did its sagging performance in the polls and the frequently furious anti-development protests that were sweeping the country. In the 1972 election, the Liberal government was reduced to a minority.

While Ottawa couldn't control Hydro-Québec's massive James Bay development in northern Quebec, which was primarily a provincial initiative, the federal government certainly recognized the need for a referee in the Northwest Territories.

Ottawa passed the whistle to Justice Thomas Berger, a BC Supreme Court judge, asking him to write his own rules to cover a very broad mandate—an inquiry into the social, environmental and economic implications of a natural gas pipeline down the Mackenzie River Valley. I would have a ringside seat—even a bit part—in the remarkable chapter in the history of the North that followed.

9

STARS IN THE NORTHERN LIGHTS

Principles Before Personalities

"Are your guys ready?" the producer for CBC's the *National* asked.

"Yes, we're ready," I said.

Considering that none of the "guys" had ever been on television before and we had only thirty minutes in which to package four on-camera reports—both the questions and answers—the schedule seemed absurd to the experienced technicians standing by, all of them about to go on lunch break. Nobody in their right mind would try to record twenty minutes of on-camera narration in a mere thirty minutes. After all, they'd spent the last couple of hours recording various thirty- and forty-second takes from Lloyd Robertson, the best in the business, for that night's *National*.

The producer put his foot down. "We are going to do this," he said, and then turned to me. "Who's first?"

Who better than Joe Tobie to launch Indigenous-language reporting on the Mackenzie Valley Pipeline Inquiry on northern television? Hollywood handsome, with streaks of silver in his jet-black hair, dark eyes and a soft, rich voice, he was made for television. Joe looked straight into the lens and spoke in Dogrib for exactly five minutes. He didn't pause, stammer or waiver, setting a benchmark that the corporation would not be able to back away from. Not that it ever tried to.

Joe then passed the microphone to Abe Okpik, who had been the first Inuit member of the old NWT council before it became known as the legislative assembly. He had also been a government administrator, trapper and trader, and only three years earlier had undertaken a project that had changed the North and that would earn him the Order of Canada.

Like Joe, he delivered five minutes on the button, with no flaws and no retakes, explaining the purpose of the inquiry, what to expect, and the key issues for Inuit.

Fort Norman's Louie Blondin, barely twenty and our Slavey-language broadcaster, wasn't even supposed to be there. A dog sled misfortune several years earlier had led him to develop severe arthritis, which paralyzed his hips and left him unable to walk without crutches.

I actually had recruited his father, John. But a few days before the inquiry began, this young guy turned up in front of me, saying, "My dad sent me. He thinks I can do the job better than he can."

I asked, "Can you do it?"

"Yes."

"Are you sure?"

"Yes," he said, looking me straight in the eye.

I believed him.

Now he propped himself up on the edge of a table, setting his crutches aside but not out of the picture. Until that point in his life, he had never spoken in public, let alone appeared on television. I pointed my finger, the camera went on, the recording light lit up and so did Louie. His voice was clear and exact, and his face, eyes and hands were animated; he radiated television confidence and presence and delivered exactly five minutes. One take!

One to go, the elder, the Reverend Jim Edward Sittichinli of Aklavik. Thirty years in the pulpit for the Anglican Church in northern Yukon and the Mackenzie Delta makes a skilled communicator. His delivery was captivating. Just when I was about to flash him a promised ten-seconds-to-go signal, he broke into English. "I just want to say good night to my grandchildren, but I have to do it in English because they don't speak our language. That is a shame, but it is also in part what this inquiry is about. This is Jim Edward Sittichinli reporting."

Four novice broadcasters had just delivered perfect performances that most seasoned broadcasters could not have equalled. In every corner of the conference room turned studio, people were applauding, including the anchor of the *National*. The technicians went to lunch on time.

The five-minute television reports, four in Indigenous languages, were one of the selling points in getting approval for a CBC Northern Service package covering the inquiry. From March 3, 1975 to November 19, 1976, we travelled up and down the Mackenzie Valley and the western Arctic, throughout Yukon and across Canada. Sixteen-hour days were common. No one quit, no one complained, and no one missed a deadline.

Television across northern Canada was in its infancy; since there were no production facilities in the North, programming came from the south. Yukon and the Northwest Territories received the Vancouver evening news. Some smart technical switching blacked out the BC weather forecast and inserted our five-minute Berger Inquiry reports, five nights a week, one in English and the rest in Indigenous languages. We took advantage of the temporary mobile facilities the network brought north for the opening day, but from then on, we recorded our reports on 16 mm film, stuffed them in a red bag and shipped them air express to Vancouver, where the film was developed, edited and packaged.

My report ran on Thursday nights, after a deep voice announced: "And now our report on the Mackenzie Valley Pipeline Inquiry. Tonight, Whit Fraser reports in English." The redundancy was amusing, but on the other evenings, it was refreshing for viewers to hear the news in Dogrib, Slavey, Gwich'in and Inuktitut.

As soon as it was announced, we knew the inquiry into the massive pipeline proposal would be a major story, and that as broadcasters we needed to be ready, even though we didn't know specifically what for. But when I answered the tiny Yellowknife newsroom's telephone one September afternoon in 1974, I wasn't expecting Raoul St. Julien, the station manager, to ask me to come to his office because Andrew Cowan wanted a word with me.

Cowan was the Northern Service director. I had never met him, just heard about him. Frankly, I was scared shitless. You couldn't get to the manager's office from the newsroom in the old CBC studios in Yellowknife. You had to go out onto the sidewalk, walk ten metres and enter through another door.

As I walked, I worried: What could he want with me? Cowan rarely visited the stations, preferring to meet his managers in Ottawa. Even more intimidating, I was aware of his name and reputation because I had heard it so many times in my childhood when my mother recalled the CBC's major radio war correspondents during the Second World War, a small list that included Matthew Halton and Andrew Cowan. I myself had heard his voice when listening to *Canada at War*, a once-popular radio series that pulled reports from the archives to document the war. One passage stayed with me from a night I spent in Frobisher Bay listening to an episode from the series. Cowan was describing the surrender of some German soldiers, in a clear, deep voice that brought his listener right into the scene: "When they came out of the bunkers, their hands in the air, the colour of their faces and the look in their eyes tell us these Germans have no more stomach for war."

I also remembered his voice from another broadcast barely six years earlier: "The Northern Service will not be successful until the Native people start bitching about our service and demand more." That impressed me too. Sounded like the voice of a radical. Believe me, at that time, nobody could say "bitching" on the CBC, except, I guess, Andrew Cowan.

Raoul made the introductions and I shook hands with Cowan, thinking he looked like the epitome of the Canadian establishment and yet wanted to hear the Native people "bitching." He was impeccably dressed in English tweeds, with mutton chop sideburns and moustache all neatly trimmed, and oh, so polite. "Thank you for coming in," he said. Then he told me he was trying to determine how we should cover the Berger Inquiry and asked whether I might have some ideas.

I was the senior reporter in a two-person newsroom in Yellowknife, responsible for covering the entire Northwest Territories. Most communities were just beginning to receive radio or television signals and basic telephone service, through a newly launched Anik satellite, and our broadcasting was at best a make-it-up-as-you-go undertaking. To that point, no one had asked me how we should go about anything, but I had some thoughts, which I shared with him. I said we needed to approach this as the biggest story that had ever unfolded in the North. I pointed to the current tensions, the strong statements made by the Indigenous organizations, and the possibility of violence if Native people were denied a proper hearing.

I sensed I had one thing in common with Cowan. We were both reporters. He lived and worked in Ottawa, but he had an ear to the chill northern winds and an old reporter's nose close to the cold ground. He also had his sources and, like all reporters, his opinions.

I said that our coverage must be done in all languages in a one-hour program every evening, giving each language about twelve minutes' airtime. I recommended a schedule where we could split our Mackenzie network lines and beam one language north to the Mackenzie Delta and Arctic coastal areas, and on the second line broadcast simultaneously to the Great Slave Lake area and southern Mackenzie, in English and Slavey. English, common across the North, would go on the full network. I also spoke of television possibilities.

Cowan began asking questions, but my mind had turned to more immediate concerns. I screwed up my courage. "Mr. Cowan, excuse me. You asked my opinion and I gave it to you. I am sorry, but I don't have the time to debate the merits—I have a newscast to prepare." I was short of material and the deadline was getting closer.

"Forgive me." The feared director was actually apologizing to me. Then he announced that Raoul would find an immediate replacement for me because I would be leaving with him for Ottawa in a few days to put together a detailed plan to bring my proposal into reality. I was once again in the deep end of a very cold pool. But this time I'd jumped, full of excitement and confidence. Andrew Cowan's words, and his presence, reassured me that I would be swimming with the current rather than against it.

In Ottawa, I began to develop a proposal setting out the political, social and economic imperatives to justify the expanded coverage and a million-dollar budget. One of my overly lengthy internal memos to Andrew and the managers outlined why we needed to pick the right people to do the job. "When I say, 'our people must be devoted,' I mean they will probably end up sleeping on the floor of the school or community hall for nights on end. Maybe they'll have to carry their pots and pans and prepare meals from tins bought at the Bay store." When Joe, Abe, Louie and Jim delivered those first remarkable TV segments, I knew I had the right guys.

After two weeks of planning and budget forecasting in the Ottawa headquarters, I handed the completed program proposal to Andrew and sat in front of his desk as he read it.

"This is good," he said. Then he shocked me by sliding the folder back across the table.

"I want you to present this to the vice-president this afternoon. A meeting is scheduled for three o'clock." Marcel Ouimet was the vice-president for special services—the person who determined what went forward and what didn't.

By now, I was comfortable with Andrew and asked him why he would send a young reporter from the boondocks to meet Ouimet. "Will he even take me seriously?"

"Marcel and I have known each other since the Second World War when we were war correspondents," he replied, and then he confessed the two of them couldn't be in the same room for five minutes without getting into an argument. He didn't want their old baggage to get in the way, but he also said he knew Ouimet would listen with an open mind. He added, "Wear your tie and when he challenges you, don't back down."

Ouimet did challenge me, and he also listened. Within a month, CBC made a formal funding request directly to the federal Treasury Board, and before the end of 1974, our million-dollar budget, a staggering amount for a broadcast venture at that time, was approved.

Berger's public hearings were scheduled to open in Yellowknife on March 3, 1975, leaving us barely two months to get ready—including hiring all the reporters—for this unprecedented and intimidating broadcast challenge. We were about to provide daily radio coverage of the inquiry in seven Indigenous languages—Chipewyan, Dogrib, North and South Slavey, Gwich'in, Eastern and Western Inuktitut—as well as English. It was a daunting task to find the people to do all of this and get them ready in a few short weeks.

Sometimes being in a remote location works in your favour. We could fly under the radar of human resource managers and unions and simply recruit the people we needed. I knew whom to hire first. Joe Tobie had impressed me from the moment we met. He was wise and gained the respect of everyone he met, and he was experienced. He was also fluently trilingual in English, Dogrib and Chipewyan, quite comfortable in Slavey and, as we would learn later, not a stranger to French.

Joe knew the politics, the players and the issues. More than that, he was known everywhere. He was already my friend and now he would become my fixer, my guide, my interpreter and my conscience.

By hiring one more great voice and mind, I covered two more languages—Eastern and Western Inuktitut. Abe Okpik, already a northern legend because of his Project Surname, was working for the territorial government in Iqaluit when he took my phone call. After he listened to my pitch, he responded with a swift "Eee" (or yes).

Abe was no stranger to the rigours of Arctic travel, having visited every community in the region to restore names to people who had been given government numbers. He met most of them in their homes, recorded their family names, and sometimes even helped them find family connections to determine the most appropriate name. Often he had to mediate family feuds when there were conflicting views about which side of a family the name choice should honour. When he returned with the inquiry, only a few short years after this remarkable accomplishment, Abe was greeted with respect, even admiration, in the Inuit and Inuvialuit communities on the Arctic coast. I certainly noticed it, and Berger must have seen it as well. Early in the inquiry, the judge nominated Abe Okpik for the Order of Canada, and he received the award from the governor general before the hearings were over.

Nellie Cournoyea, then the manager at CBC Inuvik, was the one who suggested that a seventy-year-old retired Anglican minister, Jim Edward Sittichinli, would be an asset to the team. The first time I met him, I didn't know whether to call him Reverend, Mr. Sittichinli or Sir. He was twice my age, confident and charismatic, and built like a marathon runner—fit, trim and muscular. Most importantly, he was all keyed up for the amazing race ahead.

I already mentioned that my final hire, Louie Blondin, came to us because his father, John, believed his son would be better at the job. Louie was brilliant from the start, but I did worry at first about how a man who used crutches would deal with travelling in small planes and boats up and down the Mackenzie Valley. It ended up being tougher than either of us imagined, but Louie never complained and never said, "I can't do it." Always, as we loaded him into float planes or boats, we threatened to drop him as payback for his practical jokes.

Once, though, he was in real trouble. We were in tiny Paulatuk on the western Arctic coast. It was fiercely cold—minus thirty-five—and a vicious wind, probably forty kilometres an hour, was blowing. Our sound recorder and all-round technical guy, Dave Porter, and I were making our way back to the hearings after the noon break, our heads buried in our hoods against the cold. Around the edge of the parka, I saw someone's laundry, frozen stiff, blowing in the wind at about a twenty-degree angle.

One piece of laundry looked very familiar: it was Louie, stuck in a drift under the clothesline. In the usual high winds, Arctic snow becomes as hard as wet sand or cement. Generally you can walk or even drive across drifts and not leave an impression. This time, as Louie thrust his crutches forward, he hit a soft spot and the crutches went deep into the drift. With his legs extended backward, he couldn't move, and he was also getting very cold very quickly.

Porter lifted him off the crutches, propped him up straight, and then turned and hoisted him up so he could piggyback him. I rescued the crutches. In a few minutes, the three of us were back at our desk in the warm hall as though nothing had happened.

Porter, a Yukon Dene from Lower Post, British Columbia, whom CBC Whitehorse had just hired, gave us that kind of commitment and support on the job too. He was twenty years old, ambitious and excited to move to Yellowknife and join us, recording the hearings, and doing all the technical set-ups and operations for our coverage in Yellowknife and all the small northern communities where the inquiry stopped, as well as across southern Canada. He could also do first-class on-air work, but he was hired as the technician and equipment operator. It never bothered him that he didn't share the limelight. Coordination and production duties were also often unloaded on his young but very broad shoulders, and he accepted it all without complaint. The inquiry was his classroom and he was smart enough to see Joe, Abe and Jim as mentors and respected elders in a context that was both important and relevant in Indigenous society.

Within a decade of the inquiry, Porter would be a member of the Yukon legislative assembly and a cabinet minister. He then served many years in the public service in Yukon and British Columbia, and is currently CEO of the BC First Nations Energy and Mining Council.

Our cameraman, Pat Scott, was also in his early twenties. He was born in Toronto and was working freelance in Vancouver when he heard we were looking for a filmmaker willing to work on his own for very long hours with low pay. Pat was a tremendous asset. He had the brains, disposition and character to move to a strange place, work in six new languages, as many different cultures, and most days under exceptionally difficult circumstances. His contribution to our team was enormous, and his contribution to the North and Yellowknife even greater. He found the love of his life, Gabrielle MacKenzie, a young Dene schoolteacher, at the community hearings in the village of Rae-Edzo, married her and stayed in the North. They are now grandparents.

Our inquiry newsroom was like no other before or since. Of the seven of us, only Pat Scott and I were "white guys."

The most difficult stretches for us were not the complicated engineering and environmental phases of testimony, where everyone had predicted that the Indigenous broadcasters would be completely lost, but rather those weeks when the inquiry was in recess and we needed to maintain our schedule with background reports and reviews of critical environmental or social issues that had been raised at the hearings or covering community reaction to the unfolding story.

I remember Louie, short of material and struggling to put a program together in one of those down periods. Joe got up from his small desk with a reel of tape in his hand and generously passed it over. "Here's an interview I did last week with Chief Cazon in Fort Simpson. You can have it." The interview was in Slavey, which meant Louie was in luck. He put it on the tape deck and began listening and editing.

But when Joe added up his program segments, he discovered he was now a few minutes short and slid back in front of Louie's desk. "I'm sorry, I made a mistake. I am going to need Chief Cazon." Louie stared at him and then, in stony silence, handed over the five-inch reel. Joe turned and had barely taken two steps when the tension was broken by these memorable words: "Goddamn white giver." I don't know whether Joe gave the tape back to Louie or whether they both aired it in the end, because all of us were laughing at ourselves too much to care. We were all in this together, as reporters and as best friends, and we had proved all the many naysayers wrong.

Rather than being confused or intimidated by the complicated technical, scientific and engineering testimony in which the language mostly being spoken was jargon, all four broadcasters soon found their footing and confidence, and started giving the witnesses a run for their money, because at the root of the technical issues was the environment. For instance, the engineers said that to keep the permafrost from melting as they piped the gas through the pipeline, which would cause the ground to thaw, sink or erode, they'd refrigerate the natural gas to extremely cold temperatures; in areas where there was no permafrost—and there were hundreds of kilometres where this was the case—they would freeze the ground. "It won't work," said Abe, and more than once he put his mic under an engineer's chin to ask how they expected the ground to freeze evenly. Abe's land learning told him the ground would freeze and expand more underneath the pipe and thus push it upwards, causing a rupture.

About two-thirds of the way through the inquiry, one of the principal engineers for Arctic Gas announced they had an important amendment to submit. After a review of their engineering plans, they'd found evidence that the "frost bulb" around the laid pipe would not form evenly and that indeed it would likely be "egg-shaped," resulting in such severe upward pressure on the pipe it might break. It would not be the first nor the last time at the reporters' table that I felt Abe's big elbow jab into my rib cage as he whispered, "See, I told you so!"

These men's superior knowledge of their surroundings and environment set them apart from the other reporters who covered the inquiry, including myself. As another example, the matter of burying a pipeline under Shallow Bay at the mouth of the Mackenzie River was a particularly touchy environmental issue. Nobody knew the possible adverse impacts on the beluga whales that migrate to the area every summer to calve. Moreover, nobody who was testifying seemed to know when or where the calves were born. At the inquiry one morning, questions had been going back and forth for some time, with Canadian Arctic Gas saying it spent several summers and a million dollars researching and would continue to do so until it found the answers. With some clear tension and frustration in the air, Justice Berger called a coffee break.

Jim looked at me, smiled and said, "I know where and when the calves are born." He put his finger on the route map on our reporters' table. "Right here, and usually on the second of July."

I motioned to the head of the research team, a marine biologist, and suggested Jim might be able to help. I can still see their heads together over the coffee cups and the map. When the inquiry resumed fifteen minutes later, to his everlasting credit, the marine biologist, Dr. Richard Webb, said, "Mr. Commissioner, during the break Mr. Sittichinli of the CBC was good enough to share his knowledge on this, and tells me the calves are born in this particular bay"—he pointed to the map—"and usually on the second of July." Webb went on to say the construction would be scheduled accordingly.

That evidence went into the record. To my recollection, it was the only "scientific fact" that was not challenged by any of the intervenors.

As the inquiry progressed, and the friendly discussions, debates or challenges accumulated, so did the respect for my colleagues grow among the dozens of PhDs who appeared as witnesses. In time, greetings were often in the vein of "Good morning, Dr. Okpik" or "How are you today, Dr. Tobie?"

As a testament to the quality of the work of the northern broadcasters, Berger himself often said the success of his inquiry was in part because people in the northern communities, especially the Indigenous population, understood the issues. The reporters also felt a sense of duty to their community to testify when the inquiry visited their hometowns, so Berger heard from them formally.

Jim Sittichinli was the first, in Aklavik.

> Mr. Commissioner, ladies and gentlemen, I am very glad to have this opportunity to have a few words here in my hometown. . . . I have lived here for 30 years.

> There are older people especially that are not in favour with this pipeline. They disagree with it because it is going to damage the land that they have been living on for many, many years.
>
> Now, at the time of the treaty . . . fifty-five years ago [the government people] said, "As long as the river runs, as long as the sun goes up and down, and as long as you see that black mountain up there, well, you are entitled to your land."
>
> The river is still running. The sun still goes up and down, and the black mountain is still up there, but today it seems that the way our people understand, the government is giving up our land [to the developers]. . . .
>
> You know, Mr. Commissioner, the other day I was taking a walk in Yellowknife . . . [and] I was thinking about the Berger Inquiry, walking along, and I passed a house there with a dog tied outside. I didn't notice it, and, all of a sudden, this dog jumped up and gave me a big bark, and then, after I passed through there, I was saying to myself, "Well, that dog taught me a lesson."
>
> You know, so often you see the Native people, they are tied down too much . . . by the government. . . . It is about time that we the people of this northland should get up sometime and bark and then we will be noticed.

It was natural that Abe would follow Jim. Aklavik was also Abe's hometown, its name the Inuvialuit word for "barren ground grizzly bear habitat." It sits on the Peel River channel on the west side of the Mackenzie Delta. It began as a trading post in about 1920 and prospered as the demand for fur, especially muskrat, exploded. The Mackenzie and northern Yukon River deltas were rich in fur and both Inuvialuit and Gwich'in people settled there, trapping and trading. Soon the RCMP and the missionaries arrived. Abe's roots were in Alaska. In the 1920s, when borders were not yet important, the Alaska Inupiat brought reindeer to the region. Several families followed, including his. Jim and Abe were raised in separate cultures, but in the same town, and their relationship was based on both respect and rivalry.

When Abe Okpik spoke to Berger, he reminded the judge and others that the old days that people speak about are also synonymous with hard times.

> I don't want you to be impressed that I am trying to call this country as rosy as a lot of people think it is; I want you to understand that we have our bad times in this land too like anywhere else, like the farmers do, or other parts of the world where they don't have everything as they should.
>
> Number one I got on my list, Mr. Berger, is that when we have severe cold winters in this Mackenzie Delta and there is hardly any snow, the lakes freeze to the bottom, and all the muskrats . . . disappear.

He outlined ten points on hardship that would make any northern romantic think twice, including starvation, floods, extreme cold, and living on the land in the summer, when the mosquitoes and black flies were so severe the dogs would be blinded from bites around their eyes. And lastly, a flu epidemic.

"There has been recorded in this settlement of Aklavik one year as much as 36 people died in a week because of the common flu. . . . We were not ready for it."

Abe concluded that although there were good times and hard times, despite the people's struggle with the land, it belongs to them. "I would like to say we own this land in our hearts and we like it."

Beyond giving testimony in their own communities, our broadcasters were often asked to provide translation for the locals. Thirty years earlier, Jim had served as the Anglican minister in Old Crow in northern Yukon, and when the inquiry came to town the community insisted on more than translation services. After twelve hours translating the proceedings, on a steamy, sunny, Saturday night, above the Arctic Circle and under the midnight sun, the locals pushed the meeting room's chairs and tables aside and held a square dance. After the jigs and reels of the first set, someone called for "the old preacher" to call the dance. For the next three hours, Jim was on his feet. "Swing your partner and do-si-do round the room," he called, again and again, in Gwich'in and English. The dancing went on till the very early hours of Sunday morning, and the old man put on quite a show.

Before the last dance, the inquiry brigade was told that, out of respect, they were expected to attend the church service that morning. Jim was staying with friends, but the rest of us—me, Joe, Louie, Abe, Pat and Porter—were bunking in an old mission house. We managed to get out of bed just in time to catch Berger and his staff making their way along the banks of the beautiful Porcupine River to the little log church. As we all shuffled into pews hand-carved from local wood, the organ started playing and from behind the pulpit, the old preacher stood to deliver the morning service and sermon.

Is there no end to Jim's talents? we sinners wondered. Blessedly, he did not tell any of us we were going to hell for our transgressions, which by now, he probably knew.

Only Jim lived to old age, passing away in Aklavik in the early 1980s. Joe, Louie and Abe all became part of the painful Canadian government statistic that defines Indigenous average life expectancy as ten years shorter than that of white people. When the inquiry ended, Joe and Louie and I went back to the Yellowknife newsroom. They each had their daily news program. Abe returned to Inuvik and worked the morning program, then moved on to Iqaluit. In the early 1990s cancer took him. Only hours before he passed, I spoke to him on the phone and was able to say goodbye.

Joe stayed at CBC for several more years and took an early retirement package. He had returned to work as a translator when, at barely sixty, a massive heart attack took him almost instantly.

Louie's death was tragic. On a Saturday night barely three years after the inquiry finished, he and his friends were having fun in downtown Yellowknife. Tired of the Gold Range, they bar-hopped across the street to the Yellowknife Inn. Louie's crutches slipped on black ice and he fell backward, his head hitting the concrete curb. He suffered a massive concussion and brain hemorrhage and died within hours.

Three of the four were "greenhorns." I was supposed to be the go-to guy on the newsroom team, the one with all the ideas and answers. In the end, their skills, ability and knowledge humbled me. In so many ways, they were so much better at the craft than so many of the people I would work with. I learned far more from each of them than they did from me.

They were like brothers to me, and I loved them.

10

ALL EQUAL NOW

Berger and the Winds of Change

A simple power failure plunged the windowless dining room in Inuvik's Eskimo Inn into total darkness. A room full of oil executives, lawyers, the town's business elite, and Justice Berger and his Mackenzie Valley Pipeline Inquiry staff couldn't even see the plates on their table. Not even the light of a single candle flickered.

One voice rang out in the darkness: "We're all equal now!"

The silence turned from startled to tense.

I knew the source of that wit. He was sitting directly across the table from me—my twenty-year-old colleague and Slavey language reporter, Louie Blondin.

Suddenly a laugh broke the silence—a good, hearty laugh, familiar to Louie and me and most others in the room. Thomas Berger, recognizing the ironic truth of the moment. Gradually the others joined in, some from the heart, but others with the kind of nervous, forced laughter that comes with confronting an uncomfortable truth.

This inquiry, to my mind, was a critical turning point in the history of the North, and we would need a lot more than Louie's sharp wit to break the tension that gripped the Mackenzie Valley and much of the rest of Canada. The portrait of the "True North" being painted by the Indigenous witnesses at these hearings was of a racialized colonial territory that had been subject to a century of federal government assimilation policies and practices. The current rules and regimes that governed towns, settlements and outposts across the Territories supported and sanctioned that colonial mindset.

The minority Liberal government had only appointed Justice Berger to lead the inquiry as a matter of political survival; it had been pushed to do so by the New Democrats, rather than by the opportunity to serve equality and justice. Berger had been an NDP member of Parliament; he'd also run for the leadership of the NDP in British Columbia. As a lawyer, he'd won the historic 1973 Nisga'a case in the Supreme Court of Canada that recognized Aboriginal rights in Canadian law. Only thirty-nine when he was appointed to the Supreme Court of British Columbia, Berger was just forty-one when he was asked to head the pipeline inquiry. He was considered by some to be youthful, aggressive and in a hurry. But he never appeared to be in a hurry when he sat, for twelve or more hours a day, in tiny smoke-filled schoolrooms and community halls in every village, regardless of its size, along the proposed pipeline's route. He listened intently and patiently as people poured out their emotions on matters of land, environment, community, culture and survival.

None of the many pipeline proposals before us in Canada today—all still matters of national importance—are as momentous as the Mackenzie Valley Pipeline proposal of the 1970s. The proposal before Justice Berger was unprecedented from every standpoint and in every aspect—on a par with the transcontinental railways a century earlier or the construction of the St. Lawrence Seaway. It was meant to be the longest pipeline ever built, and even the company that wanted to build it was without equal. Canadian Arctic Gas was a consortium of some of the world's largest oil companies, including Exxon, Atlantic Richfield, Gulf and Shell Oil. In all, twenty-seven of the biggest oil and gas companies in the world and all wanted to stake their claim in Canada's Far North.

Equally unheard of was the projected cost. It was a staggering $4 billion dollars at the outset, and its estimated cost rose to close to $6 billion towards the end of the proceedings. For context, the entire annual budget for the Northwest Territories at the time was a mere $100 million. Berger's three-year inquiry cost $5 million.

The proposed route was from the Alaskan Prudhoe Bay oil and natural gas fields, four thousand kilometres across the Canadian coastal plain in Yukon and the Northwest Territories, and then under the waters of Shallow Bay at the mouth of the Mackenzie River to connect to the gas fields of the Beaufort Sea; from there south up the Mackenzie Valley and into Alberta. The line would cross the most remote regions of North America and be further challenged by permafrost and the harshest winter working conditions imaginable. Then there was the steel pipe itself, measuring 48 inches in diameter—the biggest ever.

A second proposal for a far shorter line would surface from a Canadian company, Foothills Pipe Lines out of Alberta. Its founder, Bob Blair, called it the Maple Leaf Line, and it was designed to carry only Canadian gas from the Beaufort-Mackenzie region down the east side of the river; fundamentally the same route as in the competitive Arctic Gas proposal, without the Alaska connection.

Midway through the inquiry, Blair would be persuaded by American and Canadian oil interests to file yet a third application, an alternative Alaska Highway route. It became an attractive proposal because it avoided the growing and effective environmental opposition to building on the ecologically sensitive Arctic coastal plain, sometimes referred to by Berger and others as an Arctic Serengeti.

This region was and remains the domain of one of the world's great wildlife spectacles. Every year in the summer, hundreds of thousands of caribou migrate to the coastal areas to drop their calves. They graze on the rich coastal vegetation and return to the shelter of the forest areas in the fall. And every spring and summer, this shoreline, with grassy meadows, lakes, ponds, fields and swamps, is alive with millions of nesting migratory birds and waterfowl.

The Alaska Highway proposal avoided the coastal plain, running some six hundred kilometres from Prudhoe Bay straight south to Fairbanks. From there, it would parallel the gravel highway built through Yukon and Alaska during the Second World War. When it entered northern British Columbia and northern Alberta it would connect with existing pipelines and feed into the North American network.

With the benefit of hindsight, this was surely the most sensible option. But it came too late.

In many ways, the inquiry was as unprecedented as the proposal it was examining. No one had done this before, and no one has done it on such a scale since. The proceedings were divided into two phases; the first, the formal hearings, mostly in Yellowknife, where the expert testimony was presented and cross-examined. This included engineering studies, environmental assessments, financial implications, Canada's energy reserves and the national interest. Most of the hearings were in the main hall of the relatively new and modern Explorer Hotel in Yellowknife.

It was standing room only when, on that March day in 1975, almost a year after his initial appointment, Justice Berger spoke these words: "Today we embark on the future consideration of a great river valley and its people."

Berger sat at a small desk, on a slightly raised platform, a stately royal blue curtain as a backdrop. The formal setting would not change. Always dressed in a dark suit, Berger, by his count, would hear from over three hundred expert witnesses in the months ahead.

In front of him were two rows of lawyers representing proponents and opponents including the twenty-seven oil interests, "Native rights groups," environmental organizations, the NWT Chamber of Commerce, and one citizens' group that deserves special mention, the Northwest Territories Mental Health Association and its visionary director, Jo MacQuarrie. She forecast the horrific impact that several thousand construction workers could have on northern settlements and their way of life, and thus, on their mental health.

In the front row to Berger's left sat the very competent commission counsel, who would guide the proceedings. On his right were his secretary and official recorders, who repeated every word spoken into a recording mask that blocked their voices but captured everything on cassette. Every couple of hours the tapes would be sent across town to the commission office, where they would be typewritten into a daily transcript record to be available the next day.

Along the left wall was the reporters' table, more like an office for almost two full years for myself and my CBC colleagues. The only ones not wearing suits, we were identifiable by red wool vests with blue trim and polar bear and seal designs. As reporters we had full access to record and film the proceedings, perhaps the only thing the formal and community hearings had in common. Behind the rows of lawyers was a public gallery, which, no matter the weather or the time of day, always held observers.

In the second phase—the community hearings—Justice Berger would examine all proposals through the same lens and with a sharp focus on the impact on the people who lived in the small communities along the proposed route. Before he was finished, Berger would hear from more than a thousand people in thirty-five villages, towns and major cities across Canada.

Places like North Star Harbour in the western Arctic and Willow Lake in the Mackenzie Valley were not even villages, just outpost camps where people were living a quasi-traditional life and so small that there was not a building large enough to accommodate more than a half-dozen people. In these settings, the inquiry contingent was reduced to Berger, a staff member, an official recorder, at least one of our Indigenous-language reporters and a camera operator. In these hearings Berger always wore a light brown sports jacket, a knit tie and matching shirt, never white, and corduroy pants. Everybody else, including his staff and the oil executives, wore jeans and woodsy shirts. Cowboy boots were fashionable and, in summer, practical when it came to protecting your ankles from the blackflies and mosquitoes.

No two hearing rooms in the communities were the same—a school, a hall, a church, whatever building would hold the most people. There were never enough chairs or benches because every community meeting was packed. The entire village would show up, the elders often sitting on the floor among restless children, and the room would soon fill with cigarette smoke. How Berger, a non-smoker, endured it, I still don't know.

Every hearing was an adventure, often beginning with the plane ride to get there. Sometimes all of Berger's staff and our broadcast team and other media would crowd onto an old DC-3 the inquiry chartered. Other times, it would take two or three shuttle trips in a smaller Twin Otter to get into the smaller places, often taking off and landing with floats on a river or lake.

My crew and I were the first to arrive on a float plane into a small village called Trout Lake, a little southwest of Yellowknife. We landed easily on the big lake and tied up at a nice dock. Our cameraman, Pat Scott, and I were preparing one of my weekly five-minute TV reports when I saw the second plane approach. This was not a float plane. Rather than pontoons, big black tires hung down beneath the wings, and the big boulders, bushes and hummocks all around us seemed impossible for those tires to avoid. I told Pat to film it.

Somehow the pilot found an opening and we watched the plane make three big bounces, then lurch to a sudden stop. To say it taxied is misleading. Rather it laboured over the rock-riddled half-field, half-bog and then turned and stopped. Berger and the others climbed down the small rear ladder.

Pat kept the camera going for the plane's takeoff. With a reasonable wind and help from more hummocks, it bounced twice and on the third heave stayed airborne.

Later in the day, I found a tourist brochure in the community hall that doubled as our broadcast centre that warned "There are no landing facilities in Trout Lake." We all returned to Yellowknife by float plane.

On another trip in Inuvik, all hands were on board and packed into a DC-3 on a very hot, dry night. The old airplane, a veteran of the Second World War, Korea and Vietnam, rumbled down the runway for so long we began wondering if it was ever going to get off the ground.

It didn't. With the end of the runway in sight and no lift, we braced as the pilot came down hard on the brakes. The explanation came over the intercom: "It's too hot and the air is so dry and thin we can't get any lift."

The pilot made a second attempt after we unloaded much of our gear and baggage, with the same result. This time after we taxied back to the terminal, several passengers volunteered to stay behind. Third time lucky. The plane lifted, and ever so slowly, we gained altitude.

Even after we were safely on the ground, the communities were an adventure. Only a few had hotels, and even when they did, there were never enough rooms or beds to go around. Food was also often scarce. Sometimes we slept on old cots and couches, even the floor.

The hearings themselves could not have been more different from the formal affairs in Yellowknife. It seemed as though everyone wanted to speak, young or old, and regardless of language. The Northwest Territories is like no place in Canada. Its vast size contrasts with tiny places, small populations, where four races live side-by-side, white, Dene, Inuit and Métis, speaking seven different languages. Whatever their language, most of those who testified were speaking publicly for the first time in their lives.

People like Rosie Savi of Fort Franklin, an elderly woman whose voice finally mattered and whose eloquence was not diminished by the interpreters. She wanted to know "whether in a small community, where everybody is helping with each other, will that type of relationship still exist [with] the pipeline and the dam and the . . . impact it will have on the people."

Further up the Big River, in Wrigley, a young student named Martha Nayally asked, "Why do white people want to take over the Dene people's land? . . . The pipeline companies only think about themselves and the white people. They don't care what will happen to the Dene people of the north."

What was remarkable was how many young chiefs, mostly well-educated men in their twenties, were leading their communities. Chief Paul Andrew from Fort Norman reminded the judge that it came at a cost—a white education system. "There is nothing about [our] culture. There is nothing about the language being promoted. There is just continuous promotion of the white man's way of life, the white man's language. But our language, our proud way of life, our culture . . . is pushed aside entirely."

One testimony from Fort McPherson, a Dene community of a few hundred people in the Mackenzie Delta, remains burned in my memory. Phillip Blake would have been in his late twenties; he was a social worker and had been one for five years. Calmly he asked Mr. Berger why they were being asked to trust a government and a system that for two hundred years has never put the Hudson's Bay trading company in jail for stealing from the Indians, but has always put the Indians in jail for stealing from the Bay. "The system of genocide," he said, "may have become a little more polished over the past few hundred years . . . but the effect is exactly the same. We are being destroyed."

As the community hearings unfolded, a growing sense of confidence and, yes, equality—at least in this process—emerged.

Fort Good Hope sits high on the banks of the Mackenzie River, known to all Dene as Deh Cho—the big river. It was here, on a hot, dry August day in 1975, that the inquiry reached its most dramatic moments, with rhetoric that rocked the northern political climate in a way no one had heard before. The school gym where the hearing was being held was filled with reporters, TV cameras, almost the entire community and that ever-present cigarette smoke.

The band chief was Frank T'Seleie. He was only in his early twenties, but he was an imposing figure whose serious and angry eyes were framed and darkened by the shadow of his long, thick black hair. His deep, ringing voice, reverberated in the halls of government and the oil industry's skyscrapers in Calgary and Toronto, and across the rest of Canada, though in the moment they were aimed at one of the proposed pipeline builders, Bob Blair, sitting silent a few metres away from T'Seleie in the hearing room.

"Mr. Blair . . . you are the twentieth-century General Custer. . . . You are coming with your troops to slaughter us and steal land that is rightfully ours. You are coming to destroy a people that have a history of thirty thousand years. Why? For twenty years of gas? Are you really that insane?"

Then came a threat, uttered in the open and on the record. "My nation will stop the pipeline. It is so that [an] unborn child can know the freedom of this land that I am willing to lay down my life."

Thankfully, in the end, no one did lay down their life. Would they have? Who knows. My view from the reporters' table at the time, and now with the perspective of decades, is that angry young men from all cultures have always been willing to lay down their lives to defend their lands, their beliefs and their way of life.

The next day Bob Blair responded in the quiet and subdued manner that was very much his trademark.

> Chief T'Seleie, yesterday you connected my name with those of some people who are not my heroes either, including General Custer. . . . I do wish you to know that having heard the things that you said to me . . . I have not felt to take them personally . . . but to take them mainly as expressing your very great concern and anxiety, and in some cases suspicion, of the possibility of the pipeline. . . . I understand your concerns much more than I did in the past, and I regard them as serious and important.

11

BERGER'S SOUTHERN HEARINGS

Canada—Through Their Eyes

I have always loved the way the Gwich'in accent brings out the descriptive beauty of English. Every vowel is smooth and drawn out, giving you the time to feel it. The final consonant is emphasized as though to drive a point home.

"Hoooo-lee smoke, eh!

"Loo-ook at that, eh!

"I neeever seen that before!"

Those words were coming from Jim Sittichinli, more excited than I had ever seen him. He was almost bouncing up and down in his seat as we drove down the mountainside from the Vancouver home of Thomas Berger and his wife, Beverley, with the lights of downtown spread out in front of us.

It was early June 1976. Berger was fulfilling his commitment to bring his inquiry to all Canadians, with hearings in major cities across the country. His hometown of Vancouver was at the top of the itinerary, so he had invited all the staff, broadcasters and interveners, largely made up of representatives from oil companies, environmental and Indigenous organizations, for an evening dinner and reception.

Jim and I were sharing a cab back downtown, and Jim was almost breathless at the view. "It's so beautiful!" He stretched every syllable, adding the distinctive Gwich'in emphasis.

I thought, yes, it is a sight, right out of the old country song by Ray Price: "A bright array of city lights as far as I can see / The great white way shines through the night . . ."

"You've never seen lights like that?" I asked, looking at his smiling face.

"It's not the lights," he corrected me. "It's the moon." I looked again. There was indeed a big, bright full moon, rising above the brilliant city. Very much a beautiful sight.

"I never see the moon in June," Jim said. Now I knew where he was coming from.

I remembered the same sense of wonder and amazement the first time I experienced the midnight sun, which I'd seen echoed in the faces of dozens of others encountering the midnight sun in the Arctic for the first time. It's as though you have been put on a different planet. We rode the rest of the way in silence, Jim enjoying the moment, and me no doubt wondering whether my broadcast team could keep it all together as we visited ten major Canadian cities in three weeks. My colleagues were talented and hard workers, but they were also reporters, and like most reporters I had come to know, once the story was filed, they liked to tip a glass and party. I knew there would be many temptations between Vancouver's rising moon and Nova Scotia's setting sun, and the points in between.

My fears were groundless. The south brought us even closer as a team and as friends. We looked out more for one another and found new and greater respect for our sense of the country and everyone's place in it.

Our southern hearings also showed me a new side of the other "two solitudes" in Canada, the whites and the Indigenous peoples. Culturally, socially, economically and physically, John Steeves, one of the lawyers with the oil companies, and Louie Blondin, Indigenous broadcaster, were as different as Jim's first June moon and my first midnight sun.

Steeves was from Viking stock and proud of it. He filled every doorway he entered—more than six feet tall, massive shoulders, arms and hands—and always wore finely tailored suits and proper accessories. His brief was the social and economic implications of the pipeline that the Canadian Arctic Gas consortium was presenting to the inquiry.

Louie's crippling arthritis made his small frame look even smaller. I had to help lift him in and out of canoes and airplanes, and I carried him up and down the narrow ramps of float planes. I knew he didn't weigh much more than a hundred and ten pounds. At about five feet four inches, he barely reached John Steeves's shoulder. Louie was also fussy and conscious about his appearance and image. Bell-bottom jeans were imperative, bright shirts, flowered if possible, a beaded moose or caribou hide vest, and always a headband, to hold his jet-black shoulder-length hair in place. Louie looked like Willie Nelson before Willie Nelson found the look.

As the hearings progressed in Yellowknife, one could see that Louie and John had a growing friendship, often sharing the coffee break. Sometimes John would thoughtfully bring him a cup.

Berger opened his southern hearings on a sunny, warm Vancouver Monday morning in the spacious ballroom of a downtown hotel. The testimony was predictable. The oil companies stated their positions, environmentalists cast the pipeline as akin to Armageddon, and ordinary citizens, talking about fairness and justice, invariably supported the northern Indigenous position that no pipeline should be built until the land claims are settled.

What I remember most clearly about that day was our lunch break. Our broadcast gang was headed to a restaurant suitable to our tastes and budget, which is to say, quick and cheap, but Louie said he wasn't coming. When Joe, Abe, Jim and I, along with our technical crew, stepped out on the sidewalk, we saw Louie ahead of us "crutching" rhythmically along beside John Steeves. The contrast in size and style could not have been more striking.

On our way back, we passed a high-end steakhouse that catered to the executive crowd. There they were, at a table by the window covered in fine white linen, Frick and Frack, having a comradely and expensive lunch. It was a lesson for me. True friends are comfortable no matter their cultural and racial differences. Today we are calling that "reconciliation."

As we travelled across Canada, we witnessed other connections—and disconnections. In Regina, we met up with Hugh Fagan who was the head of the RCMP Training Academy there. He'd been a corporal in Aklavik many years earlier, knew Jim Sittichinli, and had arranged for us to tour the RCMP museum.

A young corporal led us to a display on the pursuit of the Mad Trapper of Rat River, which had become a part of RCMP, Canadian and Hollywood folklore. In the winter of 1932, Albert

Johnson had led the RCMP on a wild manhunt through the Mackenzie Delta after he had shot and killed a Mountie. They say that the hunt to bring him to justice was the source of the slogan, "The Mounties always get their man."

As the young corporal told the story, little did he know that the special constable and chief tracker who'd led the Mounties to Albert Johnson was Jim's big brother, Lazarus Sittichinli. Many have speculated that it was Lazarus's marksmanship that guided the fatal bullet.

When the tour guide began describing Johnson's meagre belongings, Jim interjected, speaking softly and without condescending, "Yes, I know, I packed these things and sent them here." Jim would have been about twenty years old at the time.

When we got to Toronto, I checked into a hotel room more than twenty floors above Toronto's busy downtown Bay Street. When I opened my door the next morning to retrieve the newspaper, I wasn't surprised that the headline in the *Globe and Mail* declared "Berger Inquiry in Toronto."

I began reading the front-page story, paragraph after paragraph of beautiful comparisons and concepts linking or separating north and south and all the while setting the pipeline debate in context. I was really struck by an image comparing the cars flowing along the city streets to the ice and logs that drift down the Mackenzie River when the ice breaks, and wondered where this whole piece came from. I looked to the top of the article and there was the byline: Abe Okpik.

When I went downstairs for breakfast, Abe and some of the others were there. Abe was looking particularly smug. He had likely just listened to my inferior and less descriptive offering on the CBC national radio news.

I congratulated Abe, then asked him how he got the assignment. He said that after we had all filed our stories the evening before, he'd met the *Globe and Mail* writer Martin O'Malley, who had been covering the inquiry both north and south. As reporters do, they went for a beer and compared notes. When Abe showed him the three typewritten pages of script that he'd translated into Inuktitut for the broadcast, O'Malley said, "I can't come up with anything nearly this good. Can I run it?"

Abe agreed. So did the *Globe*'s editors.

On our next stop, in Montreal, by the time we had finished our broadcast at the CBC Montreal studios, it was close to ten o'clock at night. Starving, we went to the nearest greasy spoon. As always there were questions—too many questions—about the menu. *What's this, what's that? What is that like?* We were way beyond the old English-French two solitudes here; we were now more like half a dozen solitudes.

The middle-aged waitress was doing her best, but English wasn't her strength. Finally, Joe leaned closer to her and said something. None of us understood him, but the waitress did. Joe had reached back into the recesses of his past life and spoken French; soon he was translating back and forth.

"Where did that come from?" I asked.

"Residential school," he replied, but said nothing more.

The next day at noon, Abe put his large foot down. He wanted to go to the famous Toe Blake's Tavern, owned by the legendary former hockey player and coach. He had been bugging me all week. "Whit, let's go to the Toe Blake tavern!" I kept putting him off. I was still early in my dry years and tried to avoid the beer parlours; we were also swamped with work. Finally, on the last day, I said, "Okay, but just for an hour."

He was all excited as we jumped into the cab and announced our destination to the driver in that booming voice: "Toe Blake's Tavern!" Perhaps we would even see the man or someone else connected to the Montreal Canadiens.

Inside the tavern, we found a table not far from the door. Abe was immediately rubbernecking around the room. Looking for the legend. Left, right, front, back. Then he pointed, "Look, look, there at the back, there's Toe Blake."

I never liked stargazing and felt embarrassed. "Just take it easy," I said, fearing what was to come.

Then he cupped his big hand to his face like he was getting ready to call the wild geese. Before I could protest again, the big voice was booming. "Toe! Toe Blake!"

I was barely into my cringe when a voice replied, "Abe! Abe Okpik!"

In an instant, one of the greatest hockey stars was at our table and I was being introduced by our mutual friend.

"I guess you didn't think I knew him, eh?" Abe said with a smile. It turned out that, years earlier, when Abe was living and working in Montreal, he was a frequent visitor to this particular shrine. Toe Blake, like everyone else who had ever met Abe, had never forgotten him.

12

THE SHIT HITS THE FAN

No Regrets—But Still Wrong

"I don't want the pipeline!"

It certainly wasn't the first time someone had said those words at the Berger Inquiry. Indeed, most of the people who spoke at the hearings, from the smallest Arctic communities to the largest cities in southern Canada, would voice the same opinion. As the lead CBC reporter covering that Great Pipeline Debate of the 1970s, I heard those words so often they often didn't make the news.

Except on this one day. Because the person who insisted on taking his place at the witness table, the person who delivered this heartfelt opinion, was me.

In a public hearing. On the record. A supposedly unbiased journalist.

Was I wrong? Yes, very wrong. I came as close as I've ever come to losing my job over it, but I couldn't stop myself, and I didn't want to.

Still in the the summer of 1975, only a few days after Frank T'seleie's speech, we were in the "somewhat" hostile setting of Norman Wells, an oil company town along the Mackenzie River. When I asked to speak, Justice Berger and his team tried to persuade me not to. And Whit Fraser's quote, "I don't want the pipeline," quickly became the quote of the week. Given the highly sensitive nature of the pipeline debate at that time, those five little words went far beyond the normal news cycle.

They became powerful political ammunition to try to change the direction of the coverage of the pipeline debate. Since, for months, the CBC had provided the Indigenous peoples of the North with a platform to be heard, often for the first time, about a proposal that was certain to change their communities forever, many believed that our coverage bordered on the subversive. And I didn't help matters that day. I am still so conflicted by my lapse in journalistic judgment that I haven't written or talked about it for over forty years, but I'm telling the story now.

Norman Wells was built in the 1930s when oil was discovered near where the town sits on the Mackenzie River, although the oil was not particularly hard to find, given it was often seen oozing out of the ground. The people of "the Wells" breathed the frontier spirit. A small refinery there produced oil and gas for communities farther north, along the Mackenzie River and the Arctic coast, which was transported by barge and tugboats during the summer months.

The Wells was almost wholly owned by Imperial Oil, and a passion for further development was deep in the community's DNA. Indeed, the pipeline proposal projected Normal Wells as a major staging and construction area that would house work camps for several thousand employees. The Canadian Arctic Gas consortium also projected that the construction of the pipeline would increase demand for energy supplies in the North, likely leading to an expansion of the local refinery.

Most of the several hundred residents of the Wells were employed by Imperial Oil, and those who didn't have jobs with Imperial were equally dependent on the company. That meant that in Normal Wells, we were treated to the most unchallenged support for the pipeline we'd hear, as well as the most vehement criticism of the Indigenous peoples who opposed it.

Long before the hearings were held there, I'd reported numerous stories about Norman Wells's history, character and strategic location. One would have to have one's head completely buried in the sand not to know what side the community would come down on in the pipeline issue.

But no one, including myself, or Berger or his senior staff, expected the level of loathing directed towards the Indigenous peoples of the North from the people of Norman Wells in that hot community hall on an August day in 1975. Like this comment, from a local businessman named Rick Sinotte: "I fail to see how a line approximately 100 feet wide down this well-used corridor can destroy a way of life. If the culture in question is that fragile, I suggest that it is only a matter of time before it is destroyed at any rate."

I was sitting through this at the reporters' table with my Indigenous colleagues. They were dedicated reporters who broadcast the details of every day's testimony in their languages to different parts of the North. Those days were sometimes twelve to fourteen hours long. They never let me down. They never missed a deadline. They had become my friends.

Witness Ross Laycock: "I don't think it's a lack of opportunities, but lack of initiative. Most parents are too busy drinking to worry about their children's welfare."

These friends of mine most assuredly didn't fit the image conveyed by so much of the day's testimony—that the northern Dene, Métis and Inuit were lazy, drunken layabouts who needed to get off their backsides and work. The more I listened to the racist language, the angrier I got.

Claire Barnabe: "If we want to succeed in our own way in our own happiness, we all have to learn to adapt according to how the times change, whether we are French Canadian, Indians, Eskimos or what have you."

In the early evening, there was a lull. The silence was not uncommon. Sometimes Berger would wait several minutes for people in the audience to make their final decision as to whether they would speak or not. It was also time for people to look around the room to see if anyone else was making their way to the witness chair.

Berger's composure never wavered, regardless of what we heard. It didn't waver here either, as he sat waiting to see if another witness wished to speak. Still, I think I startled him when I threw my pencil on the table, pushed back my chair, walked across the room and slammed my ass into the small school desk reserved for witnesses.

Berger looked at me and then began banging the empty ashtray that always served as his gavel. "Perhaps a break is in order," he said.

I saw him mutter something to the commission's counsel, Ian Scott. Ian was a Toronto lawyer with a brilliant mind who was totally able to handle the complex political, technical and cultural issues the inquiry grappled with daily. (In later life, Scott would run for the Liberal Party leadership in Ontario, finishing second to David Peterson, and then serve as Ontario's attorney general; he died in 2006.)

Despite his big-city background, Scott was comfortable in the northern communities. Only a few days earlier, he had given himself a proper northern make-over, buying a woodsy shirt and a beautiful moose-hide jacket, well decorated with beaded flower designs. When Abe Okpik saw the jacket in the bar in Inuvik, he barked, "Scott, you've gone Native," and then warned him he would be laughed at if he took to wearing the new duds in Toronto.

Ian Scott wasn't laughing now. Instead, he was waving at me to get out of the chair and come into the hall to talk. "Don't do this. It's dynamite and you'll regret it," he said.

I told him I couldn't back down. He was right to predict there'd be a reaction, and one even more severe than I expected. But he was wrong about regrets. I've never regretted it.

When the hearings resumed, I sat back down in the chair and told the judge in the language of the time, "I don't want the pipeline . . . because the Indians don't want it." I went on to say that in Canada's democratic system, the majority generally rules.

"It also seems to me," I said, "that if we want to live up in this country and we want to work up in this country, and they just happen to be the majority of people, then we're going to have to let them take over, and don't anyone tell me that the talent is not in this country to do it."

I named emerging young Native leaders. I spoke of the federally appointed white commissioner in the Northwest Territories who on more than one occasion boasted, "I am the government."

I pointed out that northerners should take control of their government and legislature. (Within a few years they did.)

I spoke of the respect that both the judge and I had learned for the way the Indigenous peoples care for the land. We saw proof of that every time we visited hunting camps across the northern Yukon on the Old Crow Flats, where for hundreds of years the Gwich'in gathered every spring to harvest muskrats.

I testified, "In my whole life I'd never seen an area so well-kept, so tidy. It was unbelievable [in] camp after camp. . . . I put a cigarette butt out on the ground at one camp and a lady gave me a dirty look." I deserved it. I took the cigarette and immediately put it in the fire. And I never made the same mistake again.

But as a reporter, instead of reporting, I testified. I made a mistake.

I wish it had been a great speech. It wasn't. It was too long and too rambling, uttered on impulse. Had I taken the time to prepare and think, I probably wouldn't have done it.

What I had *not* considered was that my impulse to speak out would put a critical element of the whole royal commission into jeopardy. I had fought hard for the coverage. I had made commitments to myself, to my superiors and to the team of broadcasters I worked with that we would see this through.

When I finished talking, there was a loud and encouraging round of applause. I remember thinking that perhaps my words were appreciated. What I didn't hear was the sound of the fists that were pounding desks elsewhere.

In the weeks ahead, I learned that within minutes of me speaking, perhaps even before I finished, Stuart Hodgson, the commissioner I'd referred to, was getting a full briefing. There was already bad blood between us. A few years earlier, I had uncovered a damaging story that suggested he'd abused his office by granting big game hunting permits to wealthy Europeans, the proof being correspondence leaked to me from sources within the NWT wildlife department. Hodgson's credibility was badly stung and his ability to hold a grudge was well known.

Hodgson's support for oil and gas development was equally well known, and here he saw an opportunity. By the next morning, *Edmonton Journal* and *Globe and Mail* reporters following the inquiry had filed stories that were also picked up by the Canadian Press and other outlets on how I had compromised my objectivity by speaking to the Berger Inquiry hearings.

We arrived back in Yellowknife late on a Sunday night, and early Monday morning I was woken up by a phone call. I barely managed to get the word "hello" out of my mouth, when the rant started, in a thick Scots brogue: "Fraser, the shit just hit the fan."

It was the managing editor of national radio news, Eric Moncur. Moncur was a Scot, an old-fashioned reporter who gave the profession some class just by the way he said the word "reporter," as though it was spelled with three capital *R*s. He also had a large and colourful vocabulary. "What kind of a stupid, boneheaded move was that? What kind of idiotic thinking!"

The phone in my Yellowknife home was right above the basket where we put the dirty laundry. Since I knew he was just getting started, I laid the receiver in the basket (a fitting move considering the colour of the language I was hearing), and Eric ranted on while I made the morning coffee.

When I picked up the receiver again, he was beginning to wind down, telling me that I should be fired but that would just make matters worse. When he gave me a chance to speak, I told him I wasn't sorry that I'd testified, and that I hadn't been able to help it.

"Would you do it again?" he asked.

"If I did," I told him, "I would at least resign first."

In a much quieter voice, he said the CBC would stick by me and support me, then hung up without offering any direction, instruction or advice on what I should do next. (Years later, I told him how I'd avoided the best part of his blast, and he laughed and said I had more savvy than he'd thought.)

I arrived at our CBC Yellowknife newsroom with Moncur's words still ringing in my ear, and I got the first taste of what was to come. I was the news. My colleagues, reporters Al Baxter and Jim Elson, were waiting, microphones at the ready, and they pinned me in a corner in our newsroom. They wanted a comment. They wanted a reaction, but they weren't going to get it from me—I had to make sure I didn't make matters worse.

"My comments are on the record, help yourself. I have nothing more to say."

They tried to convince me otherwise, explaining that the chamber of commerce, the Northwest Territories Association of Municipalities and others were calling for my dismissal and saying that I should be shipped out of the North altogether. They pushed the mic further under my chin—just as I had done to hundreds of others over the years, and just as I would have done had I been in their shoes—and asked for my reaction.

My response was short and consistent. I would leave it to the CBC and accept their decision.

The CBC soon stated, clearly and from senior levels, that I

had shown bad judgment and that I would be severely reprimanded, which I was. The letter of reprimand came from Andrew Cowan, leaving me in no doubt that any further departure from tradition or professional standards would be met with dismissal. Friendship is friendship but business is business.

A day or so later, I received a second letter from Andrew, this one handwritten. He said he understood my position and, yes, sometimes personal convictions are more important than professional expectations. He prophesied that over the long haul, I would be stronger because of my action and so would the CBC. I don't know about the CBC, but from a personal perspective I know he was right.

My critics continued to call for my dismissal, and so I found my own "media strategy" in an unlikely source. It had been barely a year since Muhammad Ali famously defeated George Foreman, using what Ali called the "rope-a-dope," where he hung on the ropes, protected his head with his arms, and allowed Foreman to punch himself into exhaustion. Then, in the late rounds, Ali came off the ropes to victory. In my case, I achieved survival.

I had calls from both the Indian Brotherhood and the Métis association offering statements of support. I asked them to stay quiet. Their endorsement would only further inflame the situation. I knew fighting back would only make matters worse. My colleagues on the broadcast team said if I were to be removed, they would quit. They, too, wanted to make a statement, but thankfully held back.

For the next month, I kept my guard up, stayed in my corner, covered the hearings and filed my daily reports along with my Indigenous-language colleagues. Additionally, I prepared shorter reports for the CBC regional evening and morning newscasts. If a story warranted national coverage, I would file to our newsroom in Toronto and they would air it as though Norman Wells had never happened.

The NWT Chamber of Commerce and the Northwest Territories Association of Municipalities (representing towns and villages where most of the non-native people lived) continued to demand my removal. When the CBC refused to replace me, they went the political route by writing to Prime Minister Trudeau requesting his intervention. Every move by the chamber, the municipalities and other detractors was thoroughly reported. The northern newspapers had years earlier adopted an aggressive pro-development stance and I didn't expect they would let up. Nor did I expect our local newsroom to back off from coverage or from trying to get me to speak. Had the situation been reversed, I would have also wanted to demonstrate that the local newsroom was independent of the bosses who'd refused to fire me. I felt the tension, of course, but I had a sanctuary with Joe, Abe, Louie, Jim and Pat in our Berger newsroom, a forty-foot mobile home in the parking lot that accommodated our team.

A month after I testified at Norman Wells, the inquiry was scheduled to resume its community hearings in Fort Simpson, a community of about fifteen hundred people at the forks of the Liard and Mackenzie rivers. The Fort Simpson town council passed a motion demanding that I not be permitted to report the local hearing because, in the mayor's words, I had admitted I could not be objective. He demanded that the CBC find a replacement for me, adding that I would be banned from the community.

Our area manager, Pat Reilly, immediately wrote the mayor stating that I had never admitted I could not be objective. Then he added that I had been disciplined by our director and that the CBC had examined my previous work at the inquiry and found that there was not the slightest hint that I had been anything but objective and fair in my reporting. Reilly said that Whit Fraser would be covering the Fort Simpson hearings and that he would be there too if the council wanted to take the matter up with him further.

The town councillors underlined the divide in Fort Simpson by insisting on two sets of hearings, one for the whites and another for the Natives. Berger complied in part, by setting out two different meeting halls. Consequently, the separate Fort Simpson hearings were even more racially hostile than they'd been in Norman Wells.

Gordon Erion represented the chamber of commerce. He was young, well-educated and aggressive, and he had come north to make his fortune. He told Berger, "One of the problems of our society is the permissiveness of subsidies from government. We are not doing these people any favours by giving them something for nothing."

Erion's views were in sharp contrast with those of Jim Antoine, a young leader who gave testimony at the Indigenous hearings held in the old mission schoolhouse. The chief of the Fort Simpson Dene Band, Antoine was also university educated and would soon complete his MBA. "We're the Dene nation," he said. "We are the Slavey people here and we're part of this nation." He continued:

> Members of the white community said yesterday this town is frustrated . . . but we feel that we're more frustrated. . . . We've been kicked around, discriminated against, and mistreated. . . . We live here and this is where we're going to die. . . .
>
> My people are suffering enough without the pipeline. I would stand with my brother from Good Hope [Chief Frank T'Seleie] that he would lay down his life for what he believes in, and I feel the same way. There's a lot of us young people who feel the same way.

It was not long after the Fort Simpson hearing that a short news release crossed my desk signalling that my editorial misadventure was finally over. The prime minister had responded to the NWT municipalities association regarding their complaints about me, writing, "I have taken note of your concerns, I am satisfied the CBC has adequately addressed the issue." When you seek the prime minister's intervention and he doesn't pick up your cause, you have nowhere else to go.

Amid all the demands to the CBC for my head, or at least my job, the one voice that remained silent was the voice with the most money at stake, Canadian Arctic Gas. The company had already spent tens of millions of dollars in social, environmental and engineering studies preparing for the hearings. I was to learn much later from Ian Scott and CBC's Austin Curley that as part of the network's promised investigation of my potential bias, they had contacted the pipeline companies. The senior attorney for Canadian Arctic Gas, Pierre Genest, could have done me in. Instead, he told them that neither he nor the pipeline consortium took any issue with my reporting; in fact, Genest had said I could be accused of the reverse bias.

What he meant was that in some of the Native community hearings, dozens of people spoke in opposition to the pipeline. Often there wasn't a single voice in favour. Having been taught that without context, there is no understanding, I always included the company's position in my stories. Genest and Canadian Arctic Gas also knew this decision about the pipeline was not going to be made based on what was on the CBC every evening, but rather by Justice Berger and the evidence.

That's the way it came down. Berger's hearing process, "formal" and "community," was the frame he used to set out the recommendations he presented to the government of Canada in the first of two volumes of findings and recommendations in early May 1977. He often said, "There is as much wisdom in the small communities of the North as within the walls of corporations, governments or academia," and this wisdom from the communities clearly guided his principal recommendation: "If the native people are to achieve their goals, no pipeline can be built now." He recommended a ten-year moratorium until the claims were settled.

He'd also listened to the concerns about the social impact of such a large project on small isolated settlements: "The social consequences of the pipeline will not only be enormous—they will be devastating. . . . No remedial programs are likely to ameliorate them." Equally strong was his recommendation that no pipeline should be constructed in Northern Yukon: "The risk is in Canada. The urgency is in the United States."

Berger found that the mountain of engineering, technological and environmental evidence he heard in Yellowknife supported the conclusion that, after claims were settled, the

Foothills Maple Leaf route could be built with adequate environmental safeguards through the Mackenzie Valley. (In November 1977, the second volume outlined how to build it, along with detailed recommendations and proposed regulations to protect the environment and ensure fairness in the distribution of social-economic benefits to the people living along the proposed route—if and when the pipeline was built.) Finally, Berger wrote that if the demand for the Prudhoe Bay gas was deemed to be in the "national interest," the Alaska Highway alternative route could be considered.

The irony is that by the time Berger delivered his report, after three years of hearings and deliberation, the world energy picture that had been driving the pipeline proposal had changed. Gone was the Middle East oil embargo. The dire warnings of a world oil shortage and energy crisis with fears of freezing in the dark had almost vanished. Canada's push and panic to develop potential Arctic riches were also disappearing. More than that, the projected cost of the pipeline, now close to $6 billion, was no longer considered a worthwhile investment.

In his report to the government, Berger had prophesied: "We can build a . . . pipeline at a time of our own choosing, along a route of our own choice. With time, it may, after all, be possible to reconcile the urgent claims of northern native people with the future requirements of all Canadians for oil and gas."

The pipeline remains unbuilt today, even though land claims are long settled. Since the mid-1990s, the Dene, Métis and Inuvialuit of the Northwest Territories have even sought, unsuccessfully, partners and federal financial guarantees to build a pipeline themselves, acknowledging they are now in a position to share and reinvest the benefits back into the communities.

Years after Berger made his recommendations, some northerners in business or in municipal or territory politics continued to absurdly maintain that I was personally responsible for the collapse of the pipeline proposal. The legislative assembly's former Speaker and member for Hay River, Don Stewart, even made that claim in session.

These critics gave me far too much credit. Had I been able to influence the outcome of a project of such magnitude, the largest undertaking ever proposed in northern Canada, I suspect my services would have been in considerable demand in the years to come. They weren't.

Even many of the people who were angry with me eventually changed their attitudes, including Don Stewart, whom I'd considered a friend before the inquiry. Or at least we were friendly enough that once, when he ran into me checking into a hotel in Hay River, he immediately gave me "our" plan for the day.

"I'll pick you up in a few hours, we're going fishing."

Soon we were sitting in his small boat in the channel that connects to Great Slave Lake. Stewart had an enormous personality and charisma. He was quite a big man, maybe twenty years older than me, who ran a building supply store in Hay River; he was also seen as a community builder, always fighting for a new arena or better ball fields. Out in the boat with me, he was soon tearing away at the top of the two-four of beer he had brought along.

I was confronted with a dilemma. This was only a few weeks after I had decided that the booze was killing me. This was my first real test. Stewart had been a good drinking buddy. Would I offend him?

Maybe I'll have just one to appear sociable, I thought. Newly sober drunks think that way, looking for a way to justify the drink. Then I blurted out, "Don, I can't have a beer. It's gotten out of control and I had to quit."

He looked at me. "It's about time," he said, and closed the box. I told him he should go ahead.

"Maybe later," he said, but he didn't. I really appreciated that as we spent the day fishing and telling stories, enjoying each other's company.

Fifteen years later, when a chartered DC-3 from Yellowknife arrived at the Ottawa airport with the entire legislative assembly on board in order to support the battle for Aboriginal rights in the Constitution, the first person off the plane was Don Stewart. That old redneck, who'd been so bitter about losing the pipeline bid to "the Natives," was now standing up to have their rights enshrined in the Constitution of Canada.

More years later, I saw him again in Hay River, when he was out of politics and back in business. He called me aside for a private word. "I followed you," he said. It was his way of letting me know sobriety was now a key part of his life. We hugged as only old drunks do, and a friendship came full circle.

Then and now, I found the positions taken by Gordon Erion and others at the inquiry easy to understand. He and scores of southerners had followed their dream to the "northern frontier," eager to invest what money and energy they had to make a living, build a business and contribute.

What I couldn't condone, and what, as much as anything, compelled me to speak up in Norman Wells, was their almost total disregard for people who held different values and aspirations. Indigenous peoples who'd lived there for thousands of years weren't all driven to make as much money as they could, in as short a time as possible. They have different priorities. And for that, they were treated as second-class citizens. In fact, many of these southerners didn't see them as citizens at all.

In 2007, our inquiry cameraman, Pat Scott, wrote extensively about the Berger hearings as the basis for his PhD thesis. He noted that of the twenty non-native people who testified before Berger in 1975 in Fort Simpson, only two were still in the community. Of the thirty-nine Indigenous people who testified, only three had left.

Jim Antoine is one of those who stayed. In 1991 he was elected by a huge majority to represent the community in the territorial legislative assembly and immediately became a cabinet minister. From 1998 to 2000 he was the premier of the Northwest Territories, and, now retired from politics, he continues to push for self-government and economic development, including a revised Mackenzie Valley Pipeline proposal.

Antoine and other young leaders who stood before Berger said there should be no pipeline until the land claims are settled. They added, consistently, that when the claims were settled, they would be willing partners in building a pipeline where everyone can share in the benefits and opportunities. That's where we are today.

The carving of Tootalik aiming at the polar bear commissioned by Justice William Morrow of the NWT Territorial Court to commemorate the case. *Courtesy: NWT Archives.*

Me with my brother-in-law William Tagoona and the bear that didn't get me.

Jonah Kelly interviewing Jean Chrétien on April 1, 1999, the day that marked the creation of Nunavut. The last broadcast we did together after thirty-two years.

Joe Tobie and me at tea-time on a caribou hunt, 1975.

Joe Tobie taking notes at community hearing.

Louie Blondin's first radio broadcast in March 1975.

Jim Sittichinli broadcasting live in Aklavik in 1976, with his fan club.

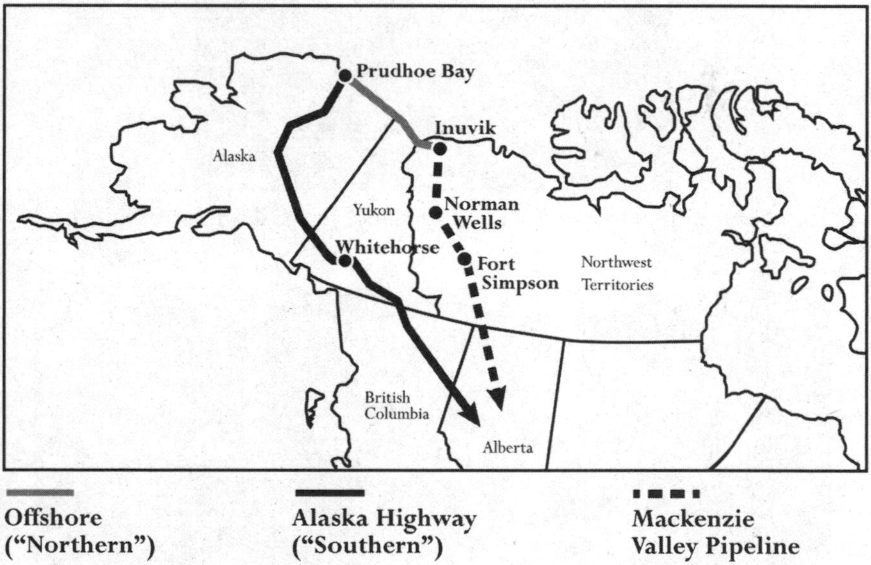

Proposed pipeline routes

Tom Berger in Old Crow, Yukon, with Chief Joe Kyikavichik in June 1975.

Berger listening to testimony in Northstar Harbour, NWT, with Inuk broadcaster Abe Okpik (at his left) doubling as interpreter. *Courtesy: Pat Scott.*

Mary May at four, on the cover of a Hudson's Bay Company magazine for the fur trade.

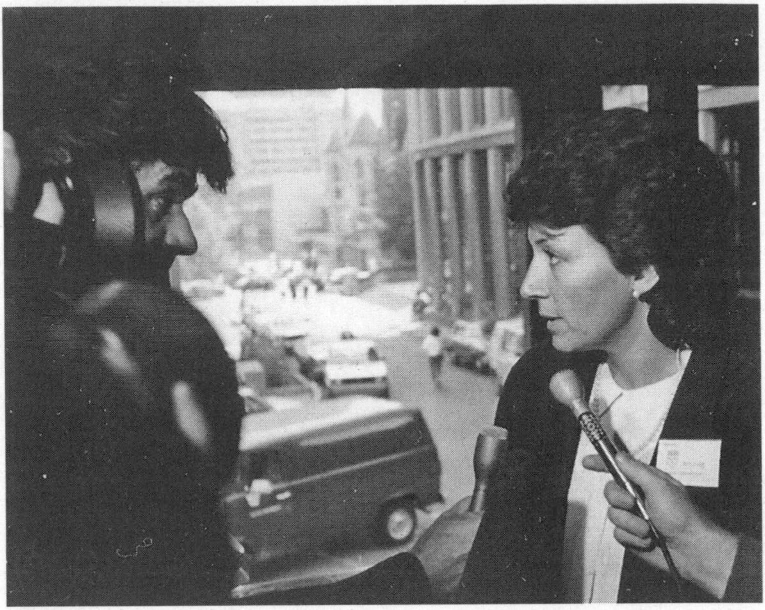

Me interviewing Mary at constitutional negotiations in Ottawa in 1984.

Mary's parents, Nancy and Bob May, in October 1994.

Waving from the window of the ambassador's residence in Copenhagen. The posting turned out to be a boot camp for a future neither of us had imagined.

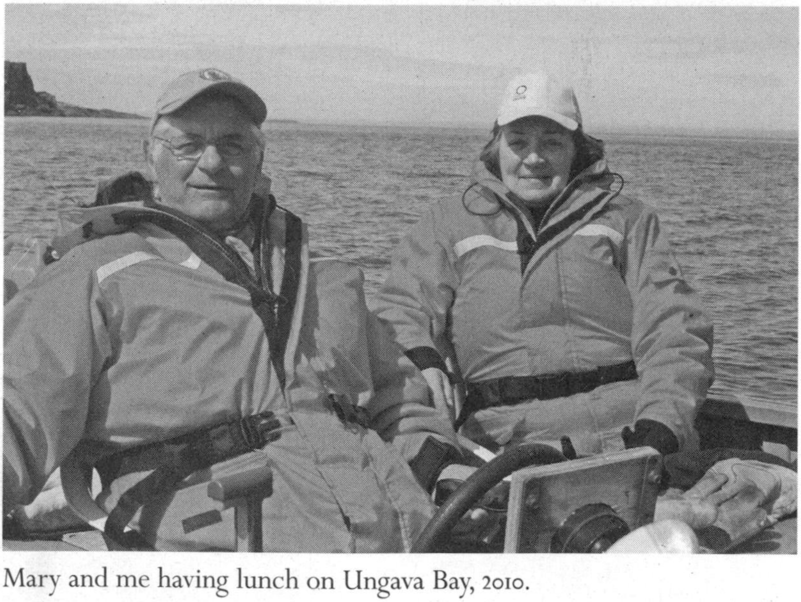

Mary and me having lunch on Ungava Bay, 2010.

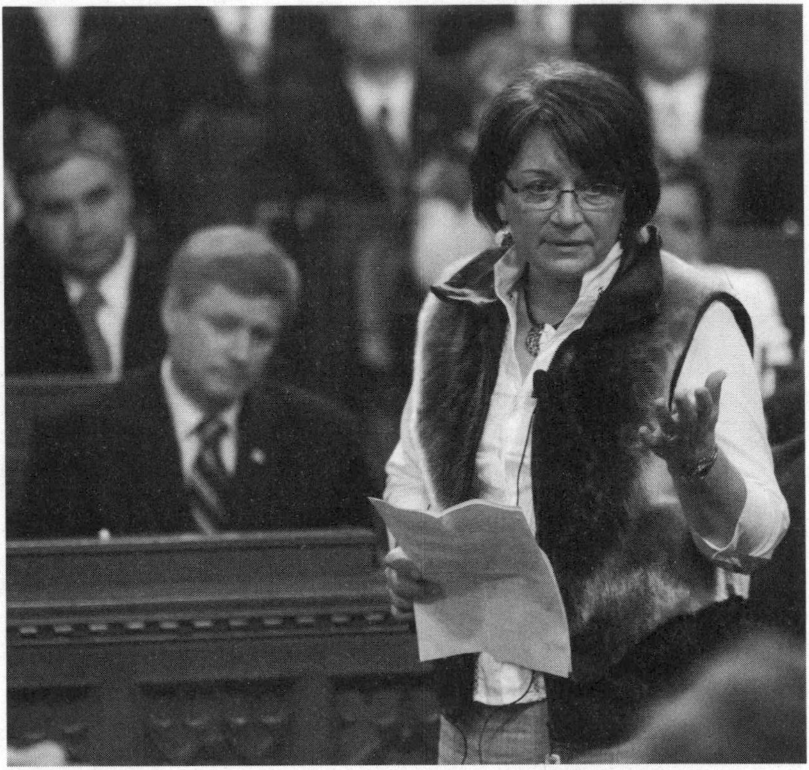

Mary accepting on behalf of all Inuit in Canada Prime Minister Stephen Harper's national apology for residential schools on June 11, 2008. *Courtesy: Jason Ransome, OPM*

Jose Kusugak unveiling the new Inuit Tapiriit Kanatami logo in 2002, which featured Inuit from four regions uniting around the Canadian maple leaf. *Courtesy: ITK Archives.*

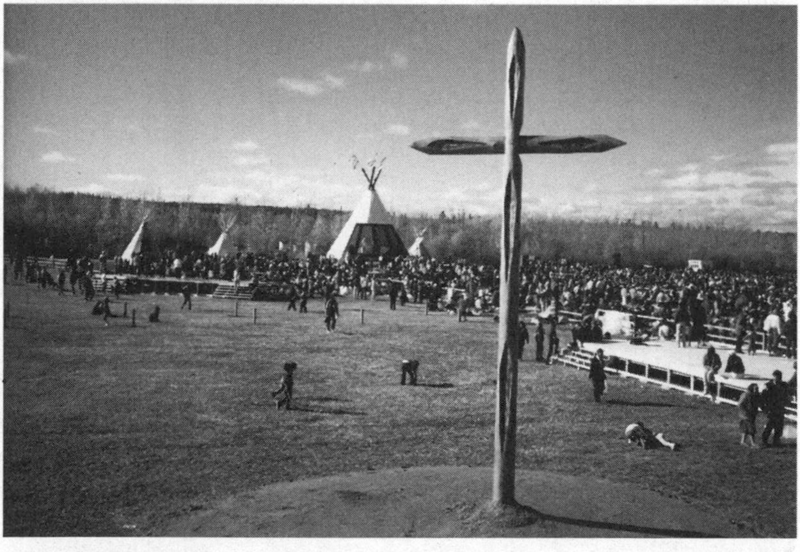

The site in Fort Simpson, NWT, prepared for Pope John Paul II's visit. *Courtesy: Herb Tyler.*

Stephen Kakfwi, Dene politician, singer-songwriter and statesman.

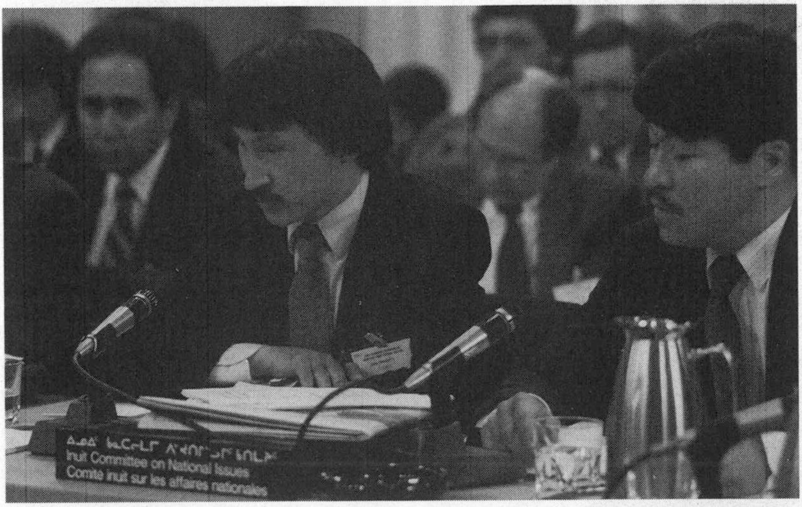

John Amagoalik (left) and Zebedee Nungak at constitutional negotiations in Ottawa in 1981. *Courtesy: ITK archives.*

Tagak Curley (centre) at the founding meeting of the Inuit Tapirisat of Canada in 1971. *Courtesy: ITK Archives.*

Airlifting dead caribou near Kuujjuaq in northern Quebec following the 1984 flooding disaster. *Courtesy: Avataq Cultural Institute; photo by Sandy Gordon Jr.*

Senate prospect Charlie Watt (right) introducing Mary to Prime Minister Pierre Elliott Trudeau at Kuujjuaq Airport in 1983.

One of Canada's foremost Arctic and Antarctic scientists, Fred Roots, hiking with students on Baffin Island in 2014.

Me with Mary at her investiture as Canada's first Indigenous governor general, on July 26, 2021. *Courtesy: Sgt Johanie Maheu, Rideau Hall © OSGG, 2021*

Builders

First Canadian, Canadian First

13

COVER GIRL

The Woman Who Would Become the First Indigenous Governor General

Some may have considered it strange that Canada's new governor general, the first Indigenous person to become the Queen's representative in Canada, would mention the family dog in her installation speech on July 26, 2021. The thing is, were it not for the somewhat hyper Labrador retriever we call Neva, Mary Simon's story could have ended in a little cottage at Caribou River, Nova Scotia, rather than extended to the new and wonderful chapters I hope Mary herself will one day write about.

Many friends have asked us, In your wildest dreams, did you ever expect this would happen? In fact, for a few fleeting months eleven years earlier, in 2010, we had been faced with that very possibility.

At the time, Mary was president of the national Inuit organization Inuit Tapiriit Kanatami. We had moved back to Kuujjuaq, Mary's hometown, a few years earlier, and had built a warm and cozy house overlooking the beautiful Koksoak

River—a place where we could imagine living on into comfortable old age.

We were tuned in to the CTV national news when Mary's picture popped up on the screen. "The search for a new governor general has begun and Inuit leader Mary Simon is said to be on a short list to replace Michaëlle Jean," proclaimed the anchor. "Where did that come from?" we said, almost in unison. It was crazy. Mary had not received any calls from either the Prime Minister's Office or the TV networks.

The weeks that followed brought more speculation; the national media were now declaring her a serious candidate and frequently paraphrasing the citation attached to her Order of Canada appointment: "Her integrity, diplomacy, and firmness of purpose have won her the respect of heads of governments and international organizations and as a respected adviser on such important issues as the environment, human rights and scientific research."

Her office made a few discreet inquiries to confirm the speculation. There was no official denial but rather a series of noncommittal responses, which are generally considered an indication that yes, something is in the wind. So Mary put a two-pronged plan in place. If the appointment came through, she would give it all her energy, but she would not campaign or lobby for it, nor would she get her hopes up and set us both up for disappointment. We didn't discuss it with our children or grandkids, but I was not surprised when she began taking French lessons. It is her nature to prepare for every possibility, and though she could read and understand some French, Mary was self-conscious about speaking it. Of course, she also wrestled with whether she wanted the appointment. She carefully considered the responsibilities, the workload and the life changes, and came to this conclusion: What better way to advocate for Inuit and all Indigenous peoples than serving as governor general of Canada?

After six months of speculation, and a determined effort not to get caught up in a political whirl, she got her answer. Again, it came without any contact from Ottawa, same time, same channel.

We were at home in Kuujjuaq and tuned in to the national news. The lead item on both CBC and CTV was that David Johnston has been appointed Canada's new governor general. We looked at each other. "Well, that's that!" There were no tears or disappointment, certainly no regrets. If anything, perhaps a sense of relief, considering the gruelling schedule a governor general is expected to maintain (and which, as we would eventually find out, is even more than we imagined). Mary was very supportive of the appointment. She'd worked with Johnston when he was at McGill University and thought that he was a good choice.

The next morning, *Globe and Mail* columnist John Ibbitson offered the opinion that "Inuit leader Mary Simon was a very serious candidate but passed over because she is not bilingual." I sent Ibbitson a short email reminding him that Mary is indeed bilingual: Inuktitut is her mother tongue and over the years she has mastered the English language. I also asked him whether Indigenous peoples would always be held to a higher standard—the expectation to be trilingual. I suggested that in the future he consider how easily the Indigenous reality is overlooked in Canada.

My question to John Ibbitson was definitively answered in July 2021, when my wife became Canada's thirtieth governor general.

When I first met Mary, I was a young reporter, covering the Canadian colonial north, where everybody knew what was best for the "Natives" except, of course, the "Natives" themselves.

It was a cold November day in 1973 when I walked into the school auditorium in Cambridge Bay on the southeast coast of Victoria Island, there to cover one of the inaugural meetings of the Inuit Tapirisat of Canada (ITC), an organization that quickly came to be the political voice of Canada's Inuit.

About four hundred Inuit from across the North were in the hall. Though I didn't know it then, some of these people would go on to change the map of Canada. But it was hard not to notice the beautiful and energetic twenty-six-year-old interpreter, Mary May, even though I wondered who she was translating for. Everybody there, except me and a handful of others, spoke Inuktitut.

It turned out that all these visionary young Inuit leaders had a message they wanted to be heard in other parts of Canada. They planned to change the North, to reclaim it for their people, and they wanted journalists and government observers to understand every word they spoke. So Mary translated into English detailed accounts of Inuit who had been stripped of control over their land and their languages, who had been threatened, uprooted and relocated—their names replaced by numbers. At this meeting, they were talking about the phenomenon of cultural genocide, long before the term found its way into the words of the chief justice of the Supreme Court of Canada, Beverley McLachlin, over forty years later.

Between the speeches, Mary also translated for me as I interviewed the delegates and provided me with spelling and pronunciation, so I didn't butcher every name and term. More than that, she also became a friend when I needed one.

These young Inuit leaders were not saints. They partied just as hard as they worked. When I found myself at one of their parties that night, I had been sober for about two years, and still felt both uncomfortable and vulnerable. This party house, as I remember it, had only one place to sit—the floor. Mary May sat beside me. She had neither a drink nor anything with ashes on the end of it, just a reassuring smile. We started talking and I told her of my unease—how and why I had quit drinking and the continuing temptations. We went on to talk about the CBC. I knew she had worked at the Northern Service shortwave bureau in Montreal with the great Inuit announcer-producer Elijah Menerak. I recalled seeing her once when I briefly passed through the studio, but she was busy preparing a program and I was too shy to interrupt.

When I told her I thought I should leave, she walked with me as far as the house where she was sharing a room. We stood on the darkened porch in a long, awkward silence, vibrating between passion and panic.

"I am married," I told her. "We have three kids, the oldest ten, the youngest two."

She said she had two children herself. She was divorced but was soon to marry a fine man, a northern pilot named George Simon.

At that point I said, "Good night—and thank you for helping me."

No hug, no kiss, and no come-on from either of us. Not then and not for a long time, although our paths would cross often during the next eighteen years.

Today I look around our home in Ottawa and I see honorary diplomas from a dozen Canadian universities plus a membership in the International Women's Forum Hall of Fame. There are photos of Mary in her capacity as chancellor of Trent University, as Canada's ambassador to Denmark, and there's one of her receiving the Royal Order of Greenland. (She was the first non-Greenlander to be given the award.) The gold medal from the Royal Canadian Geographical Society is in a glass case. Even before we got to Rideau Hall, she always proudly wore the Officer of the Order of Canada snowflake on her lapel when we went out.

There are other awards and recognitions, along with a half-dozen masterful Inuit sculptures given to her over the years by Inuit colleagues and organizations in appreciation of her hard work and dedication. My favourite, though, is her "cover girl" picture. It's a photo of Mary taken in 1951 by Dr. J. Rousseau, who was, at that time, director of the Montreal Botanical Garden, at the Hudson's Bay post in George River, Quebec, where Mary's father was the manager.

Mary is four years old in the photo. She's wearing sealskin kamiks, a homemade dress, and a tiny traditional amauti, the hooded parka unique to Inuit and designed so that you could carry a baby in the large hood (or in the case of a four-year-old, a place for little dolls or puppies). The picture was published on the cover of the April 1952 issue of *Moccasin Telegraph*, the magazine for Hudson's Bay Company fur traders. The caption is "Winsome Little Miss."

To me, this picture shows how far Mary May had to go in a part of the world where the odds were so stacked against her. I made that photo my Facebook post to mark her appointment. The response was staggering, thousands of shares and ten times that many hearts and thumbs up. It felt like a whole lot of people saw what I saw in that photo too.

Mary's father, Bob May, was a white man who joined the Hudson's Bay Company while still in his teens. He adopted the Inuit lifestyle, learned their language and life skills—hunting and trapping, living on the land, handling dog teams. Eventually he married a beautiful Inuk, Nancy Angnatuk, from Killiniq, at the very tip of northern Quebec.

But in George River in the 1940s, when Bob and Nancy pledged a lifetime of commitment to one another, there was no minister or even justice of the peace to officiate at a wedding. There was no one to baptize their first child, Johnny, when he arrived in 1945, or Mary when she was born in 1947. When an Anglican minister did come to the village, around 1949, he did the marriage and the baptisms almost simultaneously, but still the bureaucrats decreed that both Johnny and Mary were born "out of wedlock." They were also declared to be "Eskimos" and assigned an *E* disc number.

My darling wife, the distinguished Inuit leader and Canadian Governor General, is also Mary Jeannie E9-761. The *E* signifies she was born in the eastern Arctic. The 9 indicates she was born in northern Quebec and 761 was her personal number.

In the 1950s, Bob and Nancy moved twice. First from George River to the old Hudson's Bay post on the east side of the Koksoak River at Fort Chimo. Then, late in that decade, to the American and Canadian airbase on the opposite bank called New Fort Chimo. Within a few years, that base would increase in prominence as the regional administrative centre, with schools and a hospital. Today it's known as Kuujjuaq and is home to about three thousand people.

Mary's father wanted to improve his economic prospects as well as find better schooling for the children. Who would think that finding decent education would be the most challenging proposition, and one that marked Mary for life?

Her Inuit identity was never in question when she entered the federal day school in New Fort Chimo. Like every other Indigenous child who attended school under that despicable educational system, she was forbidden to speak her mother tongue, Inuktitut. At the end of grade six, when this little Inuit girl was about to become a teenager, she got a completely new message from the government. No, they decreed, she was not Inuit at all. Why? Because her mother married a white man. Such was the power of the northern bureaucratic administrators of the day.

Mary and her brother Johnny, two years older than she was, stayed at home while their friends and classmates were shipped to a residential school in Churchill, Manitoba, thousands of kilometres away. Perhaps her father could have fought the decision, but he was a proud and independent man, not prone to asking for favours, particularly from the government. Bob and Nancy were no doubt relieved, since the other parents were distraught at having their children sent away. The May family had no money to pay for a private boarding school. With no public institution she could attend, the only option was home-schooling and so her father became her teacher, relying on mail-order lessons from the Alberta education curriculum.

In the first forty years of our friendship and, later, our partnership, Mary and I had never talked about how that separation from all her friends affected her. I watched her finally confront it only a decade ago, and it was emotionally devastating.

In March 2014, I sat with more than three thousand people in the Edmonton Convention Centre and listened to Mary, having been inducted as an honorary witness at the Truth and Reconciliation Commission hearings, deliver her own deeply personal recollections of the residential school experience. The induction ceremony was the commission's way of acknowledging the contribution of several Canadians who had supported and encouraged the TRC throughout its mandate. An hour before the ceremony, Mary was still working on her remarks. She said it was going to be difficult. At least she had the comfort of knowing that she would share the stage with a dear friend of ours, TRC commissioner Marie Wilson.

This is a story of such intertwined lives. As a young reporter in 1977, Marie Wilson came to work with me in the Yellowknife newsroom of the CBC. A few years later, she and Mary became close friends. Mary championed Marie's nomination as a Truth and Reconciliation commissioner over some high-profile Inuit candidates, because she believed that Marie possessed superior communication abilities, that she was the best candidate and would deliver. Marie, in turn, supported Mary's insistence that

Inuit voices be heard by the TRC and that their painful experiences be recorded as part of a dreadful chapter in Canada's history.

I was eager to see the two women share the stage in Edmonton, but I had no idea that the event would turn into a complete emotional breakdown for Mary. Still, even through her tears, she was able to get her message out: "It is very hard to find the words to describe how moved I am now, and how this gathering is affecting me in both mind and spirit. First, my truth—when I was invited to become honorary witness, I was gripped by both a sense of guilt and apprehension. How could I understand your pain when I had never truly walked your path?"

Mary said she had shared her apprehension with members of the TRC, and especially Marie, telling them how she had been forbidden to attend residential school. She continued: "They assured me that it is the combined truth from all of our experiences and stories that will lead us toward true reconciliation. My truth is that I was denied the opportunity to attend any school beyond grade six where we lived in Kuujjuaq in northern Quebec. For the government administrators in that time and that place, I just wasn't Inuk enough."

She recalled the damage the schools caused to parents, children and the communities, and how strange it was to grow up "in a community without its older children." She said: "I saw the despair of fathers with no sons to hunt with, mothers with no daughters to sew with, and grandmothers with no children to tell stories to. I began feeling bad, even guilty, that I was spared this experience. My family was intact, and so many others were not."

She said Sundays were particularly poignant. Her mother and grandmother would take Mary and her brothers and sisters to church. After the service, they went to visit the Inuit families whose children had been taken away. Mary said she felt like a stand-in, a well-loved substitute, showered with "great expressions of love and endearments."

And finally, she confessed through her tears: "You all have forced me to recall an earlier and difficult time in my life when I felt the pressure of mental breakdown, depression, and isolation."

Three thousand people, many of them wiping their own tears, stood and applauded. In their ovation, they acknowledged that the scars of the residential school are borne by Indigenous peoples everywhere; even those who did not attend such a school share a great sense of guilt, much as the survivors of disasters grapple with why they were spared when others perished.

I cried, too, but mine were tears of pride and wonder. How was it that I had been lucky enough to witness and share and become a part of this remarkable woman's life?

Mary's journey to the stature of leader is still a marvel to me. There was a time when we sat on the same side of the table, both getting paycheques from the CBC, with Mary working in Montreal, covering national and international events in Inuktitut. After she reported on the 1970 October Crisis and the fallout from the FLQ separatist movement, her bosses at the CBC became nervous that her political interests were growing and assigned her a Saturday morning cooking show on TV. So there was Mary May, baking traditional dishes like bannock and blueberry pies—all of it in Inuktitut, her shows broadcast across the North.

She didn't know it at the time, but I was a fan. I was watching her show at home early one Saturday morning, when Dianne asked sharply, "What are you watching that for?"

"Oh," I said, scrambling, "I'm just trying to see how many words I understand."

When CBC Newsworld was created in 1989, I was transferred to Alberta to anchor the six-hour prime-time evening slot out of Calgary. It meant working every weeknight, but after twenty-five years of constant travel, it also meant I was at home every day. Which also meant that it was time to confront the fact that my marriage to Dianne had been eroding for years. Sometimes people just grow apart, and the older the children become, the more pronounced the differences are in how each spouse views the world around them. Thankfully, we live in a time when people are no longer expected to stay together in unhappy situations. Given that our youngest child was almost twenty, we agreed that a separation was in both our interests. Dianne found and made her new life in Ottawa. Hard feelings have long been reconciled: we share children and grandchildren and are both part of large family gatherings, including Christmas and birthdays at Rideau Hall.

Incredibly, and one more time, Austin Curley, the man who'd hired me in the Summerside air force base parking lot so many years earlier, would (and this time unwittingly) direct my fate. As Dianne and I were going through the early stages of separation, I got a call to speak at the party honouring him as he retired from CBC Northern Service. The party was to be in Ottawa, and I was eager to attend.

Some months earlier, I had heard that Mary and her husband George had also separated. I got in touch with her and suggested she also come to Ottawa. She knew Austin from her time with Northern Service and, like so many others, had the greatest respect for him. She said she'd be there. I think we both knew that an eighteen-year friendship was about to take a new direction.

Fast-forward three decades, and I am sitting on the viceregal consort's throne, in the temporary chambers of the Senate of Canada at the Government Conference Centre (once a stately downtown Ottawa railway station), borrowed while the buildings on Parliament Hill are being renovated.

We had both been here before. In 1982, Mary had been a part of making history while I'd documented it as a reporter for CBC's the *National*.

I tried placing where everybody had been that day, almost forty years earlier, when Mary and other Inuit, First Nations and Métis leaders took their seats at the constitutional table alongside ten provincial premiers and Prime Minister Pierre Trudeau. The Indigenous leadership firmly believed that if their rights were not enshrined in the Constitution the Trudeau government had repatriated from Great Britain, federal or provincial governments could legislate their rights out of existence. After difficult negotiations, they achieved the addition of section 35 to Canada's Constitution Act, which states: "The existing aboriginal and treaty rights of the aboriginal peoples of Canada are hereby recognized and affirmed."

Three future constitutional negotiations to define those rights, chaired by Trudeau and then by Progressive Conservative prime minister Brian Mulroney, failed. The Indigenous leadership at the time unanimously placed the blame on the provincial premiers.

Now here I am on July 26, 2021, sitting in this grand chair in the Senate, watching my wife's investiture as though it is on a split-screen. On one side, in living colour, I experience the reality of this historic moment. On the other side, in back and white, I see Mary confronting Pierre Trudeau on the matter of equal rights for men and women, with Trudeau snapping, "I wish you and your sisters would get it through your heads nobody is trying to take your rights away."

To which Mary responds in a defiant voice, thumping a finger on the table: "I am speaking for *all* my people."

Back in the full screen of this moment, I hear Mary in a much quieter voice say, "My Inuit name is Ningiukudluk." Smiling at Justin Trudeau, she adds, "Prime Minister, I need to tell you it means 'bossy old woman.'" Any ice in the room today is instantly broken by laughter from every person of every background.

When she finished her speech, in which she set out a clear priority—her commitment to reconciliation—I had to reach out and squeeze her hand to make sure I wasn't dreaming.

By now, you will have read enough to know that in my lifetime, I've witnessed too many acts of colonialism, marginalization, discrimination and genocide. Mary's priority is my priority. To the extent that the spouse of a governor general has political capital, influence and opportunity to bring about change, I will use mine in the same way.

But back to the family dog and her place in all of this. Almost a year before Mary's appointment, the two of us packed our van and headed to Nova Scotia with Neva for a long-planned two-month vacation by the seaside, in a cottage we'd rented at Caribou River, not far from where I was born and raised.

By the first of October, the COVID infection rates were continuing to skyrocket in Ontario. Nova Scotia, especially the little COVID-free coves along the Northumberland Strait, seemed like the safest place in the country, if not the world. So instead of heading home, we bought and winterized a small cottage close to the places of a half-dozen friends I had known since childhood. We had the best winter there, safe in our bubble with those friends. A few nights each week, we had fun dinners in which our friends revelled in learning from Mary about the North and Indigenous peoples.

We had also watched the misfortunes of Julie Payette unfold, followed by her resignation in late January. Considering Mary's experience from a decade past, we had no expectations. Then, within days of that resignation, Mary was asked for an interview by CBC's *Power and Politics*. She debated whether she should do it. She didn't want to be seen as someone campaigning for the job, but she did have an important point she wanted to make: it was time Canada had an Indigenous governor general, and there were many people qualified for the position. So Mary did the interview, which brought more media requests, all of which she declined.

About three months later, Mary received a formal inquiry from the Privy Council Office and a selection committee. One discussion led to another and then another. I cannot write about them because I was not part of the process. I do know that in all of them Mary addressed the fact that she did not speak French. Even though she was educated in Quebec, she was taught in English and forbidden to speak Inuktitut on the school grounds.

Between phone calls and interviews, we moved temporarily into a neighbour's cottage while ours was under renovation. At some point at the end of May, my snoring got the better of Mary's patience, and in the middle of the night, she asked me to relocate to the small bedroom at the far end of the cottage, next to the main bathroom.

I soon fell back into my deep (thundering) sleep and drifted into an unforgettable dream of wandering in a magnificent cedar forest. The smell was so powerful and so beautiful I thought this must be what heaven smells like. Then suddenly something seemed to be attacking me, paw pushing my chest, then hitting my face. Now a dog was barking. Finally, my old brain found reality and my eyes opened.

The place was filled with thick, dense smoke and the scent of burning cedar. I opened the door, then checked the bathroom, which was billowing more smoke. I could see flames beginning to lick the three-quarter-inch-thick cedar panelling. Thanking the lord for our dog, I ran to wake Mary, urging her to get dressed and head for Red and Cheryl McKean's—the closest neighbours and our closest Nova Scotia friends.

It was faster to phone Red, tell him what was happening and get him to call the fire department than to look for the number and try to explain the location myself. After he called, he rushed to our cabin, where he helped me throw water on the burning back wall. I was surprised how quickly a rural volunteer fire crew could get out of bed and mobilize two fire trucks and a dozen volunteers. Some arrived within ten minutes and ensured the flames were out and the source, a misbehaving electrical fan, identified.

We'd had a terrible scare that night that could have resulted in tragedy, but Cheryl's description of the unregal version of Canada's future governor general who turned up on her doorstep that morning allows all of us to look back with laughter. In her haste to get out of there, Mary had thrown a windbreaker over her pink pyjamas, stuffed her feet into rubber boots, slung her purse across her shoulders and grabbed her cell phone. Added to the drama and distraction, Mary was facing a critical meeting later that day with the selection committee. Somehow, she shook it all off, and for close to two hours took more questions.

On a Sunday evening in early July, the prime minister called and after a forty-minute discussion with my wife, he offered her the job. The dog and I both danced.

14

MEET THE PARENTS

Like Geese—Migratory Birds, Mated for Life

Mary and I had been together for several months when we agreed it was time for me to "meet the parents." Hers. You'll recall that their lives had connected at a Hudson's Bay post in northern Quebec. They lived most of their lives in the North. But the first time I met them was in the Arizona desert on the San Carlos Indian Reservation.

I remember turning off the main roadway, not far from the reservation's gas station, and up a barely recognizable road. It felt like I was in the opening scene of one of a hundred old western movies.

"What next?" I asked Mary, who had the letter in her hand that Bob had mailed some weeks earlier, giving us directions and telling us how good it would be for us both to come and visit. There was no obvious road, just trails, some carved during rare periods of desert rain and flooding.

Still, Bob had written that there would be signs. Just about the time our faith was giving way to fear, we saw a white paper picnic plate pegged to a cactus with the words "Bobby Aulook" (Big Bobby in Inuktitut) written on it and an arrow pointing up what appeared to be a dry riverbed. A few rough kilometres later, another plate and another "Bobby Aulook" arrow set a new course. There were several more of these at various points over fifteen to twenty kilometres. If someone had come along and taken one of those plates for whatever reason, we'd have been screwed. We could have found our way back to the main road, but we would never have located Bob and Nancy in the vastness of that desert of a million or more acres.

Then we crested another sandy gravel ridge, looked down through the cactus and spotted a little white trailer and a truck. Two small dots in the desert, not another manufactured object in any direction—one of several "winter camping" sites they had in the desert. The satellite dish and wood stove pipe sticking out of the camping trailer were unmistakable.

Despite their dedication to the North, each year for nearly twenty years they'd taken out a permit, to camp, fish and hunt small game near the large water reservoir that is part of the Apache reservation at San Carlos. Two or three times a week they purchased gas and food and filled their water cans at the trading post in the village. The rest of the time they stayed by themselves in the wilderness.

Bob May had come north from where he was raised in southern Manitoba at age seventeen. No one in his family was surprised when he applied to the Hudson's Bay Company. As a kid they'd nicknamed him "Nanook of the North" because he was fascinated with that movie and had a thirst for Arctic stories and tales. After training in northern Saskatchewan, only three months short of his nineteenth birthday, he was sent to the company's most northerly outpost at Arctic Bay on north Baffin Island, more than three thousand kilometres straight north of Montreal and even farther from his home in Manitoba. He hunted, trapped, handled dog teams, learned iglu-building, and above all, embraced Inuit values and traditions—and the language.

Bob and Nancy spoke to each other in Inuktitut even in that Arizona desert. When we were gathering firewood, his chainsaw quit working. As he fiddled and fixed it, he kept muttering to that stubborn saw in Inuktitut.

Mary's mother couldn't quite say my name. It always came out with a *V*—"Vitt." Nancy would try over and over to get it right and break out laughing every time. I was told forming the "wh" sound is difficult for Inuktitut speakers. Given that I had butchered almost every Inuktitut phrase or word I'd ever tried, I thought "Vitt" certainly better than "Twit" and many other names I had been called.

The conversation between us moved from English to Inuktitut and the reverse, depending on who was speaking. Though I only spoke English, I was warmly welcomed into their lives and their family.

There is, however, nothing warm in the story of Mary's ancestors, who experienced one of the most brutal historical injustices perpetrated by the government against Inuit. Forced relocation was the government's answer to many realities. Sovereignty in the High Arctic in the early 1950s, or the need for an instant workforce when an airbase was built at Frobisher

Bay in the late 1950s and, in the case of Mary's relatives, a settlement at Coral Harbour on Southampton Island, where there were not enough women. Today, there is only one way to describe that practice of forced relocation. It was a cruel manifestation of colonialism. For Nancy, it's a memory that burned bitterly throughout her life.

In 1942, a ship arrived at Killiniq. Men came off that ship, rounded up a group of young women and put them into a small boat with only a few belongings. Among them was Nancy's Aunt Matilda, her mother's youngest sister. Nancy said the wailing of the women coming from the small boat would never be erased from her memory.

From shore, she, her mother, Jeannie, and others watched, listening to the echoing cries growing fainter and fainter as the young captives in the boat got closer to the ship waiting to take them several hundred kilometres northwest to Coral Harbour. At the same time, Inuit from other regions were being either coerced or bribed into relocating to the growing military installation there.

Though Nancy's family had been torn apart, it speaks to their great resilience that they never lost contact with each other. At first, they relied on sporadic mail service, and much later on the telephone. Today, Mary continues to communicate with her cousins in Coral Harbour through Facebook.

But the family history is not all sad. The union of Mary's parents is a real love story, one I have heard them tell and one I have retold many times. It starts in Killiniq or, as the settlement was known to nineteenth-century whalers, Port Burwell, at the entrance to the Hudson Strait where Labrador and Quebec meet. The harbour there is quite protected, and there are still abandoned wooden whaling boats hauled high on the shore. Only a few of the old buildings remain, but at different times it was a trading post, whaling station, missionary residence, RCMP detachment, government administration centre, weather station and Coast Guard port.

The teenage Bob May was on his maiden Arctic voyage when his ship stopped in Port Burwell on a July day in 1937. When he got off to stretch his legs, he noticed a group of young Inuit children, all girls, shy and laughing and very much intrigued by this strange Qallunaaq with striking blue eyes and red hair. He motioned for them to come closer and reached into his pocket for a pack of gum. He offered each child a stick, knowing that in that place and that time, this was a great treat. The kids knew it too. They took the gum and ran away laughing. One girl, maybe ten or twelve, captured his attention—she had an incredibly beautiful smile.

At each stop Bob's ship made at the coastal communities of Labrador and Baffin Island—Lake Harbour, Pangnirtung, Pond Inlet and some other outposts, now long abandoned—the Hudson's Bay superintendent on board decided who among his group of new recruits appeared most suited for that particular post. By the time they approached Arctic Bay on the northernmost coast of Baffin Island, Bob was the last apprentice on the ship, and Arctic Bay was the end of the line—he had reached his destination.

He would spend two years there, and another three years at Port Harrison (now Inukjuak), on the east coast of Hudson Bay in northern Quebec. Then in the early 1940s, Bob was promoted to post manager and relocated to Kangiqsualujjuaq, or George River, a post at the mouth of that great waterway.

Being a manager carried some perks, among them the authorization to hire a full-time cook and housekeeper. Inquiries were made, and soon he hired the highly recommended Jeannie Angnatuk. She arrived at the post with her youngest daughter, Nancy, who was now about sixteen or seventeen. Bob immediately recognized Nancy as the child with the beautiful smile he'd noticed on the grassy banks of Port Burwell. Fortunately for him, Nancy had been equally struck by his mesmerizing blue eyes. It was love at second sight.

Neither ever gave details on just how long it took for what happened next to happen. But it did, and the lives they lived together would fill another book.

In 1948, Bob took an Inuit child suffering from appendicitis 230 kilometres by dog team across the Ungava Peninsula in the bitter cold and heavy snow to rendezvous with an RCAF crew. Upon reaching Fort Chimo, they were both flown to Halifax, where surgeons saved the boy's life.

Another time Bob and Nancy's kids were out gathering eggs. Mary was on a ledge, her small hand gently finding its way into the nest of a gull or kittiwake. Johnny was with her and would have been about twelve. He was hunting and when a duck flew past him, he swung his shotgun around quickly. He did not intend to shoot anywhere near Mary on the cliff, but two pellets ricocheted off the rock and pierced her lower jaw, lodging in her face and tongue. She didn't fall, but she was instantly in pain and bleeding heavily.

Mary's mother and grandmother gathered her up, carried her to the tent, and laid her down on her bed of spruce boughs and eiderdown blankets. Johnny had disappeared. That evening, using the high-frequency radio, they managed to contact Bob, who was with a hunting party farther down the coast. They were all concerned about internal bleeding or infection or any one of a dozen other complications. It took Bob more than two days to get back, and for most of that time, Johnny would not come back to the camp. He had convinced himself that if he hadn't already killed his sister, she would soon die, and he would be to blame. Finally, his grandmother was able to persuade Johnny to come and talk to Mary through the tent wall. When Johnny heard that she could still talk, he began to calm down.

When Bob got back, he wrapped his daughter in blankets and put her on a mattress in the bow of his open twenty-foot freighter canoe—the workhorse of the northern waterways, powered by an outboard motor—and they set off across Ungava Bay. The trip took more than fourteen hours, and for every minute of that trip, Bob gripped the throttle and tiller. One bay after another, from headland to headland, sometimes aided and other times hampered by some of the world's highest and constantly shifting tides, they moved closer to the base at Fort Chimo. Mary remembers the pain from the constant banging of every wave. Other times, she was in a complete daze.

When they made it to the clinic, the nurse—there were no doctors—judged it might be better to leave the pellets in place rather than risk additional damage by trying to remove them. Mary rested and healed for a few days, and then father and daughter made the return trip back across the sixty kilometres of the bay, though this time at a pace that was a little less hectic.

One of my favourite stories from Mary's childhood is about the full year the family spent in the bush at what locals call the "big bend" of the George River. Mary was sixteen. Her father had left the Hudson's Bay Company and was planning to build a hunting and fishing lodge. Soon after the ice cleared, he and Nancy headed upstream with all their children, along with Jeannie, Mary's grandmother.

They lived in two tents—sturdy, bell-shaped canvas tents sewn at home. The tents were large enough to stand and walk around in, with wood stoves for warmth and cooking. They lived almost entirely from the land, picking berries, catching fish, hunting caribou and gathering eggs. The children amused themselves playing Inuit games and at night listened to legends and tales that always contained a subtle message of good over evil and right over wrong—just as fairy tales do, in cultures everywhere.

It was a lonely Christmas that year, "so far away from civilization that even Santa couldn't find us," as Mary once described it. Christmas morning arrived and there were no presents. Strangely, she said, her father insisted on going outside now and again, to walk a big circle on the frozen river. Around noon, he said to them all, "Listen, do you hear it?"

They rushed outside and looked skyward to see a single-engine bush plane approaching. It circled and then landed. To the children's joy and surprise, the pilot was an old family friend. He stepped out of the plane laden with fresh oranges and candy for all. Her dad had been making circles in the snow to guide the plane to a safe landing spot on the frozen river.

Mary still talks about those times a lot. Sometimes, during a speech or presentation, when she wants her audience to better understand the context of Inuit cultural perseverance, she will speak about her life in the bush. It's always so very clear that her own strength grew from watching the example of Jeannie through that long and bitterly cold winter, going night after night with little sleep because she was stuffing more firewood into the stove to keep everyone warm. The air on the other side of the thin canvas walls would routinely drop to minus forty. Mary says, "I remember sleeping with my hat on or covering my head under the blanket to keep warm. Every day was a constant battle just to stay alive." She also says that her destiny was shaped in that tent on those cold winter nights.

I remember watching her face during one magical moment in her term as Canada's ambassador to Denmark. We were attending the inauguration of a new culture and performing arts centre in Nuuk, Greenland. The Greenland Inuit are famous for their singing, and a choir of men and women was giving us a magnificent performance. Mary was dabbing her eyes with a tissue, and I knew that she was back in that tent on the frozen bank of the George River on one of the nights when her grandmother would turn the dial on the old battery-operated shortwave radio, searching for Radio Greenland, and suddenly the tent would fill with the beautiful voices of a Greenlandic choir singing both traditional Inuit songs and ancient European classics translated into Greenlandic Inuktitut. She remembers her grandmother telling her, "Listen, Mary. Those are our people. We are all the same, one nomadic Arctic people."

If Mary's destiny was shaped living on the land, it was the schoolyard and the classroom that forged her drive and commitment to social justice and equality. It was also shaped by the strength and love of her parents, Bob and Nancy.

I still remember those two sitting in our Ottawa living room holding hands. In their seventies and eighties, they would stop for a visit on their annual spring return or fall migration to Arizona. They'd be sitting there together, and Bob would look lovingly at his wife and sweetheart of some fifty years, get a gleam in his eye, then reach into his pocket and offer her a stick of gum. She would giggle and take it.

They are still side by side, in the cemetery at Kuujjuaq. Seven of their children are still living in Kuujjuaq, all holding key positions in the community. Two of the sons are among the best-regarded bush pilots in the region. Then there's Mary.

15

VICEREGAL BOOT CAMP

Our Culture Clash

I had been out of the TV business for about three years when Mary and I went on a short holiday to the Maritimes. We encountered two elegantly dressed elderly women in a shopping district—members of the blue-rinse set and, in truth, core members of the demographic of my old *Newsworld* audience (or so said the ratings research).

One of the women approached me excitedly. "Oh, I know you from CBC. I watched you all the time and I miss you."

I thanked her and shook her hand, and that of her friend. Sadly for my ego, but happily for Mary's sense of humour, the woman didn't let it go.

"Don't tell me your name, I'll get it! Your name is right on the tip of my tongue . . . . let me think, let me think!" Then in exasperation, she blurted, "I am sure I know you. Tell me, didn't you used to be someone?"

"Yes," I responded. "I used to be Whit Fraser. Now I am Mr. Mary Simon."

We all laughed. It was the kind of moment that I hope defines how we see our relationship and marriage. Politics, particularly in the context of Indigenous rights and justice and equality, is the root and the branches of Mary's professional life and persona. And we talk about those issues. We argue about them too, and frequently they eat away at us, because we can't do more or find solutions to the enormous social and economic issues confronting northern communities, particularly the shortcomings in education and mental health care, and the scourge of suicide among young people. These are the issues that have driven Mary's actions for almost a half century. And in truth, her heart is still very much a part of the land, lakes and rivers of her homeland in northern Quebec.

For example, Mary is never as comfortable or as at peace with herself as when she's sitting on the ground in a blueberry patch, legs folded under her, picking. Every day for two to three weeks in September and early October, no matter how much her back would ache, she was berry-patch bound with her sisters, Sara, Madge and Annie, or with lifelong friends.

One year about 2005, before we built the Kuujjuaq house, it fell to me to carry the berries home to Ottawa. I placed two coolers on the scale at the airport, both of them full of handpicked berries, cleaned and frozen in resealable plastic bags, each one marked and measured, six cups or eight cups. They turned out to contain more than a hundred pounds. We had frozen berries with our breakfast cereal five days a week into the following summer.

Mary wrote about the zen of blueberry picking for *Inuktitut Magazine*:

> Picking is . . . my time, in my place. . . . We speak so easily about preserving and protecting our "Inuit Culture." Berries are part and parcel of living our culture. Yet we speak [so often of our hunting and fishing cultures and] so little of our "gathering" culture. . . .
>
> Today and for many years past, those days with my mother and grandmother are treasured memories. Their stories, their values and their work ethic greatly shaped and influenced my life. . . .
>
> As I have grown older, I have come to realize that with each passing season, both the berries and the memories that linger through my mind as I pick, grow ever sweeter.

That blueberry patch seems a world away from events like the gala evening in Ottawa in 2010 when Mary was inducted into the International Women's Forum Hall of Fame, a sorority of remarkable women that includes former British prime minister Margaret Thatcher, US secretaries of state Madeleine Albright and Condoleezza Rice, Canadian astronaut Roberta Bondar and the mother of the US civil rights movement, Rosa Parks. The award carried with it a diamond watch and bracelet from the Harry Winston company—jewellery valued at more than $10,000. Mary donated it to the Arctic Children and Youth Foundation, which offers suicide prevention and other programs to help troubled northern youth.

Mary's ability to straddle her two worlds seems effortless, but I knew that, shortly after that big Ottawa event, when we were back in our small hand-sewn canvas tent on the shore of Ungava Bay in the shadow of an ancient inuksuk, she would be in her true element—the wood stove blazing and bannock mixed with fresh blueberries in the frying pan. I loved these times too; our shared enjoyment is a large part of what defines us as a couple. That, and our mixed family of six adult children—the Frasers: Rhonda, Dianne and Whitney; and the Simons: Richard, Carol and Louis. Add in a dozen grandchildren and great-grandchildren and you get what one of the grandkids described, looking around at a huge Christmas dinner, as "our own Simon Fraser University."

By the time Mary was appointed Canada's circumpolar ambassador in 1994 and later ambassador to Denmark, she was well known in Arctic diplomatic circles. Amusingly, a few in that circle nursed old wounds.

I was attending a rather grand dinner in Washington, DC. It was the conclusion of a major Arctic conference and I was there in my capacity as chair of the Canadian Polar Commission. Nobody had taken the time to explain to the gentleman beside me, Ray Arnaudo from the US State Department, that in Canada's North, everyone and everything is connected. If they had, he probably would have confined our conversation to baseball.

We had been getting along really well until this question from him came out of left field. "Tell me, Whit, there is this very difficult Inuit woman, Mary Simon. Do you know her?"

Marianne Stenbaek, sitting on my other side, practically choked. She is as close a friend as Mary has ever had, a professor at McGill who, at the time, was president of the Association of Canadian Universities for Northern Studies. No one who knows me, including Marianne, would describe me as either diplomatic or tactful.

"Yes," I said, deadpan. "I do know her. Very well, in fact, and you are right, she can be very headstrong."

I also knew, very well, that Ray Arnaudo had been Mary's nemesis for years. When Mary had fought to ensure that Indigenous peoples would have a meaningful place in the proposed Arctic Council of polar countries, Arnaudo's job was to push the US position to exclude them. Their fight had come to a head at a meeting in Yellowknife in the early 1990s.

At the time, Mary was president of the Inuit Circumpolar Conference, representing the Inuit in Alaska, Canada, Greenland and Russia. It was a tiny organization that punched well above its weight on behalf of the people who'd lived in the Arctic for thousands upon thousands of years.

Arnaudo was attending the Yellowknife meeting with his boss, Ambassador R. Rucker (Tucker) Scully. The Americans had made it clear that they only wanted "sovereign" nations to be members of the Arctic Council, excluding the Inuit and other Indigenous peoples.

Here's how Mary describes that day: "I walked into the hotel conference room where all the tables were in a big rectangle and began looking for my chair and name card but couldn't find my designated place. I was told by Mr. Scully that I was not a participant, I was there to make a presentation to the group. The meeting was for members of the Arctic Environmental Protection Strategy group, or AEPS, only."

Mary marched out of the room and told the reporters waiting in the lobby that she had a few things to say. The reporters lapped it up. It was a good story—the headline: "Arctic Inuit Not Welcome at Arctic Conference."

Canadian government bureaucrats scrambled to move Mary away from the media. What followed was considerable scurrying about and a new set of negotiations. And Mary won not only that battle but also the war that followed. Her determination got Mary and the Inuit Circumpolar Conference a seat at the table along with additional seats for other polar Indigenous peoples, including the Canadian Gwich'in. Within a few years, she was Canada's circumpolar ambassador and chair of the new Arctic Council itself.

I admit that I have a bias here, but I often joke that just because you're biased, it doesn't mean you're wrong!

I boast about Mary's accomplishments, with good reason, but one stands apart, from when we occupied 26 Dag Hammarskjölds Allé in Copenhagen, the residence of Canada's ambassador to Denmark. Mary had been in her job as ambassador for circumpolar affairs for five years, successfully leading Canada's initiative to establish the Arctic Council. Her dogged determination had made an impression within the Foreign Affairs department, and in 1999, she was asked to accept the Denmark ambassadorship. We quickly began imagining the most optimistic aspects of the job—a chance to travel in Europe on weekends and holidays and to visit many of the great historic sites. Foolishly (and now with apologies to my fellow taxpayers),

I even brought our sixteen-foot cedar and canvas canoe to Denmark, thinking we'd have time for outdoor adventures. I should have known better.

In two years, I think we put the canoe in the water twice. The new minivan we purchased for weekend road trips accumulated no more than three thousand kilometres a year. There was just no time. Her schedule was full. Being Canada's ambassador to Denmark was more than a new job, it was also a second job, because Mary maintained her responsibilities for circumpolar affairs.

The even bigger adjustment might have been that two quite independent people suddenly had a household staff, including a cook, maids and a driver. There were two huge reception rooms with ornately panelled walls and exquisite furniture. We had a formal dining room big enough to seat twenty or more people and also housed a grand piano, which neither of us could play.

In the early days, our clothes were laid out for us in our comfortable apartment above the formal ground floor. I recall Mary saying, laughing, "Look, they've ironed my underwear." I checked out my unmentionables and lo and behold, they too were neatly ironed and folded. (But I also remembered that my kind mother had similarly pampered me when I was a teenager.) Within days Mary set out to "deformalize" our surroundings. There would be times in the months ahead when I would find her deep in the cavernous basement, ironing her clothes and some of mine—but not the underwear. It was her way of staying grounded.

She performed her diplomatic duties well. I did my best to remember my table manners and to keep my tongue in check rather than in cheek. The first big reception we hosted was a formal affair, introducing the new ambassador. We stood at the grand front door entrance welcoming each guest as they arrived, trying desperately to remember names and faces.

One gentleman with a huge presence and booming voice came through the door, thrusting his hand forward. "Lloyd, Malcolm Lloyd, professor, University of Copenhagen," he thundered, simultaneously clicking the heels of his highly polished shoes together in the old-school European style. His distinctive Nordic features instantly rang a bell.

"Yes," I said. "I believe you have a brother, Trevor, in Montreal, who's a distinguished polar scientist, and your nephew Hugh lives in Yellowknife and works for the CBC."

The professor was dumbfounded, "My God, do all you Canadians know one another?"

"Of course!" I said, laughing.

I learned that ambassadors everywhere have a tough job—indeed it's more of a lifestyle than an occupation. Although I can't speak for today, in 2000 to 2002, Canadian ambassadors paid for their food and lodging. A typical day would have Mary leaving for the office at 8:30 a.m. to take care of duties that included managing and interacting with a large staff and the complex business of relations between two countries. In any circumstance, that's a full-time job. In addition, protocol and diplomacy dictated attendance at reception after reception hosted by other consulates and embassies, which meant that rather than go home at five or six o'clock, she put in several more hours of greetings and gracious talk, cocktails and sore feet, until finally it was time to go home. On other days, she'd be the one hosting a dinner or reception at the residence, perhaps for a Canadian delegation trying to move a business deal forward.

In Mary's case, once she got back to the apartment at night, she'd start on the second job, opening the files, faxes and emails on circumpolar issues. Her circumpolar staff remained in Ottawa, in a time zone six hours earlier than Copenhagen's, and they'd be at the end of their workday, ready to brief her or ask for direction or approval.

After two years she told Foreign Affairs the workload was too much. The department agreed and let her have a choice: stay in Denmark or return to Ottawa as ambassador for circumpolar affairs. Staying in Denmark would have meant choosing a different direction in life; in another two years, a new posting would have been offered, perhaps to another interesting place. But it wouldn't be the North. I think the department was somewhat surprised when she chose to retain her position as circumpolar ambassador.

How were we to know that Copenhagen was in effect a two-year viceregal boot camp? But in many ways, it was an unscripted and unplanned education. We enjoyed it and the people we met, especially the Peruvian ambassador, Liliana Sánchez de Ríos, and her husband, Gustavo. Mary and I knew little of the complexity of Peruvian politics that they had to navigate, and we didn't ask. We just became friends.

Liliana was a gifted pianist who was well-regarded in Peru. Gustavo was a scientist and researcher quite knowledgeable on Arctic issues, but also an expert on the Antarctic. Liliana did not have a piano in the Peruvian embassy, so when they came to visit, she would occasionally play—for herself, and for us. It was marvellous: conversation and laughter and private concerts over coffee.

Liliana and Mary stole the show at a gala "talent evening" hosted by the US embassy. Liliana had to be persuaded. She was nervous, protesting that she hadn't practised and didn't have her music, but she relented under pressure from Mary and me. When Her Excellency from Peru touched the keys in front of a hundred or so other diplomats and guests, she immediately cast a spell. After Liliana finished and the applause subsided, she introduced Canada's ambassador, who would perform some traditional Inuit music. I reached under my chair and passed Mary her push-button Hohner accordion, thinking you can take the ambassador out of the North, but you can't take the North out of the ambassador.

Mary played traditional Scottish and Irish jigs and reels, passed down from generations of whalers and traders, music that Inuit, Métis and First Nations adopted and eventually made their own. She had been taught to play by both her mother and grandmother, often out on the land in tents. Mary was a great hit, and no one cheered louder than Liliana.

Once we returned to Canada, Mary remained busy. She stayed on as circumpolar ambassador until 2003, but increasingly felt that the job kept her away from the North and the issues that mattered most to her: education and mental health.

In 2007, Mary took over as president of the Inuit Tapiriit Kanatami, the national Inuit organization. We built a house in Kuujjuaq, where her siblings still lived, and for several summers, we travelled with her brother Billy and his wife, Louisa, in a twenty-two-foot freighter canoe with a fifty-horsepower outboard motor around Ungava Bay, fishing, camping, whale watching and clam digging, but mostly resting and enjoying the solitude.

I was looking at a picture of one of these trips a few years ago, while I was serving as volunteer chair of the Arctic Children and Youth Foundation, and the thought burst into my mind—for the next fundraising initiative, we should auction off one of these trips with Mary. The publicity was easy. The now renamed CBC North was keen to interview me about "selling my wife—the national Inuit leader." I knew that more than the money we'd help raise, this would also allow us to talk about the foundation and its objectives. The "sale" took place in Ottawa before several hundred people at the well-attended Northern Lights trade show and conference. We promised that on the trip, "we will be your guides and clean and filet your fish," and yes, catching fish was guaranteed. First Air, the Inuit-owned northern airline, donated return tickets from Montreal to Kuujjuaq.

The bids came in fast and furious, and then became a battle between a Toronto banker and an older First Nations businessman from the James Bay region in Quebec. In the end, it was the Cree businessman, James Blackned, who outbid the banker, but Blackned didn't want to go fishing. He paid $5,000 simply to express his support for all that Mary had done for Indigenous peoples in Canada, and sent his daughter, Emily Hester, and her husband, Hugo, on the fishing trip with Mary and me.

By the second day, Emily and Hugo insisted on helping clean up after meals. I joked with them both, saying, "Mary and I had doubts about our skills as guides, but you two clearly know even less about being guests."

On June 11, 2008, Mary went to the House of Commons to enact a moment of history. Prime Minister Stephen Harper had announced that he was going to apologize on behalf of all Canadians for abuses at the residential schools—abuses that, in his words, have "no place in Canada." Mary was there to accept the apology on behalf of all Inuit in Canada. Like millions of others across the country, I watched the event on television. After the prime minister spoke, Mary turned and faced him. In a calm voice, she said: "I need to look you in the face because what I have to say comes from the heart. We need the help and support of all thoughtful Canadians and our governments to rebuild strong, healthy families and communities. I stand here, today, ready to work with you, as Inuit have always done, to craft new solutions and new arrangements based on mutual respect and mutual responsibility."

That night she told me that she regretted not having had more time to prepare. It was only when they were all gathered in the Prime Minister's Office a half-hour before the apology that Harper and his staff agreed that leaders could respond briefly to Harper's words. Mary scribbled some quick notes that she held in her hand, but the message was certainly "from the heart." It was probably the event, and the words, that caused her to be considered for governor general.

16

AMAUJAQ

First Canadian, Canadian First

With nine words and expressive skills honed as an educator, broadcaster and politician, my friend Amaujaq defined for Canadian premiers the place of Inuit in the national conscience. "Inuit are First Canadians," he said. Then, looking around the large oval table at the men and women who represented the ten provinces and three territories, gathered in Kelowna in 2005, he added, "and Inuit are also Canadians First."

Canada and the circumpolar world knew him as Jose Kusugak, but he preferred that his family and closest friends call him by his Inuit name, Amaujaq. I use it here because he allowed me into that special circle closest to him.

Amaujaq was a gifted communicator in both English and Inuktitut. More than once he held Canada's political elite in the palms of his thick, powerful and constantly animated hands as he made his case for a stronger and more equal Inuit presence in Canada.

He was born at Repulse Bay on May 2, 1950, a community that sits exactly on the Arctic Circle. Jose was the second child in a family of twelve. "Our mother raised us as though we were eggs," he once told me. "She protected our nest and taught us to love one another."

I only met her once, but the encounter, which came after an unusual trip I'd made with her son, was revealing. At the time, Jose was president of the Inuit Tapiriit Kanatami, and I was working with him. Together we had travelled to his home in Rankin Inlet on the west shore of Hudson Bay, and he also wanted to check out his cabin, some distance from the town. When he took the wheel of his twenty-four-foot aluminum boat and pushed the throttle forward, opening up the two-hundred-horsepower engines, I remember thinking, he is finally in his element. He even wore one of those black woollen captain's hats that set off his white goatee and hair and contrasted with his sparkling dark eyes.

I said something about him looking like the "Eskimo" version of Hemingway's old man and the sea. He loved it. He didn't object to my use of the term "Eskimo," meaning "eater of raw meat" and considered by many to be derogatory. In fact, he'd often use it himself, to make a point or to reinforce the cultural and geographic characteristics that are unique to Inuit of Canada and the circumpolar world.

As soon as we arrived at the cabin, he picked up a gill net from a wooden box on the shore and passed it to his son Puujjut, a strapping young man in his twenties, a natural athlete who had played some junior hockey in Ontario. He headed off to set the net close to shore.

Jose then turned to me. "You like to fish. There's a rod there by the cabin, and a half-mile inland is a nice lake full of trout."

Fifteen minutes later I had one of those scrappy lake trout on the end of my line and then I had another and another—one for every time I cast out. A northern fisherman gauges his daily limit on what he can comfortably carry. I stopped at about a dozen of these two- to three-pound beauties. In not much more than an hour, I was back at the cabin. Looking out the cabin door to the west, I saw a big bull caribou travelling across from the area where I had just been fishing. I called Jose. He kept an old British Lee-Enfield .303 rifle at the cabin. In an instant, he'd snapped a clip with five or six bullets into the rifle and bolted out the door.

The animal was too far away for a reasonable shot, but he was moving diagonally so my friend began running to close the distance. I was amazed. Twenty-five years earlier, Jose had been fit and muscular, at about 160 pounds. He had since gained a nicely rotund shape—surely well over 230 pounds—but he closed the distance with a young man's sprint. When the big bull saw him coming, he stretched out his long legs and accelerated. By now, maybe two hundred metres separated the hunter from the hunted.

Jose stopped, grabbed a huge lungful of air and raised the old rifle.

I saw the sand fly in front of the caribou, startling the bull into a full gallop. A second shot also missed. In the half second it took to bring a new round into the chamber, Jose gulped in more air, then held his breath and pulled the trigger. I saw the big animal reel and drop almost at the same instant as I heard the third shot.

If ever there was a man who straddled two worlds, that was my friend at that moment. Fifty-five years old and eighty pounds overweight, he stood over this trophy bull caribou as naturally as he would preside over a Monday morning staff meeting in the offices two blocks from Parliament Hill. He was even wearing his white Ottawa dress shirt.

I had always thought of him as the modern Inuk who graduated from the Churchill Vocational School in Manitoba, the residential school where children from the eastern Arctic were sent for their high school education. He had described his residential school experience to me as rewarding and productive. He said it was there that he realized education is the key to Inuit cultural survival. Like so many others, he went on to work in government and organizations often far removed from the land and people these institutions served. Yet the skill and dexterity he showed dressing that animal was on par with anything I had witnessed among experienced Dene and Inuit hunters, who all somehow managed to skin, gut and butcher an animal without leaving any traces of blood.

When he got back to the cabin after stowing the meat in his boat, he told Puujjut to lift the net that we'd set no more than three hours earlier. I offered to help. We were two men in a very small yellow dingy that could not have been more than six feet long. The young man had all of his dad's confidence and ease as he began lifting the net and folding it ever so neatly into the bottom of the boat.

I could see the heads of the Arctic char that had been caught by the gills. Big, round, fat and healthy—fifteen or twenty fish, ranging from five to eight to ten pounds. These we added to the caribou and my modest catch of lake trout, as once again I realized how remarkably bountiful this land can be. Is it any wonder people have fought long and hard and over such a long period to protect it? How fortunate I am to be able to call many of them my friends.

In the early 1970s, Jose went to Ottawa to meet with the recently formed Inuit Tapirisat of Canada. He was looking for support to help develop a common Inuktitut writing system. And he also wanted to meet with the organization's new leader, Tagak Curley. The two men knew each other; they were about the same age and came from the same Keewatin region of the Arctic around Hudson Bay.

Tagak told Jose he had something bigger in mind than a writing system. The organization was looking for a land claims coordinator, someone who could travel and work in the communities across the Arctic explaining how the people had been colonized—but that they had rights, that this was their land, which they had never surrendered to anybody. Now it was time for all Inuit and other Indigenous peoples to assert their Aboriginal rights.

Tagak couldn't have found a better candidate for this job, given Jose's outgoing personality and talents as a communicator and educator. By the time I started working with him, he was in charge of the whole organization, and the name had changed to the Inuit Tapiriit Kanatami.

He hired me in 2001. I'd known him before, but as Jose. That's when we began a different friendship—the kind that lets me call him Amaujaq.

Mary and I had returned from her diplomatic posting in Denmark and I was looking for part-time work or a short consulting contract. I dropped into the office to ask Jose if he had anything I could do. His assistant said he was travelling but she would pass on a message. The next day she called and said, "I spoke to Jose and he said to tell you, you can have a real job if you want." I became an adviser on political affairs and later the organization's executive director.

On my first day, Jose and I argued. We did the same on the second day. On most of the days that followed, we engaged in what politicians like to term "full and frank discussions." After a few weeks, he stuck his head into my little office. "Let's go for lunch, just you and me." I had a sense that this was my pink slip day—probably I had pushed too hard. Towards the end of the lunch—a time when we never argued—he said, "There is something I need to tell you."

I braced myself, but what came next was not what I expected.

"I like working with you. I like our discussions. You know I have never liked yes-men."

It was a challenging time and we continued to have plenty to discuss. The new territory of Nunavut had been established a couple of years earlier. We were quickly realizing that from the government's perspective, the land claims settlements and the creation of Nunavut were the ends of a journey. For Inuit, the real journey was just beginning.

There were also growing questions from the public servants of the day. Given that the claims are settled, and considering the creation of Nunavut, they wanted to know, is there any need for the national Inuit organization? That question also surfaced at an Inuit General Assembly in Nain, Labrador. Amaujaq's response was inspiring. He casually picked up the nearest piece of paper and held it up close to his face.

"Imagine that on this page are all of the demands and issues we made to the federal government when we began our land claims negotiations," he said, then listed a few specifics: our rights, our land, health, education, jobs, training, the culture, language protection.

"Well, we didn't get most of those things in the claims settlement," he said. "We got very little of what we initially demanded." He tore off a small section of the page and held it up. "Now look at this and imagine this small piece represents all the things we achieved in the claim and remember that this is what the land claim organizations do."

With his other hand, he held the larger piece of paper, the main piece, in the air, looking around the room. "This represents all the things we did not get. These are the important issues we had to give up, including health care, education and so much more! This is what ITK does."

Making the case to the bureaucrats and politicians in Ottawa was a bit harder. Amaujaq was marvellous at explaining Inuit traditions, culture, history and customs. He'd offer a few words of language instruction, tell stories and make jokes. But when he had to deliver politically, he was brilliant. I remember a brief "questions from the floor" session in the dying moments of an academic conference on Indigenous issues, in Ottawa about 2004. Indigenous leaders were asked how they viewed themselves. Did they think of themselves as Canadians? This is tricky territory for many Indigenous peoples in Canada, given the four centuries of mistrust, broken promises and unfulfilled treaties, assimilation and marginalization.

"Let me put it this way," Amaujaq began. "Recently my daughter Aliica married a fine young man named Cedrick. As Inuit, we know we are not losing a daughter. We know that in Cedrick's family, Aliica will be placed on a pedestal. We know we will also embrace Cedrick and place him high on a pedestal in our family. Neither is less a member of either family but rather both are more. Our relationship with Canada is much like that; we are not less Canadian because we are Inuit and not less Inuit when we call ourselves Canadians."

The audience burst into applause. "First Canadians, Canadians First" was now part of a new national Inuit identity.

But Amaujaq could be tough. Prime Minister Paul Martin was preparing to put Indigenous issues on the national agenda, and he scheduled a summit breakfast with all five national organizations, now including the Congress of Aboriginal Peoples and the Native Women's Association of Canada in a room on Parliament Hill. The prime minister and his senior people were on one side of the table, the Indigenous leaders on the other, all dressed in their best bib and tucker.

When Jose (as the prime minister knew him) took his turn to speak, he asked Prime Minister Martin, "Do you remember how you applauded when the secretary-general of the UN praised Canada for its multiculturalism?"

"Of course," Martin replied. "Everybody did."

"Then how can Canada claim to be a great multicultural society and at the same time insist on a melting pot for Aboriginal Canadians?" He added, for emphasis, "Inuit are not Indians!"

Jose explained there was not a single person within the government with sole responsibility for Inuit, and within the federal spending estimates it was impossible to find a single line of spending for Inuit programs.

"Is that true?" the prime minister asked, turning to his deputy minister of Indian and northern affairs.

"Yes, prime minister, I am afraid it is."

Paul Martin promised changes and, within weeks, "Inuit specific" became a familiar and acceptable term within the public service.

As Jose's executive director, I was often obliged to sit beside my friend at these gatherings. I am not sure why, but perhaps because everybody else at the table had an official at their side. Certainly, I would never whisper in his ear or want to be seen passing him a note. Part of my job may have been to offer "political advice," which he always listened to. However, his political instincts were far superior to mine, and during a critical federal-provincial meeting on health care, he used that political savvy, and me, to drive his point home.

The meeting was chaired by the federal minister of health at the time, Ujjal Dosanjh. From his prepared text, Amaujaq set out the grim numbers from Statistics Canada that place Inuit at the extreme of every social-economic indicator: the highest rates of unemployment, the lowest per capita income, the highest cost of living, the highest rates of communicable diseases, the shortest life expectancy, the highest rates of infant mortality, a suicide rate eleven times higher than other Canadians, and educational attainment rates far below the national average. His challenge to governments was clear and consistent.

"What Inuit are demanding is a standard of living comparable to other Canadians, no more, no less." Then he broke from the prepared text and placed his hand on my forearm.

"This is Whit. He works with me. Because he was born and raised in the south, and because I am Inuk, born and raised in the Arctic, the government's statistics predict that he will live at least ten years longer than me."

He paused as an awkward silence filled the room. I was not embarrassed, though I expect my face was grim. I knew just how accurate he was. My mind flashed with memories: of Joe Tobie and Louie Blondin, people you have now met, and others, all younger than me, who died long before the "Canadian median age." (Of all his prophecies and predictions, if only he could have been wrong on that one.)

Jose and Canada's other Indigenous leaders made great headway with the Martin administration. Though people refer now to the "failed Kelowna accord" of 2005, some great work was done. Those leaders negotiated financial commitments on health, housing and education and a promise for continued First Ministers meetings to measure progress. The total financial commitments were $5 billion over ten years.

The late Jim Prentice attended the Kelowna meeting in his capacity as an opposition critic for the Conservative Party of Canada. I met him on my return to Ottawa; we were both connecting with the red-eye flight out of Calgary. I asked him for his take on the meeting. It was "positive," he said, and good work had been done. If anyone had told either Prentice or me that night that, less than three months later, the Conservatives would be in power, Stephen Harper would be prime minister and Prentice would be the minister of Indian and northern affairs, we would have said they were delusional. But three months later that was the reality, and only a few months after that, the new government withdrew those financial commitments and Kelowna was dead. The new way of doing business would be the old way of doing business.

Jose was devastated. But he was also determined and philosophical. It will come again, he would tell us. We just need to stay the course, keep the faith and always search for the silver lining.

Jose stayed on until the end of his term in the summer of 2006. I know he would have left the job even if the Kelowna deal had survived. He had simply been too long away from home, from his wife, Nellie. Trying to live and work in one city and maintain a home and family in another, more than four thousand kilometres away, took a toll on his health and his happiness.

Nothing meant more to Amaujaq than Nellie and the family. He said, "The first time I saw Nellie, I fell in love with her. When I was working on the land claim, I saw her again in her hometown of Arviat; she had a baby on her back. Oh, I thought, I am too late." He soon learned the baby was a nephew, and he made his move by going to visit her mother.

Nellie picks up the story. "He was able to charm her quite easily. My father, who was with the RCMP, was a different story. He was not impressed with Jose's long hair and old clothes."

They soon married, the skeptical father came onside, and together they raised three daughters and a son.

I left the ITK on the same day as Jose did, but on the flip side of family reasons. I could not work with the incoming president. The board knew replacing Jose would not be easy; they needed a strong, committed leader. They asked Mary to run. No one opposed her and she was acclaimed. Some on the board said I should have remained as executive director, given that she had not hired me, but neither Mary nor I wanted the constant sniping about conflict of interest that would follow us, let alone the danger of allowing work to consume our relationship. I know we would have argued every bit as much as Jose and I had, and then we would have had to take it home. Besides, with Jose, I could sometimes win.

Shortly after returning home to Rankin Inlet, Jose accepted the leadership of the Kivalliq Inuit Association. In the Inuit land claims structure, it is one of three regional entities that promote regional and local interests, priorities and input.

Jose was beginning to build good relationships and partnerships with prospective mining companies, but tragedy struck within a few short years. He was diagnosed with cancer of the bladder. He made an immediate decision to go very public, urging people to get checkups, take better care of their health and each other.

That's when I saw his relationship with Nellie in a different light. I went to spend some time with the two of them during one of his sessions at the Winnipeg cancer clinic. He was wearing his blue hospital gown. She was sitting very close to him. The nurse was asking him questions, preparing for yet another test.

"Any problems with your heart?" she inquired.

"Only when I am away from her for any length of time," was his immediate response, pointing a thumb towards Nellie, who just smiled with a "flattery will get you everywhere" look.

I was never surprised at how recognizable and respected Jose was in the northern communities, and across the circumpolar world, but during that September 2010 visit, as we walked along Portage Avenue one day, I expected he would be just another weathered and too-often-unseen Indigenous face making his way along the sidewalk.

His pace was slow. He had lost a lot of weight and he was a little short of breath. We were standing on the corner waiting for the light to change when someone began shouting, "Jose! Jose Kusugak!" Suddenly a stranger jumped out of his car and rushed to the curb. "How are you? How is the cancer treatment going? I've been thinking of you," said the man, now holding Jose's elbow and shaking his extended hand.

"I'm doing fine and thanks for stopping and asking."

After the man left, I asked, "Who was that?"

"I don't remember his name, but I met him at an antique flea market. I bought some old fishhooks from him."

The encounter was brief, just the time it takes for a traffic light to change, but it spoke volumes about Amaujaq's ability to connect with people.

Chemo didn't slow his cancer. Soon he was given only weeks to live. Mary and I went to visit him in Rankin Inlet and were delighted to see that his incredible sense of humour was still intact.

He was at his kitchen table drinking tea. Nellie and his four children were caring for him, while half a dozen grandchildren played quietly on the floor. His brothers and sisters were providing constant hugs and love. Amaujaq shook two packets of Sweet'N Low into his tea and a big smile came across his face. "What the hell am I doing with this stuff?" he said. "How can real sugar hurt me now?" Everybody laughed.

The last time I saw Amaujaq, he was in a bed in the nursing station. I hugged him, told him I loved him, and that somewhere in the great beyond, we'd connect again. I noticed that the Bible by his bedside had a bookmark about two-thirds of the way in. He said, quickly, "I am reading it. I want to read it all the way through before I go, just in case there's a test."

"How about doing something for me?" I asked.

"What's that?" he asked.

"Please read slowly."

He smiled and said, "Finally, after all this time, some good advice." Our last laugh together.

Less than a month later, I came back to attend his funeral. I had been asked by the family to deliver the eulogy. There was a plane change in Iqaluit. ITK's communications director, Stephen Hendrie, and I walked about seventy-five metres or so to get lunch at the closest restaurant. On our return to the terminal, the air was as cold as anything I had ever experienced in the Arctic. As we fought against the vicious wind and minus thirty-five temperature, I said, "Remember, this is not harsh. This is beautiful."

I was reminding him of Jose's reaction to a presentation Stephen had prepared for him a few years earlier. In the middle of the Ottawa summer, Jose had arrived in the office drenched in perspiration after a fifteen-minute walk from his apartment. When he'd cooled off and dried out, Stephen presented a release that the three of us were to go over. Jose jumped on a single line that described the Arctic climate as the harshest and the most inhospitable on earth.

"What do you mean harsh? The Arctic is not harsh, it's beautiful!" he roared, raising his big arms as though he was cradling the globe in them. "You want harsh, go outside! That is harsh."

In the eulogy I delivered, I spoke of Amaujaq as a leader, a negotiator, a mediator, a musician, a comic, and above all as a charmer, recalling our visit with a former governor general, Michaëlle Jean, who had asked him for a briefing before her first visit to the North. When we were leaving her office, Jose took her hands and said, "Look into my eyes." Still holding her hands, he continued in a soft voice, "If you're going to get to know and understand Inuit, you need to know about eye contact."

Because of Jose, when she made her first trip, Jean knew that when a child or elder raised their eyebrows to one of her questions, they were saying yes, and that if someone crinkled their nose and sort of squinted, they were saying no.

A mutual friend told me a story that illustrates Jose's constant ability to get to the heart of a matter. He was attending a conference that was grappling with social issues across the region, especially among children and youth. Jose told this audience of experts that a few days earlier, his young granddaughter was lying on his chest when she said, "Ataatatsiaq [grandfather], I hear your heart."

"What does it say?" Jose asked the child.

"It says, I love you!"

The point was made: "All you need is love." Jose—Amaujaq—the communicator!

17

STEPHEN KAKFWI—RADICAL BUT RIGHT

New Strings on an Old Guitar

Stephen Kakfwi's "New Strings on an Old Guitar" is both a good country song and a great lyrical self-portrait of the singer-songwriter—and activist and politician—himself. In the 1970s he was described as a Native rights radical and in the 1980s as an Aboriginal activist. In the 1990s, labels became titles and he was both a minister and premier in the government of the Northwest Territories. Now he's a respected Indigenous statesman. When he is doing what he wants for himself, this remarkable Dene leader, born in Fort Good Hope, is a musician, singer and songwriter. But he hasn't had much chance to live his life for himself because he still lives for a cause.

As a child, he endured horrible suffering, locked in a dark room and repeatedly abused by a Catholic school supervisor. He's confronted his twisted tormentors in the Catholic Church in the lyrics of one of his songs: "You gave me my stone face—you took me from my home and locked me in that horrible place." He doesn't hold back on the extent of the pain and suffering that shaped his life, either in music or in conversation with friends, saying, "I write of the moments of pain and longing in my life to get it out and deal with it."

Canadians have learned a great deal about reconciliation in recent years—dealing with the horrors of residential schools as documented in the TRC reports; seeing a prime minister formally apologize for the assimilation policies that served as the handbook for those who ran those dreadful schools. More recently, Canadians were horrified by the news of the discovery of hundreds of unmarked graves in Kamloops, British Columbia, and other places, and equally shocked by the realization that in the years ahead there will likely be many more unmarked graves located on the grounds of some of these former schools.

More than twenty years before Canada began moving towards reconciliation, Stephen Kakfwi was chief of the Dene Nation, negotiating and persuading Pope John Paul II to return to the Northwest Territories in 1987, after a dense morning fog kept His Holiness from landing at Fort Simpson during his 1984 visit to Canada.

I first met Stephen in the mid-1970s, when he was a young field worker with the Dene Nation, during his radical and my redneck years. Thirty years into our friendship, he reminded me of our first encounter, which I admit I had completely forgotten. After I had quoted him in a story, he came to the newsroom in Yellowknife asking if he could see a copy and, apparently, I barked at him, saying, "What for? Don't you remember what you said?" (I was relieved to learn that I eventually did rummage around, find a copy and pass it over.)

A few years later I would know him as Louie Blondin's good friend, fellow singer and guitar player. During my last year in Yellowknife's newsroom, I knew him as the boyfriend of a rising journalist, Marie Wilson; they would marry, and Marie would make her indelible mark on the North and on Canada, and so would he.

Stephen and Marie's story is a remarkable one. I can't do justice to their individual and combined commitment to today's North in a single chapter here, but I'll try.

Many Canadians will know Marie as one of the three co-chairs of the Truth and Reconciliation Commission. Northerners know her as an exceptional journalist, a former director of CBC North, a community activist and builder, and a friend to all. She is a woman of character, confidence and generosity, the same values that guide Stephen. (I was thrilled when she was appointed to the CBC board of directors in 2018. They should get her to run the place.)

Stephen's political roots are deep in the fierce northern pipeline politics of the mid-1970s, during and because of the Berger Inquiry. His hometown of Fort Good Hope is on the high banks of Deh Cho, the Mackenzie River. He was home in Good Hope on a very hot and dry day in August 1975 to witness Chief Frank T'Seleie's unforgettable testimony before the inquiry, and then to lend his own voice.

Stephen knew what the chief would say that day; he and Frank had grown up together. They were friends and they both knew that here in their little hometown of a few hundred people, they were about to step onto the biggest stage of their young lives. The fact that it was home may have even added to the drama. Years later Stephen recalled for me how he and Frank had spent days walking around the community, stopping to look out over the river, notebooks in hand, working on their speeches, trying them out on one another and measuring their effect.

Stephen's voice rang loud in Fort Good Hope on the day after Frank's, as he reinforced the message that had been heard in more than thirty other communities up and down the Mackenzie Valley, across the Arctic coast and throughout Yukon, that there could be no pipeline until the land claims were settled. He testified, "Until such time as we feel we have regained our self-respect and our identity fully, as a unique people, then maybe we would feel confident and willing enough to consider the possibility of allowing foreigners to propose such major developments like the pipeline."

The Fort Good Hope hearings changed Chief T'Seleie, Stephen Kakfwi and Bob Blair, and it changed the way they viewed each other. Stephen recalls, "We gained tremendous respect for Bob Blair then. He was advised by many not to come because there was so much anger, but he came and brought his young son with him." Blair did not believe that the Dene, whom he knew to be a respectful and peaceful people, would harm anyone, but he heard the passion with which they defended their land and their rights. And he learned another valuable lesson: Dene leaders can negotiate and hold their own with corporate leaders and others in some very high places.

Stephen's job with the Dene Nation was to carry that same message across Canada, through a Canadian Christian Church coalition called Project North. For that project, he visited pastors and congregations, explaining and advancing (in the terminology of the time) "the Native position" on the pipeline proposal. In the most basic terms, at stake in the pipeline debate were their lands, their lives, further colonization and continued marginalization.

If the congregations and preachers felt guilty over four hundred years of combined colonization, neglect, assimilation and genocide, Stephen and his fellow "northern truth" missionaries played to that as well. They soon had the churches in a squeeze play, with congregations divided like families at a wedding—on one side, those pro-development, either by instinct, upbringing or personal investment and livelihood or by business interests in the oil industry itself. Then as now, some people simply would not accept Native rights in either legal or conceptual form. On the other side, people in the Native rights pews believed that equality and justice for Indigenous peoples was just as important, perhaps more important, than oil company profits and southern jobs.

When Berger took his inquiry to major cities across Canada from Vancouver to Halifax in the early summer of 1976, the rallying cry—no pipeline until the land claims are settled—was echoed in lavish hotel banquet halls every bit as loudly and sincerely as it had been in the tiny log structures or borrowed schoolrooms of sparsely populated northern villages—at least partly the result of Kakfwi's campaign with Project North.

Later, Stephen worked tirelessly and successfully to bring the Pope to Fort Simpson, not once but twice. The initial visit in 1984 was unprecedented; it was meant to be more than a spiritual visit, with Indigenous rights also on the agenda.

Critical for Stephen and for Canada's national Indigenous leadership was that, after long and difficult diplomatic negotiations with the Catholic Church, through the Canadian Conference of Catholic Bishops and the federal government and its bureaucrats, the Pope would make a statement or declaration supporting Aboriginal rights. Stephen and other leaders wanted the Canadian government to hear this message from the Pope himself, standing at a pulpit in an Indigenous community. In Stephen's words, "Above all, we wanted it on the world stage. We wanted the rest of the world to see us, know who we are and what we stand for." There was something close to home that he also wanted to achieve: "I wanted it to be a gift to our old people. I needed for them to know that they count and their faith counts."

When fog over Fort Simpson caused the visit to be cancelled, an estimated three thousand people waiting on the ground were bitterly disappointed. Some even felt they were to blame—not worthy of the visit because divine will had somehow turned against them.

No one was more disappointed than the man who had worked to make it happen. But Stephen Kakfwi didn't despair. Immediately he began lobbying for a seemingly impossible return visit, which soon became known as "the Second Coming." It took three years and countless meetings and communications with the Vatican and diplomats, bureaucrats and politicians in Canada, including all the major Indigenous organizations to make it happen. It also took two trips to Rome and Stephen's direct plea to the Pope himself.

He invited me to cover that initial Vatican visit, and my CBC bosses agreed that we needed to be there. There were three in the delegation: Stephen Kakfwi, Jim Antoine and Jim Villeneuve, a Métis delegate who was the mayor of Fort Simpson. We (myself and a borrowed cameraman) were not granted access to their hour-long meeting with the Pope, but when Stephen and the two Jims came out, they made a short and sweet statement: the Pope had listened, and yes, he wants to return.

They were full of optimism but were once again back to square one on the logistics of the visit—needing now to deal with "officials," meaning scores of bureaucrats both in Ottawa and the Vatican, with the Canadian Conference of Catholic Bishops in the middle. Predictably, the planned visit quickly got bogged down in schedules, protocols and money concerns; too often the focus was on how not to do it, rather than the reverse.

The leaders needed another trip to Rome to seal the deal, this time with added heavy hitters. All of Canada's national Indigenous leaders made a plea and a pilgrimage and were greeted with a larger meeting and a reception. Stephen recalls, "Every chance I had, I would ask the Pope directly: When are you going to return to Fort Simpson?" The Pope's short reply never varied: "Talk to my officials."

The delegation also delivered a handwritten invitation reminding the Pope and his officials of his own statement at the end of the 1984 trip, expressing regret for not visiting Fort Simpson and adding, "Pardon me, I think I may have just invited myself to return." Stephen says the second delegation also suggested how the Pope could do it with the least amount of trouble: add it to his planned 1987 visit to the United States.

Stephen recalled there was a big group photo to commemorate the Vatican visit. As head of the delegation, he was placed beside John Paul II. As the photographer was lining up the shot,

Stephen leaned close to the Pope, careful to keep his eyes forward. Out of the side of his mouth, he whispered, "When are you coming to Fort Simpson?"

Out of the side of his mouth, the Pope responded, "I said, talk to my officials." They both broke into laughter at the very instant the photographer snapped the picture.

A few months later—almost three years to the day from the first attempt—another dense fog rolled across the little town at the forks of the Mackenzie and Liard rivers and the three thousand people gathered there asked themselves whether history was about to repeat itself. They had travelled from all across the North or driven the dusty Mackenzie Highway from northern Alberta and British Columbia to be there. Many had also spent their last cent to do so—and for a second time.

Fear swept across the grassy meadows. The fog was not only heavy, but rain was also coming down. At eleven o'clock the Pope's plane was overhead, but how much longer would the pilot be able to circle, waiting for the weather to clear? Then somehow word swept the crowd:

"He's on the ground."

"Our prayers have been answered."

The closing line that I would use in my report that evening raced from my mind down my arm to my notebook. There was a little lump in my throat when I delivered it to camera. "For a people and a land that had over such a long time had so many broken promises, finally, one treasured promise has been kept."

As the Pope's motorcade reached the riverbank, a ray of sun peeked through the thick clouds and began washing them away. When it stopped, John Paul II got out and began to slowly walk through the congregation, blessing people, touching hands and heads, and kissing small children. By his side, introducing people to His Holiness, often by their first names, was Stephen Kakfwi, easily recognized by his shoulder-length jet-black hair.

After Mass and Communion, the Pope sat in a circle in the huge "teepee temple" with Canada's Indigenous leaders and chiefs. Each leader, whether First Nations, Inuit or Dene, held a copy of the Pope's formal statement, that he delivered in halting English.

> My coming among you looks back to your past in order to proclaim your dignity and support your destiny.
>
> I am aware that the major Aboriginal organizations—the Assembly of First Nations, the Inuit Tapirisat of Canada, the Metis National Council, and the Native Council of Canada—have been engaged in high-level talks with the Prime Minister and Premiers regarding ways of protecting and enhancing the rights of the Aboriginal peoples of Canada in the Constitution of this great country. Once again, I affirm the right to a just and equitable measure of self-government, along with a land base and adequate resources necessary for developing a viable economy for present and future generations. I pray with you that a new round of conferences will be beneficial and that, with God's guidance and help, a path to a just agreement will be found to crown all the efforts being made.

Most remarkably, given what we know now, there was not a single mention of the extent to which people—many of them at the gathering, including Stephen—had been sexually abused by priests, nuns and others in the residential schools. The public time for that issue had simply not yet arrived, and when it came to the Pope it wouldn't get here until thirty-five more years had passed.

Similarly, a decade earlier at the Berger Inquiry, none of the more than one thousand people who testified spoke of the sexual abuse, though many did open up about the loss of language, the cruelty of physical abuse, the terrible homesickness and loneliness, and being forbidden to speak their language or even visit a brother or sister at the same school. What have been described as unspeakable acts against children were exactly that—*unspeakable.*

To my mind what is even more remarkable is that Stephen Kakfwi, the Dene leader who made the Pope's visit happen—twice—did so while carrying the burden of that abuse, inflicted on him as a small boy. How did he do that? I had trouble even asking the question, but finally I did.

Stephen said, "You're right. No one did talk about it until the 1990s. I thought I was alone until one morning in the early 1990s, I heard on the morning news that a priest from Grolier Hall, Inuvik, had been convicted of sexually abusing young boys. As a cabinet minister, I thought that I too had a responsibility to tell my story."

All of Canada began learning in the early 1990s about the degree and extent of sexual abuse and the decades of festering pain and scars so many carried from that experience. We also began learning of the same cruel patterns and behaviour in other countries, including the United States, Britain and Ireland.

That's when Stephen Kakfwi, and so many others who I have met over the years, began speaking out. Collectively, their voices and the torturous experiences they revealed came together in the largest class-action lawsuit in Canadian history; in addition to varying degrees of financial compensation for present-day survivors, their witness compelled the government of Canada to announce on June 1, 2008, a royal commission on what has often been called the darkest chapter in Canada's history, the Truth and Reconciliation Commission. And it was a week later that Stephen Harper stood in the House of Commons to apologize on behalf of all Canadians for a century and a half of assimilation policies and treatment of Indigenous peoples that "has no place in Canada."

The more the government apologized and compensated, the more the question grew in my mind: How could someone who had suffered that abuse carry on such high-level negotiations with His Holiness, even to the point of cracking jokes? His answers were simple and wise.

"When you grow up in an alcoholic environment, you witness people who are loving, kind and caring suddenly change in the dark of night and turn abusive and vile." Residential schools were not exempt from this human failing. In the daytime, authorities would appear kind, even generous, but in the dark of night became abusers twisted and horrid. "You learn to separate the two. You learn to tell yourself this is not the same person. I was just trying to do the best I could as a nine-year-old."

On the other side of all the abuse, at twelve he found the face of truth, generosity, humanity and extraordinary courage in a different world and a different school: Grandin College, in Fort Smith. Here he saw no difference between daylight and dark within the human spirit, and a much different priest fostered the character, strength and confidence that personifies

Stephen Kakfwi today. "Father Jean Pochat was like a father to me from the time I was twelve until I left the school at eighteen. He believed in all of us, Dene, Métis and Inuvialuit, and he helped us believe in ourselves."

Father Pochat was an Oblate priest, born in Switzerland, who came to the North in the 1950s. He served as parish priest in Fort Rae, later known as Behchokǫ̀, for about a decade before being assigned to set up and teach at Grandin College, a new school in Fort Smith. There he helped to educate a cadre of young leaders—even revolutionaries—and among the youngest was Stephen Kakfwi. Stephen said, "He taught us and gave us the confidence to stand up for ourselves, to take back our land, our culture and our history, and that's what we did."

Their friendship grew as Stephen's political career advanced. There were many Sundays when he would drive the hundred kilometres from Yellowknife to Behchokǫ̀, seeking "advice and guidance." (When Father Pochat died in 2010, Stephen and Marie were by his side. Stephen says, "We held his hand. We told him we loved him. Marie spoke to him in French and he smiled.")

The day came when the priest had to choose between the interests of the Dene and truth on one hand and the Church and deception on the other. By the mid-1990s, when the extent of abuse at residential schools was exploding in the media and across the country, a senior Catholic with the title Father Provincial asked Father Pochat to arrange a meeting with Stephen, who was then the NWT minister of justice. Pochat assured Stephen that if anything were said or raised that was untoward, he would shut the meeting down.

The Father Provincial's agenda soon became clear. "The meeting was in my home in Yellowknife," said Stephen, "and he asked me directly to denounce the allegations of sexual abuse. I said I would not and could not do that." And Father Pochat honoured his word, immediately leading the high-ranking priest away.

As I listened to Stephen recall the incident, I thought, another treasured promise has been kept. The meeting had been shut down—but it had revealed two opposing views within the priesthood when it came to facing the past with its difficult truths. And it also showed the victims were no longer willing to be silenced.

Soon the road towards reconciliation widened. It was a somewhat changed, more relaxed Indigenous statesman who called me out of the blue in Ottawa on a warm summer evening in 2013 about an idea he had to try to bring Canadians closer together. It became known as Canadians for a New Partnership (CFNP). What was exciting my old friend most was the level of support it was receiving. He told me, "Everybody I've called has been positive and supportive of this thing."

It was at the time when the work of Canada's Truth and Reconciliation Commission, where Marie Wilson was serving as a commissioner, was moving towards its conclusion. But it was not the TRC's work as much as the Idle No More movement and a challenge from his children that had Stephen all fired up.

He had been talking about the situation with Kyla, Daylen and Keenan, he told me. "I expressed frustration about the need for this nation-to-nation relationship to be built upon mutual respect and understanding between Indigenous and non-Indigenous governments and people across Canada. Without any hesitation, they challenged me to take the initiative."

As a former premier, he had an impressive phone book, compiled over the years, and so he began calling. "Everybody" he reached was supportive. Included in "everybody" were two former prime ministers and former political adversaries, Joe Clark and Paul Martin. They were followed by other distinguished Canadians, Indigenous and non-Indigenous, including the former auditor general, Sheila Fraser; former Supreme Court justice Frank Iacobucci; Phil Fontaine and Ovide Mercredi, who had each served as national chief of the Assembly of First Nations; and my wife, Mary Simon, a former president of the Inuit Tapiriit Kanatami, who, at Stephen's insistence, agreed to serve with him as co-chair.

On September 4, 2014, all of them, and dozens of others, signed a declaration to establish a partnership based on the principles of mutual respect, peaceful coexistence and equality. Within days, several thousand Canadians from every part of the country added their names. As a launch-day observer, I found it fascinating to watch two old political foes, Paul Martin and Joe Clark, making the rounds of the evening TV talk shows together, supporting and complementing one another in a common cause for a better Canada. They both addressed the political and social fundamentals shared by those who embraced CFNP, whose declaration states: "Indigenous and non-Indigenous people are bound together in an inseparable bond. But not all have shared equally in the same rights, freedoms, and benefits that should flow from inhabiting this magnificent land."

The CFNP was active until the end of 2017, when Stephen and his distinguished board agreed it had achieved its objective. That's not to say they were under any illusion that Canada had suddenly ended four hundred years of discrimination. But certainly, the political climate had changed. The government was committed to acting on the ninety-four Calls to Action outlined in the Truth and Reconciliation Commission's final report. Ottawa had also initiated direct nation-to-nation negotiations with First Nations and Métis on land and treaty rights, and social programs. With Inuit, who do not describe themselves as a nation, the new structure is known as the Inuit-Crown relationship. Add to that, new ventures were being put in place through an Indigenous Leadership Initiative and Guardians program that shares the same urgency and drive for reconciliation. Not surprisingly, Stephen has played a major role in the creation and success of both. And all the members of the CFNP remained committed to carrying their convictions forward at every opportunity, including reminding Prime Minister Justin Trudeau of his pronouncement that "No relationship is more important than that with Indigenous peoples."

From my nice Ottawa office with the Canadian Polar Commission, I had watched the North move into a new development environment while Stephen served two terms as premier of the Northwest Territories. With land claims settled, he fought hard for both diamond mines and pipelines, finding no contradiction with what he and others had demanded at the Berger inquiry: no pipeline until the land claims are settled.

In the three decades following the release of the Berger recommendations, there have been several attempts to build a line from the Mackenzie Delta up the river valley to Alberta that failed not because of opposition from the Indigenous peoples of the North, but because the federal government and the petroleum industry would not undertake the immense financial commitments required in a world where there is a declining market for natural gas and competing energy sources in Alberta.

Stephen's commitment to "take back our lands" was never stronger or more effective than with the multinational diamond mining companies that had discovered the enormous potential for large-scale diamond production in parts of the Northwest Territories. Today, the territory is Canada's largest diamond producer, and diamonds are a major part of the regional economy, with Yellowknife now selling itself as Canada's diamond capital. Stephen Kakfwi fought to make that happen.

He untangled complicated negotiations between the territorial government and BHP, one of the world's largest mining companies, after it had discovered large deposits of kimberlite several hundred kilometres northeast of Yellowknife. The government was a novice at dealing with such large multinational corporations, but Stephen, then a cabinet minister, achieved a breakthrough. He negotiated an agreement with BHP that obligated the company to guarantee that a percentage of the diamonds it mined would be polished and finished in the Northwest Territories. The agreement also allowed territorial officials to measure and evaluate the number of diamonds extracted.

At first the second major international diamond miner, Rio Tinto, was unwilling to deal with the local government at all. It took considerable lobbying and negotiation to persuade

Rio Tinto's Canadian executives to meet one of the NWT ministers. The meeting was scheduled to run for one hour at midnight at the Calgary airport.

"The minister responsible had a previous commitment, so I said I would take the meeting," Stephen recalls. "The next day I cancelled it instead and got on a plane to London, where I asked for a meeting with the president of Rio Tinto, Robert Wilson."

In Stephen's recollection, the diamond executive was most gracious. "I walked into his office, we shook hands and he offered coffee." After they sat down, Wilson inquired about his Canadian staff, and Stephen's response was direct, perhaps even brutal. "I said, 'They are dead from the arse up.'"

In his view, Stephen explained, a company that wants to do business in a country that offers resources potentially worth billions of dollars should show more respect when dealing with a legitimate government and not offer a midnight meeting in an airport.

Robert Wilson's response was equally direct. "What do you want?"

Stephen told him the territory needed a grading facility off-site so the government could monitor and evaluate the extent of production and, as with the other large mining concern, that a percentage of their diamonds be polished and finished in the Northwest Territories.

"He said, 'Is that all?' I said yes, and he agreed." A handshake sealed the deal. It was over in fifteen minutes, the time it took to enjoy that cup of coffee.

The moral of the story, whether it's the Catholic Church or one of the major producers of precious gems—go to the guy in charge.

He was radical and he was right. That line should be in a song on one of Stephen Kakfwi's CDs, which are packed with lyrics of hope, of love and family, and the kind of descriptions of honky-tonk and barroom life that feature in "Gold Range at Midnight" (in my memory Yellowknife's oldest diamond in the rough).

Of all his songs, I like "Bells of Radileh Koe" best. He wrote it as a tribute to his father, saying, "It is my way of making peace with him. I blamed him for all the years I was sent away. He died in 1975 before I got to know him very well."

I believe he made that peace when he fulfilled the ambition he had set for himself as a twenty-two-year-old Dene Nation field worker. He remembers his dad asking him what he was doing. In response, he said, "Dad, we are going to take back our land, we are going to have our own government, our own schools, and make our own decisions. We are going to take back control."

I love the song, in part, because it reminds me of the serenity I found in the sound of another Arctic bell I have told you about, and in part, because of the lyrical bond Stephen describes as father and son approach Radileh Koe (Fort Good Hope) on a dog sled on a night so cold their breath would freeze:

> *My father would sing*
> *when we heard the church bells ring*
> *Don't cry for me when it's my time to go*
> *just play the bells of Radileh Koe*

18

CHANGING CANADA

The Other John A.

Many times, I have walked the shores of Resolute Bay on Cornwallis Island, the midpoint of the Northwest Passage, and tried to imagine the hardship endured by the ninety Inuit High Arctic exiles during the winter of 1953. How were they able to survive at all? They had only tents for shelter. As the fierce winter with its twenty-four-hour darkness closed in on them, they scoured and scrounged the military base dump for food, scrap wood to burn and lumber to build meagre shacks.

Even harder to imagine is how one small boy, a tiny human flagpole in Canada's continuing assertion of Arctic sovereignty, was so shaped by the experience, he would someday play a principal part in changing Canada itself. All across Nunavut, that boy, now in his seventies, is highly respected, even revered—known by most as simply "John A." Just as the other John A., Canada's first prime minister, brought the country into being through Confederation, John Amagoalik brought Nunavut into Canada.

John and his parents, his brothers and sisters, and sixteen other families were relocated in the 1950s from Port Harrison, now Inukjuak on the west coast of Hudson Bay, to Resolute Bay and Grise Fiord, more than a thousand kilometres north. He recalls, "When we came ashore, all we could see was gravel everywhere. There was no vegetation. I remember everybody was afraid, feeling lost and abandoned, and we faced the harsh winter with nothing but our tents."

As an adult, every time he met a reporter, he told that story, so others would know of the mistreatment and deceit inflicted by the federal government on ninety Inuit, most of them children. Perhaps that's why he befriended me in the mid-1970s on one of Commissioner Stuart Hodgson's Arctic tours. I can't remember if John told me the story before, during or after he took all my money in a poker game. The relocation and hardship shaped his destiny: "One of the first things I remember is we were treated very badly by the RCMP and government, and that has stuck with me all my life, and then going to school and being punished for speaking my language. Me and my little brother, Jimmy."

His life story and the story of the creation of Nunavut itself are laced with "irony." As John A. points out, "The government did give me an education that I was able to use. It was not their intention to make a radical that would change Canada." The pain and suffering of the ninety exiles underpinned the long narrative that led to Nunavut. It was always there—that clear, gripping and unforgettable experience of what happens when people have no control over their lives and land, the experience of being dumped on that barren beach in a land foreign to them, in twenty-four hours of darkness in the coldest winter months, and expected to "instinctively" survive just because they were "Eskimos."

John Amagoalik may appreciate the education he received. But that too was a struggle. In Resolute as a kid, he began teaching himself, looking at the words and pictures in the pages of the magazines and newspapers that lined the walls of the family shelter to block drafts and keep melting water from dripping. He searched for the comic books and newspapers he says were carefully and deliberately left at the dump by the military people on the base a few kilometres away. In the 1960s, air force personnel and employees of other federal agencies, including the CBC, were forbidden to "fraternize" with the "Eskimos." But some at least remained considerate and generous.

Like the exiles, the airmen were also there for sovereignty. The United States was building North American Air (later Aerospace) Defense Command (NORAD) bases and the Distant Early Warning (DEW) radar network. Canada was a full partner in both, but at the same time, the Canadian government believed it needed to assert a clear Canadian presence. And so it planted Mounties, pilots and Inuit above the Arctic Circle. Over the years, I've heard all of them use the term "human flagpole" to describe themselves.

In 1960 or 1961, when he was around thirteen, John was sent to the Charles Camsell Hospital in Edmonton for treatment of tuberculosis. His English improved greatly, thanks to television and a teacher who regularly visited his ward. Fourteen months later, he was selected to attend the Churchill Vocational School in northern Manitoba.

"It was not the same as the residential schools we have come to know, with the violence and abuse, in other places," he says. "Churchill became a positive experience for many of us. And we got a good basic education and we became more independent and learned to survive by ourselves."

Despite all his accomplishments, the only time I ever sense even a hint of boasting from John A. is when he talks about that school: "It came very naturally. I loved learning and I was always a good student with good grades. I seemed to have this ability to speak to my fellow students. I guess the gift of the gab came naturally."

He told me that school is where he lost his Ilira. The word simply means a deeply held fear of white people. I have heard several prominent leaders, including Mary, speak of both Ilira and the freedom that comes with shaking free of it.

John would meet another Inuk in Churchill, a young man only a couple of years older than him, with whom he would share the distinction of being one of Nunavut's founding fathers. "Tagak Curley was the dorm supervisor. He came from Coral Harbour on Southampton Island. Tagak was twenty years old at the most and had been sent by his community to investigate if there were problems. He would patrol the halls, often drop in on classes and listen to the discussions, and visit with us in the dorms in the evenings."

Now a good story is destroyed by facts. John insists there were "no revolutionary discussions" among the boys, just young people talking music and sports and home and family.

After Churchill Vocational School, university was out of the question for John and all northern youth of the time. However, a new high school opened in Frobisher Bay, and in his early twenties, John enrolled to get his diploma. In an ironic twist, the high school was named after Gordon Robertson, the noted federal public servant who'd served as commissioner of the Northwest Territories when the second shipload of High Arctic exiles was sent north in 1955. The school was later renamed Inuksuk High School, after the traditional Inuit landmark.

High school delivered a bigger gift to John than a diploma. It was there that he met Evie Korgak, his wife to this day. They raised five children and take pride in more than a dozen grandchildren and great-grandchildren.

Newly married, he landed a job as a communications officer with the government of the Northwest Territories, travelling the communities and learning. By 1974, he had been recruited as a field worker by Inuit Tapirisat of Canada (often, at the time, called the Eskimo Brotherhood), which meant travelling the communities talking to people, explaining the concepts of a land claim settlement, and laying the groundwork for a new and much different North.

An air accident almost buried the dream. In November 1975, John and a couple dozen other ITC staff were on a chartered DC-3, returning from a major land claims strategy conference in Pond Inlet on the northern end of Baffin Island. They planned to drop delegates in Clyde River, Broughton Island and Pangnirtung. As they took off from Clyde River, a blizzard began to blow. They tried Broughton Island and Pangnirtung, with a plan to refuel in one of those settlements. Both were socked in.

Then there they were, over the middle of Baffin Island, and suddenly out of fuel. The windows in the cockpit immediately began to frost; with no engines, there was no heat. They made a forced blind landing in darkness, in a blizzard. Miraculously, the pilot hit a reasonably smooth valley and the soft snow cushioned the impact. There were no injuries, but everyone spent a very cold night huddled together in the rear of the airplane.

The pilot had also been able to send out his coordinates. Very early the next morning, an RCMP single-engine Otter arrived and the rescue began. The soft snow restricted the Otter's takeoff capacity. Since it could carry only four people at a time, it started with two women and two lawyers from Toronto. The other twenty or so staff members and three crew huddled for a second night in the downed plane, but at least they now had food and blankets courtesy of the Otter. The wreckage of the old DC-3 remains in that spot.

Barely two years into his job with the national Inuit organization, John Amagoalik had a title and responsibilities on the national stage. He was to appear at the Ottawa hearings of the Berger Inquiry in a setting that would become historic for Indigenous peoples—the stately old railway station that had been converted into a government conference centre. In a few short years, John would be among a group of Indigenous leaders who would fight successfully in that very room to have Aboriginal rights enshrined in the Constitution of Canada.

But on this day, John was laying the groundwork and Justice Berger was taking everything he said down, the background to John's stirring words the unmistakable scratching sound of Tom's sharp pencil. (The judge always left his mic on, just inches away from his notepad.)

> The north has been labelled as the "last frontier." Some look at it as something which needs to be conquered, explored and exploited. It has been called a "warehouse of resources." To us it is home. It is a part of us. It is where we were born. It is where we will die. It belongs to our children.

John's vision is reflected in the title of Justice Berger's historic report, *Northern Frontier, Northern Homeland.* In his testimony, John also connected essential national and native contexts:

> It was only about three years ago we were told that Canada had sufficient energy supplies to meet its own needs into the foreseeable future, with plenty left over to export to the United States. Now suddenly we are told that we face a shortage. . . . We are told that the oil companies must have more revenue so that they can step up explorations and find more reserves. The average southern Canadian must find all this very confusing. To an Inuk trapper living in Sachs Harbour or Paulatuk, it is positively bewildering.

Only a few months earlier, he, Tagak Curley, and others had presented the first draft of their comprehensive land claims proposal to the government of Canada. Now John put the Inuit vision squarely to Justice Berger. He said the North "is not a wasteland of ice and snow and it must not become a wasteland of concrete towers, railways, pipelines and a broken people."

Inuit had made a massive claim for 2.5 million square kilometres of land and ocean; to no one's great surprise, neither the government nor the rest of the country was ready for it. In the CBC archives, I found a memorable exchange between John and the distinguished panel members of *Front Page Challenge*—a program with top ratings at the time. With several million Canadians watching, John put the Inuit position in perspective.

"You cannot sell your heritage. We don't look at the land as something to be sold. We want to save our language, heritage and philosophy, and our way of life," he said, confronting three icons of the Canadian establishment, each of whom had a big presence and loud voice: Gordon Sinclair, Betty Kennedy and Yukon-born Pierre Berton. John was not yet thirty years old, and in his voice there was not a hint of Ilira, just a confidence that matched theirs and a mission that gave him an elevated purpose: "Our intent is ensuring our survival as a unique race of people in Canada."

John has a remarkable ability to lay out issues, ideas and positions clearly in English, his second language. And he was always a reporter's dream. Ask him a question and you got the ten- or fifteen-second radio sound bite, TV clip or newspaper quote you needed. In Amagoalik-speak, there is no hem or haw.

But there was a night on live TV when the interviewer's dream had nightmare flashes. After that first land claim proposal was formally advanced in 1976, the Canadian Inuit, with John as the principal negotiator, began a fourteen-year roller-coaster ride of dealings with the government of Canada and its bureaucrats. I am going to fast-forward through that period.

There were reports, proposals, counter-proposals, with added side-track issues and diversions that included a 1980 study by Charles "Bud" Drury, a former and highly distinguished cabinet minister from the Lester Pearson and Pierre Trudeau governments, that poured cold water on the emerging proposition to divide the Northwest Territories and create a new territory of Nunavut. Inuit responded to these political and bureaucratic setbacks by creating a lobby group, the Inuit Committee on National Issues. With John on that committee was Zebedee Nungak, from Arctic Quebec and, like John A., masterful at managing and captivating the media. As Nungak said, "We succeeded in informing Canadians in general who we are, what we are about, what we wanted and the place we believe we should have in this country's political structure."

From 1982 to 1987, four First Ministers Conferences on the Constitution enshrined Aboriginal rights but failed to define those rights. The meetings, carried live on national TV, allowed Canada to see bright, young, articulate Indigenous leaders who often seemed more focused and reasonable than the premiers. Finally, in 1990, almost twenty years after Tagak Curley advanced the initial land claim concept, John Amagoalik and the federal Indian affairs minister, Tom Siddon, shook hands on an agreement in principle for the largest land claim settlement in Canadian history and the creation of a new territory. It was a very big story.

By then, I was the evening anchor for the new CBC twenty-four-hour news cable channel, Newsworld. Our typical format for the major story of the day was a twenty-minute in-depth report with live interviews linked by satellite from different parts of the country. Generally, for each featured report, we'd do three or four interviews that embraced the basic five w's of journalism—who, what, why, when and where—and also how.

On this broadcast, we planned to begin with John setting out the basics of a remarkable twenty-year negotiation that had resulted in the largest land claim agreement in Canadian history and perhaps in the world, confirming Inuit ownership of a land mass in the eastern and High Arctic the equivalent of one-fifth of Canada. The Canadian government would also pay Inuit $1 billion in compensation for lands surrendered. The tentative agreement set out a schedule that included dividing the Northwest Territories and defining the boundary for a new territory through a plebiscite.

Our telecast got off to a great start, with John A. providing answers that were clear, crisp and right to the point, with no political or personal posturing or self-aggrandizement. Then in my earpiece came these few words, which I had already heard too many times on the fledgling network: "Whit, we lost the satellite link for the next interview; you need to extend."

John's seven-minute interview was about to double in length. In television, especially live television, you can't have dead air. As I began to stretch my questions to kill time, John's answers got shorter. Close to the fourteen-minute mark, I heard in my ear, "Whit, there's still no satellite link, you have to keep going with him."

My questions grew to a minute or more in length. I blathered on with things like, "Mr. Amagoalik, this is a very complex matter, creating a new territory and changing Canada, we have lots of time here to explore this . . ." He didn't get the hint, or maybe he liked watching me trying to stay afloat.

I am sure that at some point in that lopsided exchange I raised the issue of the Resolute Bay relocation of his childhood. Certainly, it was still central to the overall Inuit rights agenda, a constant reminder to Inuit of how they were once treated by Canada and a revelation to many Canadians about the extent to which their governments had marginalized Indigenous peoples. But that injustice would remain unfinished business for another twenty years. The 1990 Inuit land claims agreement was indicative of how all the claims were settled. A matter of timing and political expedience on the part of the government, or developers, and hardball negotiations by Inuit finding the soft spot.

John recalls the political reality. "The Mulroney government was in trouble after they had badly handled the Oka crisis," he says, referring to the government sending in the military to put down a Mohawk protest east of Montreal that was attempting to protect lands against an illicit golf course development. There was a make-or-break negotiating session. Northern Affairs Minister Tom Siddon was at the table. The government and Inuit had reached an agreement on the general terms of the land claim itself, but Siddon and the feds had balked on the second critical issue: the creation of Nunavut. John recalls, "We called for a coffee break and huddled ourselves. Then we told Siddon's assistant, Nigel Wolford, who I knew well because he had been my boss years earlier at Inuit Tapirisat, to tell the minister it was all or nothing. We knew that the government was down to 10 to 12 percent in the polls because of Oka."

The Inuit negotiators and John, unflinching poker players, knew they were holding a strong hand. "We said if this government is not ready to make the deal, we will wait for the next government. We are sure the next government will make the deal."

At that, Siddon went to another room and called the prime minister. Mulroney, well known for his "roll the dice" approach to constitutional issues and politics in general, accepted the Nunavut proposal.

There were now two legislative tracks. One bill, the Nunavut Land Claims Act, set out forty-two articles covering Inuit rights over land, water, wildlife, cultural protection, language, employment and education. The Nunavut Act would create the governing structure of the new territory, guaranteeing equal voting and citizenship rights for all residents.

A referendum was held in 1992 across the whole of the Northwest Territories to approve a boundary to define the 2.5 million square kilometres that would comprise Nunavut. The boundary cut north from the Manitoba-Saskatchewan border to the edge of the treeline and followed the treeline westerly. It attempted to both respect and find a compromise between the Dene and Inuit overlapping claims of traditional hunting areas.

The Inuvialuit of the western Arctic chose to remain in the Northwest Territories, given that the capital, Yellowknife, and its services were much closer to them than the new Nunavut capital of Iqaluit. The land claim was finalized in 1993.

At the same time, John embarked on a six-year journey to create the new government and public service, as chair of the Nunavut Implementation Commission. Division of the territories required more than drawing a line on the map; the complex administrative, financial and physical levers of government and public service needed to be divided or built.

There were three principal entities in the territory-building exercise: John's Implementation Commission, the Canadian government, and the government of the Northwest Territories. In my recollection, John succeeded in keeping the focus on Nunavut and the future, saying, "It's up to us now. We cannot blame other people."

On April 1, 1999, all the predictable pomp and pageantry were on full display in Canada's newest capital, Iqaluit. Prime Minister Jean Chrétien and Governor General Roméo LeBlanc were there to sign the proclamation that changed the map of Canada. Strangely, neither John Amagoalik nor Tagak Curley were on the platform, but it didn't seem to matter. Every one of the several hundred people in the crowded school gymnasium, where a new government was proclaimed and sworn in, and the few thousand more in the converted airplane hangars that hosted a massive gala, needed no reminder how Nunavut came about and who was responsible.

I will never forget the sense of pride in John's dark eyes as he sat in the audience, Evie by his side. Both my cameraman, Herb Tyler, and I had left CBC by then, but we were there shooting a documentary on the changing North. When Herb zoomed in, John A. was ready for his close-up. His smile widened as his hand came into the frame, and he gave a simple but memorable thumbs-up.

Tagak was also in the audience, and overjoyed. When once again I pushed a mic under his chin, he said, "It's unbelievable; we have done it."

The Oka standoff had other consequences for Inuit and John Amagoalik. In 1991, the federal government appointed four Indigenous and three non-Indigenous commissioners to the Royal Commission on Aboriginal Peoples. In the commission's own words:

> We began our work at a difficult time . . . of anger and upheaval. The country's leaders were arguing about the place of Aboriginal people in the constitution. First Nations were blockading roads and rail lines in Ontario and British Columbia. Innu families were encamped in protest of military installations in Labrador. A year earlier, armed conflict between Aboriginal and non-Aboriginal forces at Kanesatake (Oka) had tarnished Canada's reputation abroad—and in the minds of many citizens.

Two of the seven commissioners also knew a lot about the relocation of Inuit to Resolute Bay in 1953. Georges Erasmus, a Dene born in Yellowknife, was appointed the commission co-chair with Quebec Court Judge René Dussault. Erasmus was a former president of the Dene Nation and, later, national chief of the Assembly of First Nations. He had played a key role for First Nations during the constitutional conferences of the 1980s, while at the same time building bridges with Inuit and Métis leaders. His sharp intellect and superb communication skills, especially in the nationally televised exchanges with the premiers and the prime minister, earned their respect and the respect of Canadians in every part of the country.

Commissioner Mary Sillett was Inuk from Labrador. Throughout the 1980s she had worked on constitutional issues and land claims and served as president of both Inuit Tapirisat of Canada and Pauktuutit, the national Inuit women's organization.

The royal commission determined that its report and recommendations to the government would be evidence-based. Accordingly, the commission completed the most comprehensive research initiative ever done on Indigenous peoples in Canada. For John Amagoalik and every other advocate for justice for the High Arctic exiles, a new door opened when the commission committed to examining the relocation through both documented research and public hearings.

After almost forty years, the people forcibly moved to Resolute Bay and Grise Fiord would finally get a chance to tell their own story. Surprisingly to all, they wanted to tell it in Ottawa. I went to that hearing feeling a twinge of regret that I was no longer a reporter. I watched now elderly men and women, unmistakable in their fur-trimmed parkas and sealskin kamiks, shuffling along as old people often do, some with canes and others holding onto a proffered hand to climb the curb and steps. Still, they walked ever so confidently into the grandeur of the ballroom in the stately old Château Laurier near Parliament Hill, the very stone buildings where the decisions that had drastically changed their lives so long ago were made.

My mind switched back to the black-and-white photos that I had seen of these same people, carrying on their backs a child or scant belongings, yet walking straight and strong up the gangplank of the government ship *C. D. Howe* headed to an unknown land and a painful future. They had waited for this day for a very long time.

John A. sat with them, and among the commissioners were two familiar faces, Georges Erasmus and Mary Sillett.

The facilitator who would ask the questions and lead the testimony was Mary Simon, someone who for twenty years, in many jobs, they knew had been a strong advocate for them. Mary was part of the commission's legal research team, headed by a former federal deputy minister of justice, Roger Tassé, also a veteran of the constitutional negotiations.

Mary spoke to the Inuit witnesses in Inuktitut, her words translated for the commission by a person equally familiar with the story: Zebedee Nungak. Born in northern Quebec, Zebedee had never stopped searching for ways to make this day happen.

In the grand hall, children and grandchildren surrounded the surviving exiles. Sadly, many others did not live long enough to witness it. The testimony was gripping.

"We had to find wood in the dump to build a shelter."

"We didn't know where to hunt."

"We were hungry. We didn't have enough food to eat."

"I thought we would freeze to death."

The most frequent of all was this simple statement: "We were lied to."

But the public servants, the RCMP and even the former fur traders who testified still denied that people were either coerced or promised they could return.

The royal commission's report, released in 1994, determined there was coercion and recommended compensation and a formal apology. Three years later, in 1997, the Chrétien government negotiated a compensation package, offering a $10-million trust fund to be managed by Inuit that would pay for people to travel back and forth to their homeland and rebuild lost connections. But the government would not apologize.

The elderly Inuit signed that agreement, but again under duress. They just felt too old and too tired to fight on. John A., along with every single member of the Inuit leadership, was outraged but not defeated. They would find the next opening. As many of us had learned from the marathon process of the land claims settlement and creation of Nunavut, Inuit are a patient people.

Picture an Inuit hunter, bent over, staring down a small hole in the ice pack, a harpoon raised and poised, ready to plunge, waiting for a seal to surface for a breath of air. The wait may take hours. The hunter does not move or make a sound, barely breathes. Finally, a seal appears—and the harpoon descends like lightning.

It is survival of the fittest and the fittest is the most patient. When Stephen Harper apologized on behalf of Canadians to all those who had suffered abuse in the residential schools, he opened the door for the same government to apologize to the High Arctic exiles. It would take two more years, but John A. was on the platform in Inukjuak, northern Quebec, when Northern Affairs Minister John Duncan said the simple words no one else had been able to find for almost sixty years:

> On behalf of the Government of Canada and all Canadians, we would like to offer a full and sincere apology to Inuit for the relocation of families from Inukjuak and Pond Inlet to Grise Fiord and Resolute Bay during the 1950s.
>
> We would like to express our deepest sorrow for the extreme hardship and suffering caused by the relocation. The families were separated from their home communities and extended families by more than a thousand kilometres. They

> were not provided with adequate shelter and supplies. They were not properly informed of how far away and how different from Inukjuak their new homes would be, and they were not aware that they would be separated into two communities once they arrived in the High Arctic. Moreover, the Government failed to act on its promise to return anyone that did not wish to stay in the High Arctic to their old homes. . . .
>
> We would like to pay tribute to the relocatees for their perseverance and courage.

Duncan went on to acknowledge the contribution the "relocatees and their descendants" made to Canada despite the suffering and hardship. John A.'s legacy as "a father of Nunavut" is surely at the forefront of that contribution.

John says he has only one piece of unfinished business in his advancing years, one I share. Toronto has to win the Stanley Cup. *Go, Leafs, go!*

19

TAGAK CURLEY

The Inuit Enigma

He once showed me how to build an iglu—and even said I had potential as an iglu-builder. Years later, in the fall of 1998, he was standing under the dome of the People's Iglu, more formally known as the new legislative assembly in the new territory of Nunavut.

Tagak Curley, the man who began the long journey towards the creation of Nunavut, was pointing to the fine wood arches over the legislative chamber, wearing his construction company's head-honcho white hard hat. My cameraman and colleague Herb Tyler was just behind his shoulder following the hand and recording his comment about what the new structure signified: "The Nunavut dream realized."

To say Tagak Curley is a man of many talents is an understatement. In the 1970s, he was the young radical who marched unannounced into the cluttered little CBC Yellowknife newsroom and declared into my microphone that Inuit would demand a land claim settlement. In the 1980s, he was a member of the legislative assembly of the Northwest Territories, constantly asking questions and advancing motions and petitions to divide the territories to create Nunavut. In the 1990s, he was in business, president of Nunavut Construction Corporation, which had the contract for building much of the infrastructure for the new territory, including the building we were standing in.

After the territory was formed, Tagak returned to politics and was acclaimed for two consecutive terms as the member for Rankin Inlet North in Nunavut. He served in the cabinet during both terms but resigned as minister of health and social services in 2011, after disagreeing with Premier Eva Aariak's decision to split the department into two separate entities. No one was surprised. People across the North know him as strong-minded, even stubborn. He did not run in the following election.

Everybody, including me, also knows Tagak Curley as a successful hunter, historian, craftsman and Inuit intellectual. He was born in 1944 on the land, in a hunting camp. His earliest years were lived in a traditional way of life. Unlike other Inuit who were forced to move to Coral Harbour, Tagak's father chose to move the family to the Southampton Island community in the early 1950s so the children could attend school. When Tagak had an opportunity for education in the south, he took it, first in British Columbia and then at Algonquin College in Ottawa.

From our first encounter, we always got along. I appreciated his directness and his focus. I accepted that, come thin ice, hell or high water, he would get his way. Tagak could be very charming and persuasive. How else could a young man with a transparent agenda to remake the Northwest Territories and assert the unheard-of concept of "Native rights" wriggle his way onto so many free government flights to the most inaccessible communities throughout the Arctic?

Twice I was on one of those tours where Tagak had obtained passage and was marching to the beat of his own drum rather than that of his host. One of them was through the western and central High Arctic, a trip where the senior federal government civil servant at the time, Frank McCall, was hopping from place to place to explain to Inuit the government's new resource development policy and the benefits that would soon flow from it. The other was one of Stuart Hodgson's expeditions in the eastern High Arctic.

On both junkets, Tagak was the exception. He would attend the events and accept introductions, listen politely and attentively to the government pitches, and then work the room and the community in his way and especially in his language, sowing the seeds for a new and different kind of "northern development."

On one of the stops on the Hodgson tour, we were stranded by a fierce blizzard in a now-forgotten destination. Since we had time on our hands, at breakfast I asked Tagak about the intricacies of building an iglu. He searched the hostel's kitchen and selected a foot-long butcher knife—a lot different than an Inuit bone snow knife, but he said it would do.

He led me outside, where he quickly found hard-packed snow and began cutting out blocks and setting them in a neat row. Soon he was laying them out. He shaved the top of the first one on a slight angle, another followed with the same angle, and soon a dome was taking shape.

By now we had been joined by Hodgson's assistant, Don Johnson. After about three rows, Tagak said we were on our own. I followed Tagak's pattern, trimming and skinning the sides and bottom of the blocks at slight angles so they fit firmly on top of the previous row.

As we worked, an elderly Inuk came close and carefully eyed our construction project. He wore sealskin kamiks up to his knees. His weathered face and pullover parka told me here was a hunter and landsman who had likely built hundreds of iglus in his time. After watching us for a while, he walked back to a nearby house. A few moments later, the old man reappeared in front of us, pulled up his parka, raised a Polaroid camera, aimed and clicked.

The camera made that unique purring sound as it coughed up the instant photo. He stood there smiling, waiting for the thirty-second magic of Polaroid to take place under the thumbs of his sealskin mitts. Then the smile got bigger. "Eee!" he said, and then he turned and walked back to his house. I'm pretty sure that the old man tacked that little snap on the wall, where it became a conversation piece about the two Qallunaat who built an iglu in his front yard.

There was a lesson for me in those carved snow blocks. The new, southern-educated generation of Inuit and Dene leaders were often disdained by colonialists. "They could never survive on the land," they'd say, or "They talk of a way of life they know nothing about." In my experience, I found that all the young Indigenous leaders were highly competent in traditional life and survival skills. As years went by, I came to learn that traditional and cultural confidence also prepared them as twenty-some-year-olds to survive in southern cities and corporate boardrooms, and to overcome myriad government barriers and layers of bureaucracy.

When Herb and I were producing our documentaries on the creation of Nunavut, Tagak invited us into the tidy workshop behind his home in Iqaluit to view his remarkable collection of harpoon heads and traditional hunting tools. It looked as much museum as workshop. Dozens and dozens of finely carved and surgically sharp killing instruments were carefully laid out on display. On the bench, a carver's tools were visible, files, grinders and sharpening stones alongside several harpoon heads in varying stages of development. They were all sizes and shapes, but each carried the weight of generations—centuries—of meticulous observation on effectiveness and efficiency.

Many had jagged edges designed to penetrate deep into the flesh of a marine mammal and withstand the strength of a fighting whale or walrus. Some of the heads measured five or six inches in length, others might be only a fraction of an inch, but each had a unique design and application depending on the animal—mammal, bird or fish—being hunted. Most were made from ivory or caribou antler. Some were brass or stainless steel, adapting ancient knowledge to new technologies. Thirty years later, when I asked Tagak if he was still collecting and crafting traditional tools, he said, "Of course. When I look into a hunter's boat, I always look to see what kind of harpoon he has. That tells me what kind of hunter he is. These are how we survived."

Tagak is remarkable in so many ways it's hard to figure out which is the most remarkable. Is it his astonishing success in establishing a new national Inuit organization that almost overnight captured the attention of Canadians and their government, or his shocking decision to walk away from it after only a few years?

The Inuit Tapirisat's three formative years, 1971 to 1974, were exceptional, as Inuit from all across Canada united behind Tagak Curley. The climate was ripe for change and a break from the colonialist federal and territorial governments. The organization's formative conferences, in Pangnirtung in 1972 and Cambridge Bay a year later, were full of energy, conviction and excitement. You knew the winds of change were gathering here and there would be no turning back. They were the beginning of the Inuit movement that would soon capture first Inuit specifically, then the whole territory, and then Canadians across the country. It did not take the government in Ottawa long to recognize it was in its political interest to listen and pay attention.

In addition to recruiting the best and brightest young Inuit, people such as Jose Kusugak, John Amagoalik and Mary Simon, Tagak also attracted a cadre of well-educated, non-Inuit legal and political advisers equally committed to change and social justice. With so many idealistic, energized and pissed-off young minds on board, there were angry debates and bitter disagreements as to tactics and strategy in those early years, but always behind closed doors. Lena Pederson, who was born in Greenland and emigrated to Canada in 1959, was a member of the first ITC board of directors. (She also became the first woman elected to the NWT legislative council.) After Nunavut was declared on April 1, 1999, I asked her what she remembered most about that time. She said, "We always spoke with one voice, that was the key to our success." In public, at least.

Tagak recalls that the biggest challenge in the formative years was getting money—core funding—from the government. After months of meetings and negotiations, including sessions with both Canada's secretary of state (a cabinet post that no longer exists) and the minister of Indian and northern affairs and their top officials, Tagak says he was both disappointed and discouraged: "The government was providing core funding to six hundred other organizations but refusing Inuit." One more make-or-break session with the two ministers and their officials failed to win a funding commitment from the government; as is often the case when people push for major change to the way things have been done in the past, most of the resistance came from the senior bureaucrats. After Tagak announced that he was ready to return home to his family, Jean Chrétien, then minister for Indian and northern affairs, suggested the two of them have lunch the next day. That lunch and Chrétien's personal involvement finally turned the tide; from that point on Inuit would receive government money to pay the rent, keep the lights on, hire staff, and above all begin researching their land claim and legal positions.

In 1974, James Arvaluk, in his mid-twenties, replaced Tagak as president of Inuit Tapirisat of Canada. Arvaluk was bright, charismatic and a good communicator. His term was also three years. (He eventually moved into territorial politics, but his career ended after convictions and jail sentences in 1995 and 2003 for sexual and physical assault.)

Tagak's career and his outlook shifted. "I went back home to Repulse Bay," he says, "to spend more time with my father." He took over as executive director of the Inuit Cultural Institute, which was a natural progression, given that the preservation of culture, language and basic rights were also at the core of the ITC mandate.

In 1979, Tagak ran as a Liberal candidate in a new federal riding called Nunatsiaq, which comprised roughly the territory now known as Nunavut. He was defeated by Peter Ittinuar, the NDP candidate. In my view, that was fate stepping in, and both Tagak and the North were the better for it. Instead of heading for Ottawa, later that same year Tagak was elected as a member of the NWT legislative assembly for the Keewatin South riding.

There were no political parties then or now in the Northwest Territories, and this consensus style of government was also adopted by Nunavut. However, there were informal and often effective political alliances, and Tagak brought the Inuit members of the assembly together in the equivalent of an opposition. The largest caucus in the assembly, it began setting the stage for dividing the Northwest Territories and creating Nunavut. It also immensely strengthened the Inuit voice. As far as Tagak was concerned, since there was no government representing his people, "it was up to us to take up the fight for the people and the issues, like health."

These became stormy times in the assembly and across the North. Soon the Inuit caucus and Tagak Curley pressed for a plebiscite on division. The first of two plebiscites was held on April 14, 1982, asking the straightforward question "Do you think the Northwest Territories should be divided? Yes or No."

A bookmaker would have looked at the population split, east and west, and probably given odds that the Nunavut dream would be defeated. Consider that two-thirds of the voters lived in the western Northwest Territories and had little or nothing to gain from division. The majority living in the larger towns and in Yellowknife were opposed. People in the smaller Dene communities appeared evenly divided.

What upended the odds was the voter turnout: low in the west and extraordinarily high in the east, where more than 80 percent voted in favour. The final count: 56 percent in favour, 44 percent against. Only one Dene politician, Stephen Kakfwi, argued in favour of division. If the Dene were seeking a homeland, how could they oppose the Inuit drive for their own land? Also, Kakfwi didn't look at it as dividing, but rather as building and growing. "It is a unique opportunity to finally shape, with the active participation of all northern residents, a truly northern system of government, one which incorporates the needs, aspirations, and cultures of the original peoples into its fundamental character," he said. "We can meld the historic collective rights of the Aboriginal peoples with the individual rights of all its citizens."

It took ten more years for Inuit to bring the federal government around to finalize the Nunavut Land Claims Agreement and the parallel agreement to create Nunavut. Ottawa did set a clear condition: the people of the North would need to choose and vote on a boundary.

Tagak wanted all Inuit included in the new territory, but the boundary line, as drawn, left the Inuvialuit living in six western Arctic communities—Aklavik, Inuvik, Paulatuk, Tuktoyaktuk, Ulukhaktok and Sachs Harbour—in the west. The boundary proposal shattered Tagak's vision and he was forced to oppose it: "We simply do not wish to sell ourselves out for a cheap little version of what some people call Nunavut."

The Inuvialuit are Inuit, but they prefer to be known by their Inuktitut dialect, which is different from that spoken in the eastern and central Arctic. And they were practical. They lived in the west. Their historic transportation and economic ties were in the west. Put bluntly, they preferred a capital in Yellowknife, a thousand kilometres or so away, rather than one in Iqaluit, more than two thousand kilometres away.

Also, their fate had been decided as far back as 1976, when they were forced to abandon the land claim quest directed by the Inuit Tapirisat and pursue their own claim. With Beaufort Sea oil and gas development at a fever pitch and the Berger Report calling for land claim settlements before development, the Inuvialuit simply couldn't wait. Like the Inuit of northern Quebec whose land was affected by the massive James Bay hydro project, they negotiated the best deal they could.

The Inuvialuit settlement, signed in 1984, confirmed Aboriginal title over large parcels of land and waters, provided financial compensation for lands surrendered and protected Aboriginal hunting and fishing rights. It also provided for a level of local government that appeared to be working well for the people in the region. Accordingly, the boundary that was approved in a second plebiscite in May 1992 kept the Inuvialuit in the west, with 54 percent in favour.

As a reporter, I learned that I could give my stories an added edge by pointing out the contradiction or irony that was almost always present. Rarely was it as clear as in this situation. The visionary who had laid the groundwork, set the political and legal frameworks, and worked so hard to make Nunavut happen watched Inuit voters embrace someone else's "cheap little version" of the new territory over his much bigger vision.

"I have no regrets," Tagak told me later. "The people of the west did what they thought was best for them."

In his life so far, Tagak has made history in more ways than one. If you were to ask him about Charles Dickens, author of many English classics, including *A Christmas Carol*, he would not respond with a salute to either Scrooge or Tiny Tim. More likely, you'd hear a rant about a pen-for-hire opportunist who slandered and vilified Inuit.

Around the midpoint of his life, Tagak developed an interest in the history of the English explorers. Like many in the North, he observed with passing interest the continuing, sometimes obsessive quest to find the remains of the Franklin expedition. And like many, he knew that Sir John Franklin had embarked from Britain in 1845 with two ships, *Terror* and *Erebus*, and 129 officers and crew, in search of the Northwest Passage. He had provisions for two years but disappeared, with ships and men. Franklin's earlier expeditions had made him a living legend in England; the British admiralty and his widow, Lady Franklin, spared no expense in financing new expeditions to find him. All they discovered was bones, many of them on King William Island in the High Arctic.

Tagak began reading some of the accounts of the extraordinary efforts to find Franklin. He laughed aloud when he spoke about it. "I remember turning one night to my wife, Sally, and saying, 'Why am I doing this?' She replied, 'Someday it will become useful.'"

Then he came across an attack Dickens had written, at the request of Franklin's widow, on findings by Dr. John Rae, one of the many British seafarers and explorers who set out to determine Franklin's fate. Rae had encountered two groups of Inuit, and each had told him about seeing white men, some years earlier, struggling overland, starving and mad. Inuit he consulted also reported seeing many corpses and evidence of cannibalism.

Rae travelled to the areas in question on King William Island and the Boothia Peninsula to investigate. He reported his findings in considerable detail, including an observation no one in the British Admiralty was willing to accept. Some of the starving, shipwrecked crew, Rae reported, had indeed resorted to cannibalism. In defence of Franklin and his men, Dickens turned his ire upon Inuit:

> We believe every savage to be in his heart covetous, treacherous, and cruel; and we have yet to learn what knowledge the white man—lost, houseless, shipless, apparently forgotten by his race, plainly famine-stricken, weak, frozen, helpless, and dying—has of Esquimaux nature.

With Dickens's help, the Admiralty dismissed Rae's conclusion emphatically. No Englishman would resort to cannibalism. Rae's findings were no more than "the wild tales of savages."

In response, Tagak researched Inuit oral history—the accounts of witnesses passed down from one generation to the next, including the same accounts that Rae had heard more than 150 years earlier. His own cultural-values knowledge told him that Inuit would not resort to the barbaric acts the Dickens defence alleged.

The accuracy of Inuit and oral history was confirmed recently, when an Inuk of Gjoa Haven, Louie Kamookak, after spending much of his own life researching Inuit oral history, provided the critical information that led to the discovery of both of Franklin's ships. Sadly, Louie died of cancer in 2018 at age fifty-eight. Before his death, he also gave Parks Canada additional clues for its future search for Franklin's grave. By now, it is safe to say the British Admiralty knows Louie's story and his contribution.

It is also well acquainted with Tagak Curley, who became the key figure—even the "star"—in a fine National Film Board of Canada documentary directed by John Walker called *Passage*. It's the story of Franklin and Dr. John Rae, the Scottish surgeon turned explorer who set out to find him and became one of the few to come back with answers. The film follows Tagak into the historic halls of the Admiralty in London, where he confronts the learned historians, among them the great-great-grandson of Charles Dickens. Tagak, like them, has read all of Rae's reports, including the examination of the remains of the bones and limbs of members of Franklin's crew and the observation made by Rae. The bones revealed scars that could only have been made by sharp steel knives, in a pattern consistent with removing flesh from the bone.

Throughout the lengthy exchange with the historians, Tagak is as sharp as every harpoon head he had ever constructed and as confident as any hunter could be, knowing he has his prey at his mercy. He is also respectful. He neither condemns nor judges the English sailors for their last desperate attempt at survival. In the end, so moved is Charles Dickens's descendant, he extends his hand and apologizes.

It is one thing to make history. It is something else to challenge and correct it.

20

CHARLIE WATT

The Comeback Elder

With thousands of dead caribou surrounding him, Charlie Watt didn't fit the stereotype of an honourable Canadian senator. First, he was just thirty years old. Second, this was not the Red Chamber; it was a river shoreline in northern Quebec. But the senator *was* taking charge, wearing a baseball cap, hip waders, lined wool shirt and well-worn work gloves. He wrapped strong hands around the legs of a drowned caribou and, in tandem with another young man, hauled the heavy carcass out of the water, across the gravel shore and up the bank.

It was 1984, and Charlie Watt had been a member of the Senate for only ten months; his hometown of Kuujjuaq had never seen anything like this wildlife tragedy. The caribou that littered the river here were part of an estimated ten thousand animals that had been swept over the roaring Limestone Falls on the Caniapiscau River, about 150 kilometres south of town, on their annual migration.

Their story found me, rather than the other way around, when my phone rang in the Parliament Hill CBC bureau. It was one of the hunters from the village, calling to tell me that he'd seen dead caribou everywhere along the river. Within a couple of hours, I, along with a camera crew, was on a small chartered jet skimming over the river staring down at what, at first, looked like driftwood lining the riverbank. Then heads, antlers, hindquarters and white tails came into focus. It quickly became apparent that there were thousands of animals washed up here.

Moments after the plane landed at the small terminal in Kuujjuaq, I'd hired a pilot and his helicopter to get out to the river. Stuart Luttich, a biologist and caribou specialist with the Canadian Wildlife Service, had also received a report and I invited him to come along. All of us were shaken by the number of dead animals. We filmed in several locations until darkness moved in. Stuart's view was that these deaths were not a natural disaster. "These are animals in their very prime. This is not how nature works," he said into the camera, with dead caribou behind him as far as we could see.

We flew back to Ottawa that night to prepare a report for the next night's *National*. By the time it went to air and was relayed worldwide, we were back on the river covering the cause and the cleanup. The big concern now was protecting the water from the serious contamination that would result when those dead animals began rotting.

Senator Charlie Watt and every other able-bodied person in the village joined in to drag most of the animals several hundred metres away from the river. Other crews pulled the caribou into clusters of three or four and tied their hind legs together, so a helicopter could hook, lift and carry them several hundred metres away, dropping them on the high ground. The sight of those animals in free fall from the helicopter seemed to double the impact of the tragedy. The only positive in the situation was that it was autumn, with cool days and nights, so the animals had not yet begun to decompose.

Since we'd lost our ride, the crew and I were now in the hands of legendary bush pilot Johnny May, who flew a red single-engine Beaver plane named *Pango Pally*. The translation, "I miss you," is a sweet message for his wife, Louisa. (This was another case where in the North, everything and everybody is connected. When Mary and I married a few years later, Johnny would become my brother-in-law.)

Charlie Watt and the cleanup workers travelled up and down by canoe, all of them knowing both the wide Koksoak River and the Caniapiscau that flowed into it like the back of their hand. Both of these rivers have long, shallow, boulder-strewn stretches, twisting channels and rapids, and every few kilometres, a sweeping sand-bottomed bay with water deep enough to accommodate a small float plane. Johnny had one of those tried and true landing spots just below Limestone Falls, the source of the disaster, and he easily and smoothly tucked us into position to shoot there. The line to cap off my follow-up report came easily: "When you stand near these falls and feel and hear the force, you don't wonder how thousands and thousands of caribou could have drowned, but rather how any survived at all."

Many did survive. We watched a small herd at the bottom of the falls wandering back and forth to the water's edge, shell-shocked and afraid to go back into the river. They remained that way for several days but eventually took the plunge to once again follow the migration. We also saw countless others limping along the shoreline, slowly recovering.

At any other time, every man or woman along the shore would have been hunting them, given that the George River herd, at that time estimated to be about 200,000 animals, was their main source of food. As he worked, Charlie and everybody else from the village pondered the waste. The animals were waterlogged, badly bloated, bruised and broken, unfit for human consumption. To no one's great surprise Charlie soon began hatching a plan.

Prime Minister Pierre Trudeau got to know the young Inuk up close and combative just a few years earlier, in the historic negotiations to patriate the Constitution from Britain. In the November 1981 constitutional negotiations, four days under the bright television lights with a nation watching, Charlie Watt was one of those articulate young Indigenous activists who fought to ensure their rights were written into the Constitution.

When the prime minister flew into his home village in 1984 for a visit, Charlie knew it was not just a social call. "I knew there was talk of the Senate, but I couldn't say anything and thought, if I did, I'd jinx it. But I never knew for sure until the announcement was made."

Trudeau also knew Charlie through his role in negotiating the first comprehensive Inuit land claim in Canada. And he would have had to be impressed by the fact that before he was thirty years old, Charlie Watt challenged both Hydro-Québec and Quebec premier Robert Bourassa over their plan for the massive James Bay hydro project. The James Bay Project was to hydro development what the Mackenzie Valley Pipeline was to petroleum development—unprecedented in size, money and scope. It is fair to say that in 1971, Charlie Watt, Tagak Curley and a handful of other Indigenous leaders with the National Indian Brotherhood, the Cree of northern Quebec, and the prairie Métis organizations had a better grasp of Aboriginal rights and treaties than did Prime Minister Trudeau, Minister for Indian Affairs Jean Chrétien or Premier Bourassa.

The difference was that the government lawyers were either not paying attention to Aboriginal legal precedent, or were simply telling their political masters what they wanted to hear, whereas the Indigenous peoples had good lawyers studying and researching legal "Native law" precedents and rights in treaties and British Crown proclamations going back two hundred years. But with Ottawa still struggling with how to address the growing unrest among Indigenous peoples and to develop a national land claims policy, intentionally or not, the actual land claim negotiations were in limbo. The uncertainty forced Inuit of northern Quebec and Inuvialuit of the western Arctic Beaufort Sea area, who were facing major oil and gas and pipeline developments, to break from the national land claims initiative and pursue their regional claims.

In November 1973, after three years of protests, demonstrations and continued government rejections, the Cree of northern Quebec, led by Chief Billy Diamond, and Inuit, led by twenty-one-year-old Charlie Watt, filed an injunction in Quebec Superior Court to halt the construction. Charlie remembers, "It was the magnitude of the development that made me think we should have been challenging these issues long before, because we had been losing our rights over our lands going back as far as 1912 when Ottawa extended Quebec's boundaries into our lands."

The judge who heard the case was Albert Malouf. For six months after the hearing, the judge researched law and precedent while the bulldozers tore at the vegetation, traplines, salmon rivers and beaver dams that lay in their path. Thousands of workers living in huge construction camps worked around the clock.

Then the ruling came. *Stop construction!*

The decision was a shock to the politicians, the industry and the public. The media coverage was wide and predictable: either a David and Goliath battle and little David wins, or a handful of Natives paralyze Quebec's economy. It was also a very big story in faraway Yellowknife. I was following it closely for the light it shed on the six-month-old Berger hearings.

A week later, a setback. The Quebec Court of Appeal lifted the injunction stopping construction but upheld Justice Malouf's ruling that the province had a legal obligation to negotiate a treaty covering Inuit and Cree lands. Charlie says, "That gave us a bit of an edge. It didn't confirm the existence of our rights one hundred percent. We could have appealed to the Supreme Court of Canada, but we chose to negotiate."

As land claims negotiations go, this would be quick work. Both sides had to make deals and compromises. And always, as they negotiated, heavy equipment continued to transform waterways, traplines and lifelines into high-voltage power corridors. Where once there had been hunting camps, construction camps returned. There was pressure on both sides for a quick settlement. For the government and Hydro-Québec, it was about energy and money. Charlie believed the stakes were even higher for the Inuit and Cree: "It boiled down to, are we going to survive?"

The negotiations took less than two years. On November 11, 1975, the first comprehensive land claim in Canadian history was signed. Northern Quebec Inuit received $100 million in cash and maintained land and hunting rights throughout the claim area. In addition, they maintained title, including subsurface and royalty rights over about 20 percent of the land from the Quebec/Labrador border, around Ungava Bay and west to the Hudson Bay coast—in all, encompassing fourteen villages and more than a million square kilometres. The agreement also gave Inuit broad responsibilities over social development, education and regional government.

It was a historic and monumental achievement, but Charlie Watt, and many other Inuit in northern Quebec, were left with one lingering regret. "We had to extinguish our rights."

I had watched Charlie's "Trudeau audition" in 1984 from the back row of a twin-engine Otter on the way to Kangirsuk, formerly Payne Bay. They were sitting together up front for the forty-five-minute flight; at our destination, the prime minister would hold a small town-hall-style meeting that would be chaired, directed and translated by Zebedee Nungak, who had been prominent in both the constitutional and land claims battles over the past decade. Trudeau would have been well aware of Nungak's credentials, and there was speculation among the press and the locals that he was also being considered for a Senate seat.

Sitting beside me was the president of the Makivik land claim corporation, Mary Simon. She had also been a force in the constitutional conferences and had defeated Charlie in the election for the job of president a year earlier. Trudeau Senior did not share the "feminist" and "gender" values his son would later proclaim. Thankfully, because otherwise, things may have not worked out as well as they have. At least for me.

There is no doubt the Senate changed Charlie. He had moved from radical and successful activist to loyal member of the Liberal caucus. From the time of his appointments onwards, he picked his fights carefully and fought his battles "within the system." But through it all, he never fully accepted the extinguishment provision in the land claims agreement as the last word, vowing that it was "unfinished business."

Over his thirty-four years in the Senate, Charlie dug away at legal research, convinced that the complex issues surrounding Aboriginal rights need to be reopened, challenged and legally and constitutionally defined. In 2018 he quit the Senate in order to reopen the constitutional debate with the federal and provincial governments. He went so far as to state that he would again resort to the courts if necessary.

My initial reaction was that Charlie was taking on an impossible task. But then I remembered some of his other "impossible" challenges, including, back in 1984, finding a way to dispose of those ten thousand drowned and rotting caribou. His solution: sell the meat for dog food.

Charlie negotiated a price with southern pet food manufacturers and got a very low freight rate on Inuit-owned airlines, whose flights usually returned south daily with empty cargo space. For most of the winter, local crews hauled frozen carcasses out of the bush and back to Kuujjuaq, where they were put onto airplanes and sent to the rendering plants in the south.

The larger question was how the drowning disaster happened. Certainly, everything pointed to the very power project that Charlie and so many others insisted would destroy the environment, when they'd protested against the massive James Bay development a decade earlier. The Caniapiscau River is one of the large northern Quebec rivers that was diverted by the project to serve as a release valve when the water levels became too high.

There had been unusually heavy rains that fall of 1984. The water levels in both the Caniapiscau and Koksoak rivers were very high. On top of that, we'd heard rumours that Hydro-Québec had released large volumes of water that fall, raising levels even further. That soon became my story.

My camera crew had not been the only ones taking photos. The biologist, Stuart Luttich, was also busy checking levels at fixed periods and sending photos to hydrologists and other scientists with the Canadian Wildlife Service. In our pictures, taken on the day we arrived, we recorded caribou in thirty to forty centimetres of water three to five metres from the water's edge. A few days later the same caribou were now high and dry. After three days on the river, constantly stepping over dead caribou everywhere, I recall standing in one spot and watching the water recede ever so slowly, as though the tide was going out. Which was impossible, given we were many kilometres above the tide level of the Koksoak. I had also been able to file a story with information from hydrologists who had calculated that the river levels appeared to begin dropping at the same time as our first pictures were shown on television.

The Quebec government allowed Hydro-Québec to do an internal environmental assessment. Its report acknowledged that volumes of water were released, but not to a degree that would cause the high water and extreme river volumes. Hydro claimed the cause was the excessive and prolonged rainfall that fall, and no one was able to prove differently.

Seeing, let alone stepping over, thousands of dead animals day after day can make you feel sick. It would be a long time before I thought of hunting caribou again.

Between 2009 and 2016, when Mary and I were living in Kuujjuaq and Senator Watt and I saw each other more frequently, we'd talk about caribou and other things. We'd chat in the grocery checkout line or he would stop by our house to see how the construction was going. Other times we would find ourselves on the same flight between Montreal and Kuujjuaq. Wherever, we would talk politics, weather or caribou and reminisce a bit. Until the Truth and Reconciliation Commission held a round of hearings in Kuujjuaq, I thought I knew Charlie well. In the testimony of several of the witnesses, I found a new and greater respect for him.

As in all hearings of the TRC, people recalled the abuse, the loneliness and the terrible fear they experienced because of the residential schools. But several here also spoke of being reassured and comforted by the presence of a young man in his late teens. Two students who had gone to school in Montreal said it was their first time in a big city. They were afraid, but Charlie was at the airport to meet them, take them to their new residence and generally help get them settled. Others spoke of a similar encounter when they arrived at the residential school in Churchill, Manitoba. The testimony boiled down to: Charlie Watt met me and Charlie Watt helped me.

Since the mid-1990s, Charlie has run unsuccessfully for re-election as president of Makivik Corporation at least four times—always campaigning on the theme "There's more work to do." He lost every time, sometimes badly, a sign that the beneficiaries of the land claim believed his time had come and gone, that when it came to northern issues he was washed up like those dead caribou.

Charlie Watt had been a founder and the first president of the organization, with the mandate to administer the funds and terms of the land claim he'd helped negotiate in 1975. He had also served two terms as president in the early 1990s. After a defeat in 1996, he attempted a comeback in just about every election. Then suddenly, in 2018, a man with more than fifty years of political and community experience behind him won again. After his victory, I went to hear Charlie speak to several hundred people at the 2018 Northern Lights trade show in Ottawa.

As we shook hands, he said, "You didn't think I could do it, did you?"

"Charlie, you're right," I replied. "I didn't think you could win, but from now on I am going to call you the comeback kid." We both laughed.

How did Charlie Watt suddenly become today's man? Here's one old reporter's assessment. Very recently, forty years of northern Quebec Inuit history had been gathered and produced into a well-made documentary—a project championed by a man soon to be the former president of Makivik, Jobie Tukkiapik, a very well-liked and respected pilot and administrator who wanted the land claim history finally on the record. It may have cost him his job. A great many young people who'd viewed Charlie Watt as an old fart senator suddenly discovered him as the energetic, articulate and courageous young leader who had stood up to Pierre Trudeau, Robert Bourassa, René Lévesque and Hydro-Québec.

The video documentary is comprehensive, recounting the stories of fourteen members of the Inuit negotiating teams, most of whom were still alive when the program was produced. Charlie was the leader, and everybody in the documentary gave him credit for the historic accomplishment. Even more importantly, the video, in both Inuktitut and English, was shown in every school in the region, on local TV, in theatres and on DVD in most households.

Charlie also told me he'd campaigned for the presidency harder than in the past, spending extra days in several communities on the Hudson Bay coast that had opposed the initial agreement all those years ago because it forced Inuit to extinguish their Aboriginal title. His energy impressed me. I said, "You sound like you're 'born again' in the political sense."

Charlie wasn't sure he liked the term, but he did add, "I now have more confidence in myself. After seventy-three years, I am the new kid on the block."

In his speech to the North's business leaders, many of them Inuit, the former senator committed to reopening the land claim to reverse the hated extinguishment clause. I didn't think it went over well with such a pro-development audience, including Inuit, but I didn't count him out. Still, Charlie was to discover a comeback can be a fleeting thing. Like an old boxer, his best days were behind him. Today's generation, concerned with issues like health care, education and the cost of living, didn't respond to his desire to reopen old political battles. Charlie was badly defeated in the 2021 election of the land claim organization.

Across all northern and Indigenous societies, there is a clear and respected role for elders and their accomplishments, large and small. I know it's a shared value in our southern societies too. I hope Charlie, who helped change Canada and Quebec, eventually shakes off his defeats and savours his many victories.

21

MEET MY ELDERS

Duck Soup Is Not on the Menu

Chief Glenn Grady, of the Ta'an Kwächän Council at Lake Laberge, Yukon, a little village north of Whitehorse that sits at the widest part of the Yukon River, was an impressive young man with the build of a football player. Handsome face, big-boned hands and wide shoulders. He wore a baseball cap that shaded his dark eyes, which made him even more intimidating. He fit the mould of the 1990s northern First Nations chief: young, athletic and articulate. You'd think he'd have a posse of like-minded youth around him, but as was the custom in almost every meeting I held with First Nations and Inuit leaders, Chief Grady said, "I want to introduce my elders."

There were about six of them, all older men with weathered faces and bright, alert eyes, all of them smoking, and all content to remain silent. Make no mistake, there was tension in the air, some level of discomfort, and why not? I was there on tour with the directors of the Canadian Polar Commission, but as seen through the eyes of the chief and his councillors, we must have seemed like yet another gang from the government, wanting to ask God-only-knows-what questions. Their body language spoke for them: Do these people think we don't have other things we would like to be doing?

The young chief had suggested we meet on the outside deck of the band council office. It was a beautiful, warm autumn day overlooking the magnificent river. Our chairs were arranged in a semicircle so we could see each other and also the majestic view.

"Thank you," I said when he finished introducing his elders. "Now, may I introduce you to my elders?"

I'd never presented them that way before, but these directors were indeed elders. They were on the commission board because they brought their own experience and wisdom to any meeting, just as the Band Elders from Lake Laberge brought theirs.

Marc D'Allard Tremblay was a distinguished Arctic scientist from Laval University. Jon Grant, at the time president of Quaker Oats Canada, was a committed environmentalist with a passion for the Arctic. Michael Kusugak, an Inuk from Rankin Inlet, was the author of beautifully illustrated children's books and the older brother of Jose Kusugak—borderline as an elder, being barely fifty, but he looked the part.

The person we all regarded as the elder statesman of our group was John Stager, dean of the geography department at the University of British Columbia. He had travelled and studied the northern boreal forests of the western provinces, the Yukon and the Mackenzie Valley for four decades and was one of the people who pushed hard for the establishment of a polar research commission. Many, including John himself, thought that he was the natural choice to chair the commission after it was established. But that didn't happen. I got the job.

The day after I was appointed both chair and CEO of the Canadian Polar Commission, I sat in a temporary office in a downtown Ottawa hotel, without even a working phone, holding a full staff meeting. Which means I sat down with myself and looked ahead. If I had been hired for my communication abilities, then I had better start communicating with the board of directors.

I knew I had to begin with John Stager. We arranged to meet for dinner in a downtown Vancouver hotel. He would have been in his early sixties at the time, very distinguished and professorial. I was a few years short of fifty, and I saw him as older and wiser. The air between us was more than a little tense. As soon as we were seated, the waiter came to take our order for drinks.

"Are you going to have one?" I asked him.

"Glenfiddich," he said.

The waiter looked at me.

"I'll just have water," I said.

John looked puzzled.

"I quit drinking years ago because I couldn't handle it," I told him. "The only thing that bothers me now is if people who enjoy a drink refuse to do so because of me."

There may have been one or two more Scotches that followed, but even before his first glass arrived, he came directly to the point—the polar elephant in the room. "I had my heart so set on the chairman's job," John said, and admitted that he'd had to think very carefully about accepting when he was offered a board seat instead. Then he said, quite graciously, "I decided I want to be a part of it, and I will support you all the way."

There was no more tension at that table that night.

John Stager proved to be a man of his word; for the six years we worked together, I had his support and the benefit of his experience. We frequently disagreed, but we always found the middle ground.

There was a moment on that Yukon trip when I saw just how much he loved the North. We had extended our meeting in Dawson to include the traditional First Nations village of Moosehide. We'd viewed the old site and the pioneer cemetery, and then did some board work. When we stopped for lunch, John drifted away from the group. I saw him settle on an old handmade bench crafted from small shoreline willows that overlooked the river. After he'd been there a long time, I became concerned and walked down to see if everything was okay. When I came up behind him, he still didn't move, just continued staring at the sweep of the majestic river and the westerly and northerly hills and mountains.

"Are you okay?" I asked. He still did not move.

I put my hand on his shoulder and asked again. That's when he turned, his scholar's eyes watery. He told me he was fine and that he just wanted to enjoy as much of the day, the land, the river and the beauty as possible. Then he added words I have never forgotten: "I fear I may never see it again."

In my Arctic travels, I have encountered two kinds of people—those who are captivated by the North and those who are not. All of us on the Canadian Polar Commission recognized at some point that we had been captured by what Robert Service, so long ago, called the spell of the Yukon. We also knew that most people from the south regard it as a vast and cold land with no appeal; they wouldn't understand our Arctic passion even if we were capable of putting it into words.

The Canadian Polar Commission was created by the Mulroney government in 1991 to build a bridge between those born and still living in the North, and those who'd been captured by it, whether for romantic reasons, scientific research or as a great storehouse of natural resources. Western research and scientific inquiry were nothing new to the North. Mapmakers sailed with the first whalers and scientists; explorers and fortune-seekers came with the traders, missionaries and administrators who followed. By the late 1960s, there was a common joke across the North that the average Inuit family consisted of a father, a mother, four and a half children, three dogs and one anthropologist.

Throughout my term, the polar commission heard horror stories of Inuit whose faces had been plunged into ice water for several minutes, while some "scientist" measured their response to see "if Eskimos feel the cold." We came into being as a commission at a fascinating time in the North, a time of growing development programs and an unprecedented search for oil and gas. Then there were the military exercises, the seismic exploration across traditional lands and traplines, and the expanded staking of claims for new mines.

Northerners had a reasonable suspicion of northern research. Common questions were asked of us countless times in every part of the North: What are you looking for and why? Why don't you ever talk to us about what you are doing? And most importantly, what did you learn and how can it benefit us?

At the first board meeting of the Canadian Polar Commission, the late Lloyd Barber told us that we had been set up to fail. Having Barber on our board gave the commission instant credibility in the North. In the mid-1970s, when he became Canada's first Indian claims commissioner, Barber made sure people knew that the demands being advanced by Indigenous peoples were not only fair but were based on law. (He was also president of the University of Regina and served as a board member on an impressive list of large national companies, including banks.) Barber told the rest of the board that he had looked at our mandate and then at the budget. "It's like they've given us the keys to this great big Cadillac—it's all decked out, but there is no money for gas."

Our mandate was to promote and disseminate information about the North. We were to host conferences and seminars. We were also directed to hold half our board meetings in the North. All of this was to be achieved with an annual budget of $1 million. Lloyd was right: it was a paltry sum, but given the time it took to get the government to agree to establish a commission that would no doubt start asking hard questions, we accepted our lot and decided to do that—ask tough questions: Why is the suicide rate among northern Indigenous youth more than ten times the national average? Why is the overall life expectancy of Indigenous Canadians more than ten years less than a southern Canadian? And when we spoke to communities, leaders and elders in places like Lake Laberge, we could ask for their ideas. We really weren't there to explain a government agenda.

I remembered moving our Lake Laberge meeting from the deck to the muddy shore of the Yukon River, where I walked with Chief Grady (who I was saddened to learn passed away in August 2021), while each of our board members paired up with one of the community leaders. The people here had already been told by federal health authorities that, as a result of global pesticide use, the fish they were eating from the Yukon River system contained high levels of toxaphene contamination. We would learn that the threat to northern health was by no means confined to Lake Laberge. Fears about contaminants in the Arctic fish and wildlife food chain were raised in every place we visited, from Yukon eastward to Baffin Island and Labrador.

On a sunny autumn afternoon in the southwest corner of the Northwest Territories along the Liard River, board member Joanne Deneron took us to visit Sue and Edwin Lindberg, a First Nations and Métis couple, living about as close as you can to harmony with nature. They had a vegetable garden. They fished and hunted, and the family pet was a noisy and attention-starved mallard duck that they'd found injured a few years earlier. After they nursed him back to health he refused to leave. When we arrived at their dock, the duck came running up excitedly, like a little puppy, and then followed as our party of eight walked to the house to accept the generous invitation of afternoon tea.

The log house was snug, with a bright, sunny living room offering a view of the river and valley. Michael Kusugak picked up the guitar that was sitting beside his chair, plucking at it very gently as he softly tuned it. Then he began to play, shifting into a classical guitar melody ever so tenderly, and the chatter stopped. His sound was magic, harp-like, his fingers working in unison across the strings and frets. For ten or fifteen minutes, he held us quite spellbound.

"Where did you learn to play like that?" I asked when he stopped.

"I taught myself," he said, explaining that as children they always had music in their home, all kinds of music, including classical.

Sometimes, when people talk about Canada's diverse cultures, I think back to that afternoon, when ten or so people, English and French, Dene, Métis and Inuit, sat in a log home on the Liard River mesmerized by an Inuk playing classical guitar, while a lovable and smart duck waddled and sniffed diverse feet and socks, leaving nothing on the floor for us to worry about.

On our northern tours, it was common for commission members to cook us meals in a borrowed staff house or vacant school dorm. We often carried our food into communities where supplies might be scarce, and we ate in cheap restaurants more often than fine ones.

I recall a period in the mid-1990s when the government's spending was under scrutiny by the media because of outlandish expense claims made by some heads of agencies. Sure enough, an access to information request came in for all "dinners, lunches and entertainment" expenses submitted by the chair of the Canadian Polar Commission. Me.

Our accountant assembled the receipts and claims and put them in order, then showed me the file before he sent it out. I couldn't resist reaching into the bundle and bringing one receipt to the top: lunch for the entire board and three staff, ten people in total working for the Canadian Polar Commission, at McDonald's in Whitehorse for less than eighty dollars. My reporter's mind was calculating that maybe there would be some good publicity here for the commission, that someone might write a piece to contrast the commission's style to the excessive misuse of public money elsewhere that Canadians had been reading about. Alas, it was not to be.

In April 1994, we hosted a major conference, with carefully picked partners—the Canadian Arctic Resources Committee, the Inuit Circumpolar Conference and the now-defunct Canadian Centre for Global Security—to begin developing a northern foreign policy for Canada. Every Indigenous organization from Yukon through the Northwest Territories was at the table, along with colleagues from northern Quebec and Labrador. Two cabinet ministers were also there, Minister of Indian Affairs and Northern Development Ron Irwin and Foreign Affairs Minister André Ouellet.

In his opening remarks, Minister Ouellet both "scooped" and delighted us. We had expected one of our principal recommendations would be the creation of a special ambassador, to represent Canada's arctic interests with other polar nations. The minister scooped us: "I am announcing today the government's intention to create the position of Arctic circumpolar ambassador within my department. We are joining our Nordic neighbours in creating a special ambassador."

The instant Ouellet said the words "Arctic ambassador," John Amagoalik, who was sitting beside Mary Simon, raised his hand over her head and began pointing to her. Everyone in the hall saw the gesture and no one objected. Mary had already served two terms as president of the Inuit Circumpolar Conference and had worked extensively with other polar nations. She was well known in Greenland, Scandinavia, Alaska and Russia.

Not even Ouellet was surprised to find her approaching him with her characteristic directness as he left the podium. "How do I apply for the job?" she asked.

"Write me a letter," he said.

Six months later, only a few days after our wedding, she was appointed to the job. The appointment was one more indication that times were changing. I think that even a few years earlier, a federal bureaucrat would have been quietly put in the position.

Of my own time as head of the Canadian Polar Commission, I take the most pride in a conference we held in Yellowknife in May 1994. We used facilities and staff donated by both CBC North and Television Northern Canada (a consortium of Indigenous communication societies) to link Indigenous leaders in Inuvik and Whitehorse into the conference room, where three leading Indigenous leaders from Yellowknife joined them. It was a big undertaking, and it was equally groundbreaking for the broadcasters. A conference on northern science policy was turned into a TV program that was being broadcast live across the North.

When the camera zoomed in on the charismatic Norma Kassi, a young Gwich'in environmental activist from Old Crow, I knew we were in for an earful. "There are about six hundred to seven hundred abandoned mine sites and tailings ponds in the Yukon alone and abandoned military sites," she said. "What about all those chemicals that have come to the Yukon and are buried? There are tremendous rates of cancer in all of our communities. What are we doing to research why it's happening, and how are we trying to prevent it?"

Those of us on the commission knew it was a turning point to watch Kassi and a dozen or so other Indigenous people dominating an academic and bureaucratic policy conference while the whole North was watching.

Any good TV program has its lighter moments, and ours was not entirely without humour. John Stager had organized most of the conference, and I remember him telling the attendees (and viewers) that when Norma was still a "young girl," he was conducting geographical studies in the Old Crow area of northern Yukon. He always reported his findings directly to the band council. Such generosity was the exception and everyone knew it, including Ben Kovic, who joined the panel by satellite from Iqaluit. Ben was a hunter, a carver and chair of the newly established Nunavut Wildlife Management Board—a man determined to have a voice in setting the research priorities in the vast area that would soon become Nunavut.

Several speakers followed John, until finally it was Ben's turn. He said, "I want to go back to the previous comment by the elderly scientist."

The room erupted in laughter and, when it began to subside, Ben drove home his point with the force of the strong-armed hunter sinking a harpoon into a whale. "I would like to see more of that and, as well, [researchers] should use more traditional knowledge from the people in the community. I think we can work together for the good of future generations."

(For the rest of his time on our board, John was referred to as "the elderly scientist.")

Ben had one more point to make. When his turn came around again, he spoke for about a minute in Inuktitut and then let twenty seconds of silence follow. When the room and audience began to stir slightly with the discomfort that silence can bring, he returned to English, saying, "This is just an example of the kind of silence people of the North feel when a scientist does a report." Too often, he pointed out, the language of the researchers cannot be understood by the very people who are affected.

Hand in hand with the building scientific evidence of the extent and dangers of contaminants was an increasingly urgent cry from the communities we visited: Why are there so many cancers now? What is happening to our fish and wildlife? Are our fish safe to eat? Sadly, the same questions are still asked today.

For all the good work we did on the commission, it's most often the small gestures that remain with me. Our whole commission and staff made a trip to Broughton Island, now Qikiqtarjuaq, on Baffin Island. We had asked the settlement manager and the hotel manager before we left Ottawa if we could host a dinner for the residents of the seniors' home and other elders in the village. "Wonderful idea," they replied, "but you better bring the food. We have nothing here except fish."

So in our baggage, as we landed on the gravel runway on the frozen shores of Baffin Island, were half a dozen or more big, fat turkeys. I was looking out the window and spotted a polar bear, lazily sauntering along the shoreline parallel to the runway. No matter how many times you have been in the North or how many polar bears you've seen—and not just the frightening close-ups—it's always a special feeling to see such a bear and you like to talk about it.

An hour later, we were in the settlement council chamber, a very efficient little structure with a round table, conducive for meeting and talking. "What a wonderful community," I began, recalling that I had been here a few times, including once, almost twenty years ago, doing a piece for the national news, when they had "hauled that big gasoline storage tank from the old DEW Line fifty miles overland on a series of qamutiks towed by a dozen or more Ski-Doos." Some nodded approvingly, remembering the feat.

Then I said how pleasant it had been to see that beautiful Nanook along the shoreline as we were landing. Without a word, in either English or Inuktitut, the entire settlement council rose and rushed out the door. I was never told the fate of the bear; my guess is he never had a chance.

In the meantime, the cooks at the hotel had the turkeys in the oven, and some fresh fish as well. It was quite an evening. We had set it up with half a dozen tables, about six people at each table, including one or two of our board members. A few of the elders and a high school student agreed to interpret. The dinner was buffet style, and every man and woman—and a teenager from Broughton—piled their plates with roast turkey and trimmings. Every member of the commission and its staff loaded up on the freshest Arctic char you could ever hope to taste. At the end of the night, every elder left with a wrapped plate of turkey piled high.

As the evening wound down, the elder sitting across from me, Ouviyuq Natsipik, said he had a little something to say.

We had talked all evening through the interpreter. He told me he remembered seeing me on TV and he even commented on my reports on those ten thousand caribou drowned on the Caniapiscau River near Kuujjuaq.

Then these words were translated by the student for me from Inuktitut: "I want to thank you for tonight. This was a very special night for me and others. I am over eighty years old. Tonight, this is the first time in my life that anyone has ever taken me out to dinner."

I almost cried. I could only offer one of the few Inuktitut words I had mastered.

"Ilaali." You're welcome.

22.

GLACIERS, GRADS AND GEEZERS

Climate Change You Can See and Touch

Six teenagers are at the rail of a ship. Though it's summertime, they are bundled in warm clothing and life vests. They are far above the Arctic Circle and looking out over water that's as blue as the sky. In every direction, there are pure white icebergs the size of skyscrapers.

The teenagers line up with two elderly shipmates, one in his early nineties, the other in his mid-eighties. One after the other, they climb down into a sturdy, stubby, black rubber Zodiac that will ferry them to an Arctic experience none of them will ever forget. As they settle into the Zodiac, the teenagers know that they are sitting shoulder to shoulder with two of the world's most decorated scientists and explorers. They are even on a first-name basis with Fred Roots and Don Walsh, who have each been awarded the Explorers Medal by the prestigious Explorers Club of New York, an honour they share with Neil Armstrong, the first person to step on the moon, Robert Peary and Roald Amundsen, the first to reach the North and South Poles, and Edmund Hillary, the first to climb Mount Everest. What's more, their guide and the driver of the Zodiac, a grizzled man in his early seventies, is Ian Tamblyn, a musician that every fan of Canadian folk music would recognize. Welcome to Students on Ice.

I watch them from my place in a nearby Zodiac. We are all of us sliding over glass-blue Arctic waters, manoeuvring around floating ice mountains that have broken away from the Greenland Icecap. As we pass between two of them, I look to the bow and see the ice-sculpted likeness of a frozen hand towering twenty to thirty metres above the water. The lyrics of Stan Rogers's great Arctic anthem come to mind, is this "the hand of Franklin reaching for the Beaufort Sea"?

A moment later, as we circle another iceberg with steep, eroded walls, the light suddenly changes and the image of a face appears. It is a big face, solemn, with a furrowed brow and wide eyes. It makes me think of every likeness of Buddha that I have ever seen.

For five years, I participated in this remarkable educational undertaking. I have met hundreds of students from big Canadian cities and small Arctic settlements, as well as teenagers from the US, Europe and Asia. Their distinguished northern educators have led them on explorations of Arctic and subarctic areas, from Labrador northward into the Northwest Passage, to the High Arctic and Greenland. Students and scientists become shipmates, mentors and friends. It's a special bond connecting elders and youth: a free exchange of curiosity, wisdom, knowledge and unwavering mutual respect.

One of the elderly explorers in that first Zodiac is a good friend of mine. You might think that Fred Roots, one of Canada's foremost polar scientists, has very little left to learn about the North, but he is as animated and engaged as his teenage companions. Decades ago, in 1950, he set a world record, completing a 187-day solo dog team trip across the Antarctic on a mapping expedition. Imagine his determination; a six-month-long, daylight-to-dark expedition in the most deserted place on earth. Just one man and a dog team.

For the rest of his life, Fred wore a belt that he made from the traces of his lead dog, Rachel. He never missed a chance to show it to the students and to praise his loyal husky. The only thing I ever heard him boast about was that dog—certainly never his own accomplishments.

Fred is one of those people who moved in and out of my life at critical times, beginning with the Mackenzie Valley Pipeline Inquiry in 1975, where he served as a science adviser. In 2014, when Fred was ninety-one years old, I watched him hike several kilometres across the rugged, boulder-strewn bed of a receding Baffin Island glacier. Though his back and shoulders were bent over, he kept up with kids seventy-five years his junior.

On a later expedition, when we spotted the first of more than a dozen polar bears we would see on that trip, Fred provided an impromptu lecture on the bears. He lamented that not much is known about polar bears, saying: "Unfortunately, mostly, the polar bear is viewed through binoculars or the sights of a rifle . . . It's the nomadic nature of the polar bear," he told us, "that makes it so difficult to study and understand."

When Fred sat down, a student from Qikiqtarjuaq on Baffin Island stepped to the front of the ship's lounge, which had been turned into the evening lecture theatre. Lindsay Evaloajuk nervously picked up the microphone. She looked out over the group, including her peers, two dozen other Inuit students. "I bet you're asking what a nineteen-year-old little girl would know about polar bears?"

Lindsay knew quite a bit. She showed us how to tell the difference between male and female bears. The science journals only tell you that males are larger, which is not very helpful if you're looking at a single bear or if you don't know if it's fully grown or not. Lindsay said, "Look at how they walk." Spreading her arms wide and turning her hands inward, she demonstrated how the female will turn her paws that way while a male's paws will be more in a straight line. Spotting such differences is basic life-and-death knowledge for Inuit. A female bear may have cubs nearby that a hunter can't see, which will make her more aggressive and unpredictable.

Lindsay's short lecture wasn't a put-down of a distinguished Arctic scientist. It was a gentle reminder that scientists would know a lot more about the Arctic and its environment if they spent more time talking to the people who live there. Lindsay also said that she, citing Fred's words, had "observed a polar bear through the sights of a rifle," recounting that on a recent hunting trip with her father, she had shot a ten-foot male bear. This is the kind of teaching that Students on Ice offers.

The Greenland town of Ilulissat, at the head of Disko Bay, is the centrepiece for Students on Ice expeditions. It sits a full 350 kilometres north of the Arctic Circle, but the warm Gulf Stream provides it with a much different climate than that of

Baffin and Ellesmere islands in Canada. The endless Arctic sunshine in June and July brings the temperature into the mid-twenties Celsius range.

In Disko Bay and Ilulissat, there are icebergs everywhere, peeling off the Jakobshavn Glacier and Greenland Icecap. On a single day in this bay along the coast of Greenland, I counted more than two dozen. In 2015 a massive iceberg, surely the largest I have ever seen, towering several hundred metres above the water, drifted out of Disko Bay, slowly melting and shedding as it travelled. We marvelled at its size and beauty.

Our captain's radar and sonar gave him a good picture of the two-thirds of this floating mountain that lay underwater as he turned the ship and sailed a tight circle around it. There were moments when we were probably no more than fifteen metres from the sheer ice walls. We felt we could almost reach out and touch it. It's such a contradiction—the beauty that results from the collapse of a critical part of the world's environment.

If there's a Students on Ice ritual, it unfolds like this. We sail to the head of Disko Bay and anchor at Ilulissat and then walk to a majestic, even magical, place at the foot of the Jakobshavn Glacier. It is nature's cathedral; rocks formed billions of years ago provide a natural amphitheatre where we can watch and listen as icebergs peel away from one of the world's greatest glaciers. We are all directed to sit in silence for several minutes, to look at and listen to what lies before us.

In the silence, we hear nature's language and warnings. Sometimes there are soft tones and, at other times, almost musical notes from meltwater cascading from frozen ledges into the still pools below. Then suddenly there are the raised voices of the icebergs groaning and grinding and the angry sounds made as ice sheets peel from the edges and crash below. We sit in silence, but our eyes and ears hear and see the world changing.

It's no wonder Students on Ice founder Geoff Green describes these expeditions as the "Greatest Classroom on Earth." Teaching these classes are two exceptionally skilled professors and communicators: Eric Mattson and Bianca Perren, who speak with the melting and receding glacier as their backdrop, offering both a eulogy for a great glacier and a prophecy for the climate and our environment. Bianca and Eric are experienced in handling the rigours of the outdoors and comfortable operating Zodiacs in choppy water. They can also be seen standing sentinel with a shotgun while scanning the horizons for the wandering polar bears that are a threat every time the expedition goes ashore.

Eric is a professor at Nipissing University in North Bay, Ontario. For the past twenty-five years, he's studied and measured melting glaciers and their impacts on the climate. Bianca works for the British Antarctic Survey, studying how the ecosystem is responding to climate change. The two have done the math: the Jakobshavn Glacier is losing an estimated sixty metres every single day. A hundred years ago, it was losing less than a kilometre in a year—now it's losing more than that in a single month. They estimate that this glacier, which is eight hundred to a thousand metres thick, will, within a decade, stop grinding and sliding its way down the ice-choked fjord, and instead stop. The face of the glacier will continue to break away and the meltwater will feed a glacial river roaring down a rocky gorge to the harbour, where we now sit. Bianca and Eric, and now all their students, know how special this place is in the unfolding climate change era. Few places on earth offer a more graphic daily barometer of our changing climate.

A boardwalk about three feet wide that appears to float over the grassy meadows connects the town and the glacier's exit into the harbour and Disko Bay. A few decades ago, the Illulisat Icefjord was named a UNESCO World Heritage site, and Fred Roots was one of the scientists who played a role in that decision. I joined him on the boardwalk as he began the five-kilometre walk back to town and our ship. We were alone, still mesmerized by both the receding glacier we'd just witnessed and the gripping presentation by Eric and Bianca that put it all in today's context. Some distance ahead of us were small groups of students, educators and chaperones, moving steadily, perhaps even rushing back to town to beat the lineup for the locally advertised "world's best soft ice cream."

"Whit, you don't have to hang back here with me," Fred said. He knew his pace had slowed, but I marvelled that at ninety-three he could make the trek at all.

"What if I want to hang back with you and enjoy the geezer pace?" I said. Then added, "I'm glad you made it this year, Fred."

"It was a little tricky to manage." He confessed that his wife, June, who had watched him leave to do field research every summer for more than fifty years, was less than enthusiastic about this trip.

I offered my annual compliment on his stamina and fitness, and ended with the predictable, "How do you do it?"

"Having a dog helps," he replied. Which I knew, given that Mary and I had recently had to put down our faithful Labrador retriever.

It is a simple but cherished memory, the two of us walking slowly over a boardwalk traversing a lush Arctic meadow, where sites of ancient Inuit camps can be seen, reminiscing about old dogs and loving wives. There was one other moment I shared with Fred, at the end of the 2018 expedition, that I'll always cherish. It was on the shore of a sheltered fjord on Greenland's coast; soft mossy ground and billion-year-old rocks. (That number is correct—a Fred fact.)

We all had about an hour to ourselves. Some of the kids lay on the moss; others sat on the rocks looking at the mountains or valleys or staring across the blue waters of the fjord. So many energetic teenagers and yet not a single sound except the occasional bird or whisper of wind. Fred and I were in the same group, led by Jessica Bolduc, a twenty-something First Nations community development activist from the Thunder Bay area.

At the end of our quiet hour, Jessica asked people to talk about how the trip might change their lives and their futures. A few hesitated, but others talked freely about being awakened to a wider world, with a greater appreciation for the environment and wildlife. A few wept openly, allowing honest emotions to pour out while vowing to become better, more open, productive citizens. It was as though they had experienced a spiritual awakening.

Fred was beside me. We were the last two in the small circle. When my turn came, I looked at him and said, "I think I speak for both of us. Fred is in his nineties. I am in my mid-seventies. It's difficult to look ahead and say what this will mean in the future. I think, instead, we look back, grateful to have seen so much of this northern world, and we just hope that we will be able to see it again."

The old scientist was visibly moved. There were tears in his eyes as he grabbed and squeezed my arm. Here is a man I had met more than forty years ago, a man I had travelled with and shared podiums with at conferences. Now, on a green and rocky hillside in a quiet fjord on Greenland's north-west west coast, I felt I finally knew him.

Sadly, that was Fred's last expedition to the High Arctic. A few months later, he died peacefully in his sleep in Victoria.

Each expedition of Students on Ice has its moments. One such trip, in a previous year, almost didn't happen. The students, the scientists, the crew and others such as Mary and me, recruited as educators, were all in Iqaluit. From there, we'd planned to make our way out to our ship, the Russian-owned *Akademik Ioffe*, a 117-metre research vessel. But that summer brought some of the worst ice conditions in recorded memory. The *Akademik Ioffe* was several kilometres from Iqaluit's shoreline, close enough for us to see, but unable to move any closer because of the broken pack ice.

One simple solution came from a sixteen-year-old student from Pond Inlet, Tyson Angnetsiak, who asked the founder of Students on Ice, Geoff Green, "Why don't we just walk?" If ever a question framed the cultural divide between Inuit and southern Canadians, surely this was it. Tyson's proposed "walk" would have taken about sixty teenagers, a few geezers like me, and about twenty-five adult educators and chaperones over three kilometres of broken Arctic ice pans. In Tyson's mind, such a walk was no more difficult and certainly not as dangerous as crossing a busy street in downtown Toronto or Vancouver, not to mention the home cities of other students from Russia, China, the United States and even Morocco.

I knew where Tyson was coming from. I had spent enough sleepless nights in High Arctic villages, listening to the noisy, happy children playing endlessly under the brilliant light of a summer sun that does not set. I can still see them running along the shoreline, hopping over the white carpets of ice pans that that drift and shift lazily along the shore. This is their natural playground, just as it had been for their parents and grandparents. Yes, of course, they fall asleep at their desks in school the next day, but no one, especially their parents, dares to deny them this ancient rite of spring.

Geoff, our leader, was not attending his first Arctic rodeo. He, too, knew where Tyson was coming from. But he paused, careful not to immediately dismiss the idea. Then, smiling, he said, "Somehow, Tyson, I don't think our insurance will allow that."

But Geoff was in a tight spot. Students on Ice was landlocked. As we sat, stranded in Iqaluit, the capital of the new territory (but in my mind, still the town of Frobisher Bay, where I'd first lived back in the 1960s), I tapped my broadcasting memories to entertain the students as Geoff and his team searched for ways to get this group across the ice that was jamming the bay. For four days, we waited in far less than ideal lodgings in the old Federal Building that sits just off the runway at the north end of the Iqaluit Airport.

The three-storey metal-sided building had been constructed by the US Air Force in the Cold War era as a Strategic Air Command base for B-52 bombers. I had lived here for a few months in 1967, while I was waiting for a house to become available. I told the students that I could guarantee that the sheets had been changed since then, but that the beds, mattresses and lamps were original.

Our real problem was that the Russian vessel we were waiting for had only set aside ten days for us. After that, the captain had another charter in Greenland. There was another vessel nearby—a Canadian Coast Guard icebreaker. But the slightly smaller 98-metre *Des Groseilliers* was part of the annual Arctic patrol, there for emergencies. Geoff contacted the Coast Guard captain, Sylvain Bertrand. Though he was sympathetic, he was not authorized to move people from the shore to ships. There were liability and insurance issues. He would need authorization from Ottawa.

Every one of us with political contacts began making calls. Mary called Leona Aglukkaq, a federal minister at the time, and Premier Eva Aariak. I contacted some reporters, and a few news stories began to emerge. We are not sure what took place in Ottawa, but soon Geoff got a call from Captain Bertrand. He said he had clearance, but the plan would require strict timing and coordination.

The captain told us that the tide would be high just before midnight, and a full moon that night would raise it to about twelve metres, which was above normal and would allow the Canadian vessel to get closer to shore. (We learned later that no ship of that size had ever come so far into the bay.) We had a three-hour window to plunk eighty people into small flat-bottom barges and ferry them to the icebreaker. For that evening we were not only Students on Ice, but students in and around the ice, as skilled handlers steered their boats between dangerous ice pans. Hundreds of pictures were snapped of young hands reaching up and touching the passing ice. Even Tyson admitted this was better than walking.

Onboard, the *Des Groseilliers* crew offered us fresh-baked cookies, soft drinks, hot chocolate, tea and coffee, all laid out in the crew's lounge. One crew member played a few tunes on the accordion and two of the Inuit students, Donna Lyle from Cambridge Bay and Ashley Burton from Rankin Inlet, reciprocated with traditional Inuit throat singing.

Then the *Des Groseilliers* began to move, slowly and softly slipping along for about twenty minutes until it was a few hundred metres from the *Akademik Ioffe,* anchored in a stream of open water. In the combined Arctic midnight and twilight that prevails in early August, we could easily see jet-black Zodiacs from the Russian ship pulling up alongside the gangway. Within an hour, we were all aboard and following the *Des Groseilliers* through the last of the ice-choked waters of Frobisher Bay. Occasionally, as we lay in our comfortable berths, we heard and felt the crunch of the remaining ice giving way beneath the hull.

The Students on Ice "classrooms," in my view, also bring out the best in the northern and Inuit students, who now comprise about one-quarter of the student participants. Northern governments, businesses and land claim organizations have recognized the value of the program and offer generous scholarships for Inuit and other Indigenous students to participate. Sometimes, these students bring a much different and more practical perspective on the lectures. They are certainly the students most comfortable getting in and out of the Zodiacs, considering that water travel remains a key means of transportation in most of their communities.

It's also common for the Zodiacs to be in the company of whales, including humpbacks, minke and fin whales, the second largest of all the species. As the whales or other mammals move near the ship or the Zodiacs, marine biologists will describe their size, age, migration routes, impact and contribution to nature's cycles. Invariably, the young Inuit men aboard will offer their experience about where and how to properly place a harpoon. Usually one or two of them would have already participated in a community whale hunt.

Long ago I was taught that, without context, there is little understanding. Most of the southern students were likely raised to shudder at the idea of killing a whale. Yet here they recognize that when Arctic youth look at the whale, or the walrus, the seal or the polar bear, it is in the context of food and survival in a way of life that maintains harmony with the cycles of nature. In all this vastness and beauty, no matter the season or climate, all there is to live on is wild. In my experience, the southerners, regardless of age or background, come to accept that reality.

The second renowned explorer involved with the program, alongside Fred Roots, is Don Walsh. In 1960, as a US Navy submarine captain, Don also set a world science record when he piloted a submersible to the bottom of the Mariana Trench, the deepest part of the world's oceans, nearly eleven kilometres underwater. You can find Don's weathered face in the archives of *Life* magazine, photographed before he and his teammate, Jacques Picard, closed the hatch on that submersible. Their feat was not equalled until 2013, when the Canadian film director James Cameron made a similar dive. It is with pride that Don tells students he was the person who closed Cameron's hatch and bid him a sailor's adieu.

To the students, Don Walsh describes himself as a sailor first, and an oceanographer who became a senior adviser to two US presidents second. He has published more than 150 scientific papers and articles on Arctic and Antarctic Ocean science. I once overheard a seventeen-year-old student, Jack Patterson of Ottawa, talking to his dad at the end of the expedition and saying, "Don Walsh is the coolest guy I have ever met." When I passed on the compliment to Don, he responded with a smile, and two simple words, "No shit?" Still the sailor.

Ian Tamblyn is a musician at home operating a zodiac. As well as his years of writing and recording thirty-eight albums, Ian is also a fellow of the Royal Canadian Geographical Society, an honour he earned for his years of guiding and writing and singing in the Arctic. Ian has written more songs than he can remember and nature, the environment and the High Arctic are the inspiration for many of them.

We are on the still blue waters of Disko Bay in northern Greenland in mid-afternoon, when a voice cracks over a walkie-talkie. For an instant it seems like a rude interruption, until we register the words "pod of humpbacks." We're told the whales, only a kilometre away, appear to be having some playtime, rolling, blowing, diving and singing their songs. In a flash, we are a fleet of a dozen of Zodiacs, moving like geese in a V formation.

As we get closer to the whales, Ian and the other Zodiac operators cut back their motors. Ian's hands seem as familiar and sure on the outboard as they do on his guitar. We ease a little closer, then everyone kills their motor and we drift silently on the ocean with the frolicking whales. At least six are visible, and perhaps there are more—there's really no way for untrained observers like us to tell if it's the same whale that dives and then resurfaces a few minutes later.

It doesn't matter how many times I witness whales at play, I still find that the experience borders on the indescribable. One moment, they appear oblivious to our presence; the next, they seem to welcome us to their performance. As they breach and rise, the rushing sound from their blowholes and the swirling of the water from their tails are the only sounds.

From our Zodiac comes a response, as Ian lifts his guitar to sing his personal salute, "Humpback Whale Song," whose lyrics and melody match every stirring sound and sight we are witnessing. One by one, several other exceptional expedition musicians join in. Tim Baker, a recording artist from St. John's, is followed by fellow Zodiac driver James Raffan, who has a fine voice and a well-tuned guitar. Then to everyone's delight, the expedition's doctor, Andrew Bresnahan, who was born and raised and practised medicine in Labrador, pulls the wraps off his cello. Doc Andrew's gentle touch and steady bow find low, resonant sounds that blend beautifully with nature's stunning choir of whales. An armada of mountain-high, pure-white icebergs drifts by in the distant background on a quiet blue, seemingly endless, ocean.

Despite any challenge I face in life, these sounds and images give me serenity and peace of mind. Along with the people I've grown to love and experiences only a few have shared, they form the inner Arctic Circle of my soul. A treasured place, and all of it within my own nation, Canada.

POSTSCRIPT

I was leaning on the rail of the Students on Ice classroom, enjoying an early morning cup of coffee, looking out over the unusually quiet waters of the Davis Strait as we sailed towards Baffin Island. In the distance, mountainous icebergs dotted the horizon of Greenland. One of the students joined me to share the view and the moment. Then he asked, "How many expeditions have you been on, Whit?"

I began counting on my fingers and was about to say five. Then I thought again and replied, "Just one—it began in 1967, and I am still on it." After more than fifty years, I hope the expedition continues.

You now know I became a reporter on my very first day in the North in what was then Frobisher Bay. Although I've also done other things, I've never thought of myself as anything but a reporter. In my early days with CBC, I believed I had stumbled on the best unfolding story in Canada. I haven't changed my mind.

But if I could have one wish at this point in my life, it would be that the story I've been reporting for so long concludes with a happy and fulfilling ending. It doesn't. Many chapters still need to be lived, documented and reported.

The social and health challenges facing northern communities are detailed in the government's own mind-boggling and heartbreaking statistics. Suicide rates among young Inuit remain ten times the national average. Tuberculosis, almost eradicated in the rest of Canada, is a northern epidemic, with active cases reported in more than half the communities. Poor housing, overcrowding and poverty are as prevalent today as fifty years ago. Water supplies are contaminated. Social and family breakdown is compounded by alcohol and drug abuse, resulting in rates of violent crime and incarceration far above the national average. Add to those, climate change and melting ice: these are challenges not even heard of when people began shaking off the colonial bonds in the late 1960s.

Certainly, I do not have solutions for any of these daunting challenges, just a belief that the strength is there in northern communities to turn this terrible tide of social destruction. I am encouraged by the fact that every year, I see increasing numbers of young people—the majority of them women—graduating from post-secondary institutions with the determination to bring about change. I believe today's and tomorrow's emerging leaders will find within themselves the same inner strength, determination and conviction that drove the people I've written about here, who accomplished so much.

But these new young leaders cannot do it alone. These challenges will require vast amounts of federal government money.

As I searched old tapes and scripts and memories in order to write this book, I identified a consistent contradiction. The federal government barely hesitated when it came to pouring hundreds of millions of dollars into multinational oil companies, yet it was almost impossible, then and now, for territorial governments and Indigenous organizations to get clear government commitments to provide adequate housing, education and health care. Today, if a predominantly Inuit or First Nations region documents the urgent need for five hundred houses, a typical government response may be to provide fifty. Rather than tackling the full magnitude of the humanitarian crisis, the government's response is to negotiate downwards.

In recent years I have become more optimistic, in part because Justin Trudeau has identified Indigenous issues as his national priority. He is also the first prime minister to establish a direct working relationship with organizations that represent all Indigenous peoples in Canada.

The painful and tragic social issues will remain a part of the unfolding story of our rising North, but so will the new leaders who are emerging and are the growing hope for the future. As I used to ask of radio listeners, I will stay tuned. I pray that all of us do.

ACKNOWLEDGEMENTS

This book has been born again in this new edition thanks to the commitment of my agent, Rick Broadhead, and the generosity of Tim Gordon, who published the original manuscript at Burnstown Publishing House. Rick believed that recent events—including the swearing in of a certain new governor general—meant that *True North Rising* should be exposed to a wider Canadian audience, and then convinced me and two publishers that he was right. I especially want to thank Tim and Burnstown for relinquishing the rights in favor of the superior marketing and editing capacity that Random House Canada, an imprint of Penguin Random House Canada, provides.

I am also forever grateful to Doug Ward, an old boss of mine at CBC's Northern Service, who set aside all the grief I may have once caused him and encouraged me to write these stories about an emerging and sometimes turbulent true North and its rise from colonialism.

Finally, my thanks to Anne Collins at Random House Canada for her editing skills and the polish she added to this old reporter's rough edges.

INDEX OF PROPER NAMES

Courtesy Students on Ice

WHIT FRASER went north to Frobisher Bay (now Iqaluit, Nunavut) in 1967 to work for CBC's Northern Service. For the next thirty-two years he travelled to every community in Canada's three northern territories, reporting on the historic events that shaped today's North, including the Mackenzie Valley Pipeline Inquiry, the negotiations that enshrined Aboriginal rights in the Canadian Constitution, and the progress of land claims from the initial demands of Dene and Inuit leaders through to the ceremony that inaugurated the new territory of Nunavut in 1999, which he co-hosted as his last broadcast for the CBC. Fraser has also served as the first chair of the Canadian Polar Commission and as the executive director of the national Inuit organization, the Inuit Tapiriit Kanatami. He is married to Canada's first Indigenous governor general, Mary Simon. His memoir, *True North Rising*, won the NWT Northwords Book Prize in 2019, and Nunavut's paper of record, *Nunatsiaq News*, called it a "must-read for anyone interested in northern Canada."

www.whitfraser.ca